Making Time

Making Time

Time and Management in Modern Organizations

Edited by

RICHARD WHIPP, BARBARA ADAM,
AND IDA SABELIS

OXFORD

UNIVERSITY PRESS

Great Clarendon Street, Oxford OX2 6DP

Oxford University Press is a department of the University of Oxford.
It furthers the University's objective of excellence in research, scholarship,
and education by publishing worldwide in

Oxford New York

Auckland Bangkok Buenos Aires Cape Town Chennai
Dar es Salaam Delhi Hong Kong Istanbul Karachi Kolkata
Kuala Lumpur Madrid Melbourne Mexico City Mumbai Nairobi
São Paulo Shanghai Singapore Taipei Tokyo Toronto

with an associated company in Berlin

Oxford is a registered trade mark of Oxford University Press
in the UK and in certain other countries

Published in the United States
by Oxford University Press Inc., New York

British Library Cataloguing in Publication Data
Data available

Library of Congress Cataloging in Publication Data
Data available

ISBN 0-19-925369-2 (hbk.)
ISBN 0-19-925370-6 (pbk.)

1 3 5 7 9 10 8 6 4 2

Typeset by Newgen Imaging Systems (p) Ltd, Chennai, India
Printed in Great Britain
on acid-free paper by
Biddles Ltd., Guildford and King's Lynn

FOREWORD

Gabriele Morello

When we were children, my sisters and I used to follow two orders of time prescriptions: Mama's time and Papa's time. Our mother (who as I write is 104 years old and mentally in perfect shape), born to a German family, expected us to be punctual, precise, and exact. Duty came before pleasure, treats had to be earned, meals and bedtime were fixed and had to be respected. Our father, a very creative Sicilian, was more flexible, approximate, and adaptable. With him we did not need to be rigorously on time. Excuses were easily accepted; sometimes he himself forgot what he had told us to do.

We stayed in the city of Palermo during the winter, and lived in the countryside on a farm in the summer months. Although the farm is only 30 kilometres from the city, time habits there are different. In both places, the concept of time does not seem to be of great concern to local people. Attitudes towards it differ, however. In the city, appointments have a more precise meaning than on the farm. The city-dwellers claim that 'punctuality means to foresee the delay of the others', but this does not stop people following schedules and procedures. At school, classes due to be given at 9 o'clock start—when 'punctual'—at 9.15. This fifteen-minute delay rule is known as 'quarto d'ora accademico'. On the farm, a delay of up to one hour for any appointment is acceptable. '*Un'ora è puntamento*' expresses this idea in local dialect.

I do not know if farmers' time follows everywhere the cyclical pattern based on seasonal rotation described in many books. On our farm it was certainly perceived as more moving and flowing than in the city of Palermo, where past, present, and future are more clearly experienced in the mind as separate entities. In the city, when we say 'next year', this may be any time between the following year and the next three years; on the farm, 'next year' depends on normal weather conditions: rainfall, temperature, the sirocco wind, and so on. Since weather conditions are never normal, 'next year' does not mean very much.

In the traditional Sicilian culture, greater importance is given to human wisdom and experience than to the notion that time is money. 'Everything has its own time', 'Every time comes and goes', are more popular proverbs than

'Lost time is never found again', 'Time and tide wait for no man', and similar sayings indicating that time is an economic resource not to be wasted. Recent research shows that, while Sicilians exhibit little tolerance when faced with short hold-ups and irrelevant delays (hence our antipathy to queuing and our frequent use of car horns), we are more likely to accept long delays, as if we were participants in a long story with a far-off end. The Teatro Massimo, one of the finest theatres in Europe, was closed for twenty years for restoration.

To be sure, although a background of enduring customs still exists, in the 1990s much was being done in terms of economic development and cultural change, and a 'new Sicily' was rapidly emerging. Ideally, the community should preserve and conciliate the best features of tradition with innovation and progress.

Profane time and sacred time also had different rules when we were children, as to some extent is still the case in 2001. Carrying out errands, attending sporting events, or going to a movie do not require any special dress, while festivities, going to church, and public holidays do. Santa Rosalia, patron saint of Palermo, is still commemorated on 15 July, and celebrations tend to be drawn out over two days before and two days after.

I finished high school and went through university earlier than my schoolmates. It was in those years, I think, that my biological time tended to internalize rhythmic changes, following a faster tempo than my peers. I skipped three years at school and achieved two degrees in the time it normally takes to get one. Given the fact that I was eager and impatient, this was perhaps due more to restlessness than to intelligence.

I soon developed the habit of doing several things at the same time, rather than one after the other. Such behaviour fitted well to my work environment, where it was normal for people to interrupt what they were doing and do something else, give different appointments for the same time, and talk over the phone while dealing with visitors. This is the most striking difference in conduct to which I had to adapt when commuting between Italy and other countries years later. It was not so much a problem of punctuality, which certainly had a different meaning for me in Palermo, London, and Amsterdam, but rather the monochronic versus the polychronic mode (in the sense of Hall (1983)) that was to be adapted in Northern Europe.

My interest in research on time started in the late 1950s with a project called the International Research Project on Evaluation (IRPE), funded by the Ford Foundation. This project attempted to assess the effects of management development programmes at Istituto Superiore per Imprenditori e Dirigenti di Azienda (ISIDA) and in seven other European graduate schools of business administration. We conducted an experimental design aimed at measuring what cognitive effects, if any, management programmes had produced on students' time perception, duration, sequence, periodicity, timing, and tempo. As a professional statistician, I saw the fascination of 'measuring the unmeasurable', as my Dutch colleague Peter Nijkamp calls this kind of exercise.

Indeed, incidences of numerical logic applied to time have been many and diverse, dating back to before the days when Plato held that 'the forms of time, mobile image of eternity, revolve according to the law of numbers'. Distinctions between different dimensions and meanings of time always attract our attention—clock time versus social time, mental time versus biological time, personal time versus Newtonian time, physical time versus metaphysical time—and it is never clear when and where observed relations support the speculation of the theorists. In my own studies I have concentrated mostly on the way people perceive time in different cultures and professions, and on the relationships between time and behaviour in the area of management and consumer behaviour. In doing so, my main instruments for measuring time perceptions have mostly been of a quantitative nature, including the measurement of attitudes towards the past, present, and future using Semantic Differential techniques.

Now that the time span in front of me is shorter than the time span behind me, and experience and wisdom tend to have more space, I am no longer sure that this approach best enables scientists to achieve valid results in the advancement of the study of time. Throughout the history of science, as we all know, debates on quality versus quantity have been long and fierce. It seems that even the difference in approaches has to do with different attitudes towards time. As Ilja Prigogine (1994: 17) puts it: 'Scientists do not read Shakespeare and humanists are insensible to the beauty of mathematics ... this dichotomy exists for a much more profound reason, which lies in the way in which the notion of time is incorporated into these two (scientific and humanist) cultures.'

Whatever the scope of the debates on time and temporality, and no matter which research methodologies are used, it seems to me that scientists are increasingly sharing the view that the understanding of social time—not to mention the operational possibilities to use it in 'better' ways—cannot be frozen into any rigid or schematic form that leaves out whatever has to do with attitudes, feelings, emotions, hopes, fears, and the other forms of human expressions that make up the existential nature of time. This is the reason why this book, which does not fall into the trap of unilateral thinking but gives an account of different viewpoints and experiments, should be read with interest and pleasure by all those who want to take the time to understand more about time.

Gabriele Morello
Palermo, 7 June 2001

ACKNOWLEDGEMENTS

This book arose from the long-standing interest of the editors in time and management, but it was the helpful prompting of our editor at OUP, David Musson, that proved so timely in identifying a suitable publishing opportunity. We are most grateful for both his enthusiastic support and his good-humoured guidance. The short-term origins of this volume, meanwhile, are found in a clutch of academic events in 2000. We record our thanks, therefore, to both the organizers of the meetings and, in particular, those who contributed to the discussions that arose. The events in question were: the third 'Time and Management' conference in Palermo hosted by the Istituto Superiore per Imprenditori e Dirigenti di Azienda (ISIDA) (co-organized by Morello, Adam, and Sabelis), the working group on 'Organization, Management and Time' at the European Group for Organization Studies (EGOS) conference in Helsinki (convened by Whipp), and the all-academy symposium on 'Timescapes in Management' at the US Academy of Management in Toronto (involving Adam, Purser, and Whipp). Acknowledgement is also given to Blackwell Publishers for their kind permission to use in Table 1.1 an adapted version of the Evolution of Corporate Strategy from R. Grant, *Contemporary Strategy Analysis* (1998). We also acknowledge the comments of the three referees used by OUP, which proved extremely useful in the development of the final version of the book. The work of Lesley Plowman at Cardiff Business School in helping to liase across an international project, and the technical support from Gwen Booth at OUP, are much appreciated.

CONTENTS

LIST OF FIGURES, TABLES, AND BOXES

Figures

Tables

Boxes

NOTES ON CONTRIBUTORS

Barbara Adam is Professor of Sociology at Cardiff University and a leading authority on social time (her Ph.D. was on Time and Social Theory). She is Founder Editor of *Time and Society* and author of some 100 publications on the subject. Her key publications include *Time and Social Theory* (Polity 1990); *Timewatch: The Social Analysis of Time* (Polity 1995); and *Timescapes of Modernity: The Environment and Invisible Hazards* (Routledge 1998).

Peter Anthony is a Professorial Research Fellow at the Management Centre, King's College, University of London. His research interests include management learning, the moral order of management, and the management of employee cooperatives. Publications include 'A Dialogic Analysis of Organisational Learning', *Journal of Management Studies*, 37/6 (2000), 887–901 (with C. Oswick, T. Keenoy, I. L. Mangham, and D. Grant).

Emma Bell is a Lecturer in Organizational Behaviour at Warwick Business School. Her research expertise is in culture, consumption, and spirituality in organizations. Recent publications include 'The Negotiation of a Working Role in Organizational Ethnography', *International Journal of Social Research Methodology*, 2/1 (1999), 17–37; 'Investors in People and the Standardization of Professional Knowledge in Personnel Management', *Management Learning*, 32/2 (2001), 201–19; 'The Social Time of Organizational Payment Systems', *Time and Society*, 10/1 (2001), 45–62.

Dirk Bunzel is Lecturer in the Department of Management at Keele University. He has a special interest in ethnography and critical management studies and his research focuses on issues of power and identity in organizations. He has recently completed his Ph.D. thesis on the discursive construction of customer service at the University of Western Sydney and is involved in researching the 'Future of Work' within call centres and software firms across Scotland.

David Grant is a Senior Lecturer in the Department of Work and Organizational Studies, University of Sydney. His primary research interest lies in applying an organizational discourse perspective to a range of employment issues; his research includes studies of the social construction of HRM, the psychological contract, and various aspects of trade unions and industrial relations. Publications include *Discourse and Organisation* (Sage 1998) (edited with T. Keenoy and C. Oswick); 'A Dialogic Analysis of Organisational Learning', *Journal of Management Studies*, 37/6 (2000), 887–901 (with C. Oswick, P. Anthony, T. Keenoy, and I. L. Mangham); 'From Outer Words to Inner Worlds', *Journal of Applied Behavioral Science*, 36/2 (2000), 245–58 (with R. Marshak, T. Keenoy, and C. Oswick); and 'Discourse, Organisations and Organising: Concepts, Objects and Subjects', *Human Relations*, 53/9 (2000), 1115–24 (with C. Oswick and T. Keenoy).

Laurids Hedaa is Director of the Thomas B. Thrige Center for Applied Management Studies (CAMS) and research professor at the Department of Management, Politics, and Philosophy at the Copenhagen Business School (MS Graduate, School of Business, Stanford University; Ph.D., Copenhagen Business School). Recent research includes parastatic heteronomy in networks (1997); atoms of interaction (1998); black holes in networks (1998); frequent flier programs (1998); owner managers in Denmark (1999); and kairology (2000). Publications include 'Customer Acquisition in Sticky Business Markets', *International Business Review*, 5/5 (1996), and *Afsætning og samarbejde: Teori for praksis Handelshøjskolen Forlag* (Copenhagen 1997) (edited with N. Foss).

Tom Keenoy is Reader in Management at the Management Centre, King's College, University of London. His primary research interest lies in understanding the social processes through which the employment relationship is constructed, managed, controlled, and accomplished. Current work includes discourse analytic studies of HRM, organizational timescapes, academic identities, and the management of employee cooperatives. His expertise is in discourse analysis, work organization, HRM, and employment relations. Publications include *Discourse and Organisation* (Sage 1998) (edited with D. Grant and C. Oswick); 'HRM as Hologram: A Polemic', *Journal of Management Studies*, 36/1 (1999), 1–23; 'A Dialogic Analysis of Organisational Learning', *Journal of Management Studies*, 37/6 (2000), 887–901 (with C. Oswick, P. Anthony, I. L. Mangham, and D. Grant); 'From Outer Words to Inner Worlds', *Journal of Applied Behavioral Science*, 36/2 (2000), 245–58 (with R. Marshak, C. Oswick, and D. Grant); and 'Discourse, Organisations and Organising: Concepts, Objects and Subjects', *Human Relations*, 53/9 (2000), 1115–24 (with C. Oswick and D. Grant).

David Knights is Professor of Organizational Analysis and Head of the School of Management at Keele University. He is the editor of the journal *Gender, Work and Organization* and his most recent publications include *The Re-engineering Revolution: Critical Studies of Corporate Change* (Sage 2000) (edited with H. Willmott); *Management Lives: Power and Identity in Work Organizations* (Sage 1999) (with H. Willmott); 'A'int Misbehavin'?: Opportunities for Resistance with Bureaucratic and Quality Management Innovations', *Sociology*, 34/3 (July

2000), 421–36 (with D. McCabe); and 'Autonomy-Retentiveness! Problems and Prospects for a Post-Humanist Feminism', *Journal of Management Inquiry*, 9/2 (2000), 173–86.

Paul Sergius Koku is Associate Professor of Business at the College of Business in Florida Atlantic University, Boca Raton, Florida, USA. He holds MBA (mktg), MBA (fin), MA (Applied Economics), and earned his Ph.D. in Finance and Marketing from Rutgers University. His research interests include the finance–marketing interface, information economics, health economics, and strategic marketing management. He has numerous peer-reviewed publications.

Heejin Lee is a Lecturer in the Department of Information Systems and Computing at Brunel University. His field of expertise is information systems, time, and IT. He was a guest editor of a special issue on *Time and IT* for the Information Society. He has published several articles on time and information technologies in journals such as *Organization Studies, Accounting, Management and Information Technologies*, and *Time and Society*. Recent publications include 'Time in Organizational Studies: Towards a New Research Direction', *Organization Studies*, 20/6 (1999), 1035–58 (with Jonathan Liebenau); and 'Temporal Effects of Information Systems on Business Processes: Focusing on the Dimensions of Temporality', *Accounting, Management and Information Technologies*, 10/3 (2000), 157–85 (with Jonathan Liebenau).

Jonathan Liebenau is a Senior Lecturer in Information Systems at the London School of Economics and Political Science, where he works on fundamental concepts of information (temporality, semantics, transactions, etc.) and on the political and economic character of information and communication technologies. He has written numerous books and articles on these topics and is currently working on an integration of concepts, policies, and economics of information infrastructure at various levels. Recent publications include 'Time in Organizational Studies: Towards a New Research Direction', *Organization Studies*, 20/6 (1999), 1035–58 (with Heejin Lee); 'Temporal Effects of Information Systems on Business Processes: Focusing on the Dimensions of Temporality', *Accounting, Management and Information Technologies*, 10/3 (2000), 157–85 (with Heejin Lee).

Iain Mangham is a Professorial Research Fellow at the Management Centre, King's College, University of London. His research is conducted from the dramaturgical perspective on organizational analysis, and current work includes research on corporate theatre, the scripted nature of management performance, and emotion in organizations. Publications include 'A Dialogic Analysis of Organisational Learning', *Journal of Management Studies*, 37/6 (2000), 887–901 (with C. Oswick, P. Anthony, T. Keenoy, and D. Grant).

Gabriele Morello is the founding director of the Istituto Superiore per Imprenditore e Dirigenti (ISIDA—the Institute for Management Development) in Palermo, Sicily. He is also Professor of Business Statistics and Marketing Research in the Faculty of Economics at Palermo University, and Professor Emeritus of Marketing in the Faculty of Economics and Econometrics at the Vrije Universiteit (Free University) of Amsterdam. He has lectured and conducted research in private and public, national and multinational organizations in all European countries, in the USA, Latin America, the Middle East, India, China, South Africa, Japan, and Australia. He is currently cooperating with the University of Havana for the development of a Master in Business Administration in Cuba. He has served as President of ESOMAR, the European Association of Management Training Centres (EAMTC, now EFMD), the Italian Marketing Association (AISM), and the Italian Association of Business Schools (ASFOR). He has published numerous articles on time and cultural differences in several languages. With Dawn Caseby he was the editor of *Between Tradition and Innovation: Time in a Managerial Perspective* (ISIDA, vol. 14; Palermo 1997).

Nishimoto Ikuko received her Ph.D. from Manchester University and currently teaches English at Saitama University. She is interested in the theory of the democratic order of time and space. Her articles on time include 'The "Civilization" of Time: Japan and the Adoption of the Western Time System', *Time and Society*, 6/2–3 (1997), 237–60; ' "Harmony" as Efficiency: Is "Just-In-Time" a Product of Japanese Uniqueness?', *Time and Society*, 8 (1999), 120–40; and an essay on time discipline in the Japanese educational system in a joint research 'The Origins of Tardiness', *Japan Review* (forthcoming).

Christian Noss is Assistant Professor at the Department of Management, Freie Universität Berlin, Germany. He specialises in systems-theoretical concepts of management, theories of institutional dynamics and change, and time and management studies. Publications include *Zeit im Management: Reflexionen zu einer Theorie temporalisierter Unternehmenssteuerung* (*Time and Management: Reflections on a Temporalized Theory of Managerial Action*) (Wiesbaden: Gabler 1997); and 'Reframing Change in Organizations: The Equilibrium Logic and Beyond, in S. J. Havlovic (ed.), *Best Paper Proceedings of the Academy of Management's 2000 Conference* (Toronto 2000) (with G. Schreyögg).

Pamela Odih is a Lecturer in Sociology at Goldsmiths College, University of London. Her specialist areas include gender, consumption time, and social theory. Recent publications inlcude 'Gendered Time in the Age of Deconstruction', *Time and Society*, 8/1 (1999), 9–38; 'The Women's Market: Marketing Fact or Apparition?', *Consumption Markets and Culture*, 3/2 (1999), 1–29; ' "It's a Matter of Time": The Significance of the Women's Market in Consumption', in D. Brownlie, M. Saren, R. Wensley, and R. Whittington (eds.), *Re-Thinking Marketing: Towards Critical Marketing Accountings* (Sage 1999), 126–44 (with D. Knights); ' "Discipline Needs Time": Education for Citizenship and the Financially Self Disciplined Subject', *School Field*, 10/3–4 (Autumn–Winter 1999), 127–5s (with D. Knights); and ' "Just in Time": The Prevalence of

Representational Time to Marketing Discourses of Consumer Buyer Behaviour', in P. Daniels, J. Bryson *et al.* (eds.), *Knowledge, Space and Economy* (Routledge forthcoming) (with D. Knights).

Cliff Oswick is a Senior Lecturer in Organizational Analysis at the Management Centre, King's College, University of London. His research is conducted from a social constructivist perspective and is focused on organizational discourse and language use in organizational change processes; current research includes studies of discursive tropes, the social construction of globalization, and ageism. Publications include *Discourse and Organisation* (Sage 1998) (edited with D. Grant and T. Keenoy); 'A Dialogic Analysis of Organisational Learning', *Journal of Management Studies*, 37/6 (2000), 887–901 (with P. Anthony, T. Keenoy, I. L. Mangham, and D. Grant); 'From Outer Words to Inner Worlds', *Journal of Applied Behavioral Science*, 36/2 (2000), 245–58 (with R. Marshak, T. Keenoy, and D. Grant); and 'Discourse, Organisations and Organising: Concepts, Objects and Subjects', *Human Relations*, 53/9 (2000), 1115–24 (with T. Keenoy and D. Grant).

Ronald E. Purser is Associate Professor of Management in the College of Business at San Francisco State University. He is currently Division Chair of the Organization Development and Change (ODC) division of the Academy of Management. He is the co-author of four books, *The Search Conference* (Jossey Bass 1996) (with M. Emery), *The Self Managing Organization* (Free Press 1998) (with S. Cabana), and *Social Creativity*, vols. i and ii (Hampton Press) (with A. Montuori). He recently chaired a featured symposium 'Timescapes in Management: Exposing Contradictions, Exploring New Possibilities' at the 2000 Academy of Management conference. His recent paper, 'The Coming Crisis in Real-Time Environments: A Dromological Analysis', was selected for the Best Paper Proceedings of the 2000 Academy of Management meeting.

Alf Rehn completed his Ph.D. thesis on hypermodern gift economies at the Royal Institute of Technology/Department of Industrial Economics and Management, Stockholm, Sweden. In addition to the work on gift economies, he does work on moralization processes and the question of frivolity in management and technology.

Ida Sabelis is Lecturer at the Department of Culture, Organization, and Management at the Vrije Universiteit (Free University) of Amsterdam. She is Review Editor for *Time and Society* and a member of the advisory board of 'Kantharos'—an international organizational consultancy for Managing Diversity—Amsterdam. Key publications include *Contradictions in Context: Puzzling over Paradoxes in Contemporary Organisations* (Free University Press 1996) (edited with Willem Koot and Sierk Ybema); *Over-Leven aan de Top: Top managers in complexe tijden* (*Surviving at the Top: Top Managers in Complex Times*) (Utrecht: Lemma 2000) (with Willem Koot)

Jan-Åke Törnroos is Professor of International Marketing. Åbo Akademi University, Finland, with expertise in international industrial marketing and networks and intercultural marketing management. Key publications include 'The Role of Embeddedness in the Evolution of Business Networks', *Scandinavian Journal of Management*, 14/3 (1998), 187–205 (co-authored with Aino Halinen), and *Developing Business Activities in Eastern Europe: A Learning and Network Perspective with Case Studies* (Kikimora Publications 1999) (co-edited with J. Nieminen).

Alan Tuckman is currently a Senior Lecturer at Nottingham Business School. With a background in Industrial and Political Sociology he has a research and teaching interest in new management strategies, employment flexibility, and employee representation. He has written on a range of subjects including TQM, and his recent research interests focus on the chemicals and auto industries. Publications include ' "All Together Better?" Single Status and Union Recognition in the Chemical Industry', *Employee Relations*, 20/2 (1998), 132–47, and 'Affirmation, Games, and Insecurity: Cultivating Consent within a New Workplace Regime', *Capital and Class*, 76 (2002), 65–93 (with Michael Whittall).

Richard Whipp is Professor of Human Resource Management and Deputy Director of Cardiff Business School, Cardiff University. He is the current Chair of the British Academy of Management. He has published widely in the fields of history, innovation, and strategic change. His book publications include: *Innovation and the Auto Industry* (Pinter 1986), *Patterns of Labour* (Routledge 1990), *Managing Change for Competitive Success* (Blackwell 1991) (with A Pettigrew), and *A Managed Service* (Wiley 2002) (with I. Kirkpatrick and M. Kitchener).

Choreographing Time and Management: Traditions, Developments, and Opportunities

Barbara Adam, Richard Whipp, and Ida Sabelis

INTRODUCTION

Time is an essential feature of social and organizational life. It is our prime organizing tool. People use time in order to create, shape, and order their worlds. And yet, despite its importance, we take our time values and uses of time largely for granted. This not only applies to one's daily life but is also true for academic theory and business practice alike. *Making Time* is concerned to bring time to the forefront of management theory and practice. It seeks, accordingly, to make explicit what are currently the many implicit temporal assumptions that underpin management thought and action. It emphasizes the richness of the temporal dimensions involved and the wealth of competing attempts to order, regulate, and control time in the act of managing. The point is to describe and explain this temporal complexity as it occurs in management by working with a variety of specialist perspectives, such as strategic management, organizational theory, decision making, industrial relations, and marketing. Furthermore, a deliberate attempt is made to set the experience of more traditional industrial settings alongside those at the forefront of the 'new economy', such as the computer industry.

Time is currently a fashionable motif. A popular time consciousness has emerged from public attention to the millennium—seen, for example, in the accounts of the evolution of timepieces or the exhibitions on the establishment of the Greenwich meridian. During the 1990s, the notion of 'time management' become a central feature of management training, and the business shelves of bookshops are populated with self-help texts on how to manage an individual's time. In contrast to these guides, *Making Time* provides neither instant recipes nor simple personal blueprints. Rather, its contributions offer insights into a much broader temporal domain, extending concerns to encompass the more complex and paradoxical nature of temporal relations in both the theoretical and practical spheres of management. Many commentators regard the time line on the x axis of their graphs, uniformly calibrated by the calendar and clock, as a sufficient means of capturing time in their work on management. The major theme of this collection is to challenge that assumption. The authors in the volume recognize the pervasiveness of industrial time in both management and academic discourse. Where they differ is in giving full recognition to the way that people create their own sense of time alongside the official temporal apparatus of the clock and diary.

Making Time aims to spark a debate in the field of management that does justice to the richness of the temporal features of contemporary organizations. Importantly, the volume represents the chance to share a more developed language of time for describing and understanding organizations and their management, using broader concepts such as 'rhythmicity' and 'timescape'. Equally, the book has relevance to practitioners. The conventional thinking locked within the industrial time framework offers little to organizations that are trying to come to terms with the problems raised by new technologies and seeking to release the potential of those technologies through unconventional work patterns. On a wider scale, the contributors to this volume share the central belief that developing an understanding of the social relations of time and management is a precondition to securing practices that are sensitive to the changing conditions of a global economy and its inherent paradoxes.

In this first chapter we introduce readers to key time and management issues and locate *Making Time* in its wider academic and public context. We take two routes to this end: the first takes us along the historical path of time in management studies. The second guides us through the tracks that have been opened up by time studies and theoretical perspectives on the social relations of time. Next we consider some of the methodological issues that arise from identifying time in management as the explicit focus of attention. The last task is to introduce the chapters with their authors' disciplinary location and particular time focus.

APPROACHES TO TIME IN THE STUDY OF MANAGEMENT

Any attempt to summarize the subject of management requires caution. The study of management has become a huge sector of economic endeavour in its own right. Estimates in 2001 identify an $8 billion global industry that embraces a wide range of actors. These include not only management scholars and educators but also consultants, commentators, and policy-makers. As the popularity of management as a subject and qualification grew in the late twentieth century, so an interesting phenomenon appeared: what once had been a subject investigated largely by academics became less exclusive. Those being studied in various industries and sectors began to capture and record their own experience and knowledge of management. The corporate university and the writings of managers and consultants now sit beside the more conventional academic forms.

At the same time, the diversity of the management area has continued to grow from its inception in the USA in the middle of the twentieth century, through its take-up by Europeans in the 1960s and its wider international spread from the 1980s. The subject has always born the imprints of its parent disciplines: economics and psychology in the early phase in the USA, with a marked contribution from sociology and anthropology during its expansion in Europe. The result is that management has produced an elaborate collection of writers who draw from contrasting intellectual traditions. The scope of its specialisms is striking. An exercise by the UK's Economic and Social Research Council (ESRC 2001: section F8) on research training in business and management in 2001 highlighted the existence of competing orientations to research (positivist, realist, interpretative, and post-structural) and the presence of a catalogue of established specialisms such as accounting and finance, strategy, marketing, organizational behaviour, operations management, and international business. On the one hand, such a profile cautions against easy generalization given the scale and scope of both the subject and its adherents. On the other, it also gives a sense of the opportunities for the exploration of time within the field of management.

Engagement with a Dominant Time Rationale

In spite of this heterogeneity, a first look at the work of management writers produces a clear impression. During the development of management as a formal field of study, a strong temporal dimension has been present, anchored to an essentially linear understanding of time. Until the last two decades of the twentieth century, rationalism predominated. This outcome is entirely consistent with the character of management as a subject and its evolution. The expansion of the modern economy in its Western context gave rise to a particular form of organization, with an emphasis on management as the means of controlling resources in order to secure certain organizational goals. Time was a potential barrier to achieving those goals (Thompson 1967), as Dirk Bunzel (this volume) shows in his identification of the 'centrifugal forces' that organizations produce. The undisputed aim of management has been to control time not to problematize it.

The same imperative has informed most management research, as seen, for example, in the work of Taylor and then Fayol in the first two decades of the twentieth century, through to the human-relations school in the inter-war years, and the rise of planning in the post-war era. During the twentieth century scholars progressively investigated every aspect of the functioning and circumstances of management. It is understandable that they should have worked predominantly within the temporal framework that both informed the actions of those who were the subject of their research and suffused the industrial society of which they were a part (see Pamela Odih and David Knights, this volume). The same point could also be applied to most Western historians. Thus, as Alf Rehn (this volume) reminds us, the dominance of linear time, as embodied in the clock and calendar, may appear somewhat narrow and limited as a way of conceiving of time, but it has provided an essential element of a major socio-economic form.

It would, however, be inaccurate for time scholars to categorize the broad field of management as entirely monochronic in its approach to time. Important exceptions exist in all the main parent disciplines and the specialisms within management (see Das 1991). Some indicative examples reinforce the point. In psychology, McGrath and Kelly (1985) in their work on what they call 'time and human interaction' embrace both 'dominant' and 'variant conceptions of time' (1985: 17–42) and a 'network of time frames' (1985: 50) as they build their framework for a social psychology of time and work. Thrift (1996: 220–30), from geography, uses notions of time consciousness and social theory to open up the jointly temporal and spatial components of, for example, international finance. Economics too has scholars who argue for alternatives to the overarching neo-classical paradigm. Shackle (1972), for example, presents a broad critique that challenges the rational temporal core of market equilibria, while others, such as Langlois (1986), operate in the 'new institutional' framework that gives primacy to the operation of time in the context of institutions in economic processes.

The record of sociology as a contributory discipline to the management field in relation to time is different in a number of respects. Some sociologists have pioneered the joint use of time and social theory in order to understand the operation of specific types of organizations. Zerubavel (1981), for example, in trying to make sense of medical institutions, uncovered an array of 'hidden rhythms' that permeate the work of health-care staff in the USA. The French tradition of industrial sociology has similarly produced alternative accounts of the time-ordering patterns of work and domestic life (Grossin 1974). Until the late 1990s, however, management was not regularly the principal object of this kind of study. Yet a concentration on the way time is experienced by people, which does not fit neatly with managerial preoccupations, has produced important results.

Perhaps one of the most notable outcomes from this vein of research has been the formation of a network of time specialists who operate on the boundary of sociology and organizations. Clark, for example, played a lead role in linking the temporal frameworks found in both anthropology and industrial sociology and part of the French Annales school, in his studies of organizations (1985). The assumption of a dominant, singular clock time was directly challenged when he demonstrated the plurality of chronological codes, for example, that coexist both within and between organizations (1990). Others (see e.g. Starkey 1988; Whipp 1990; Hassard 1996) used such findings as the starting point for their own empirical investigations of how people in different sectors attempt to construct and order time (see also Bluedorn and Denhardt 1988; T. C. Smith 1988; Das 1991). By making use of the critical orientation of organization studies, Burrell (1998) has confronted the received wisdom in organizational thinking in relation to time and its shaping by the broader Western preoccupation with linear images of life and death. Other specialisms within management have made their own use of the notion of the subjective construction of time in order to question the orthodox temporal assumptions behind, for instance, industrial-relations systems (Blyton *et al.* 1989).

Masking Time and Making Time in Strategic Management

One area of management studies that came to represent, and some would argue dominate, the entire field during the last two decades of the twentieth century was strategic management. Its growth has been prodigious and the results of work in this specialism have touched virtually all others. As Lyles (1990: 363) noted, the strategic dimension had become pervasive across not only management but also other social sciences. The appearance of a clutch of millennial 'Handbooks on Strategic Management' reinforce the centrality of this specialism (see e.g. Faulkner and Campbell 2002). Strategic management is, therefore, an appropriate candidate to inspect more closely in order to show what role time plays in one of the core aspects of the study of management. As will become clear, while time may be officially represented in a way that apparently conforms to the industrial time model, a more diverse sense of time is richly but implicitly present.

Various overviews of the character and evolution of the strategic management domain charted its multi-phase development from the 1940s to the close of the century (Whipp 1996; R. Grant 1998). Table 1.1 offers a summary and outline introduction to the subject. The route travelled by the writers in this area is instructive in relation to the role of time in two senses: the changing subject matter of strategic management and the varying conceptual orientations that have been employed. As Table 1.1 indicates, the agreed content of strategic management in the 1950s and 1960s was essentially planning and forecasting. During the 1970s and 1980s emphasis shifted to a wider analysis of, first, the

Table 1.1. The evolution of corporate strategy

Key dimensions	Period					
	1950s	1960s	1970s	Late 1970s to early 1980s	Late 1980s to early 1990s	Mid- to late 1990s
Dominant theme	Budgetary planning and control	Corporate planning	Corporate strategy	Analysis of industry and competition	The quest for competitive advantage	Strategic innovation
Main issues	Financial control through operating budgets	Planning growth	Portfolio planning	Choice of industries, markets, and segments, and positioning within them	Sources of competitive advantage within the firm	Strategic and organizational advantage
Organizational implications	Financial management	Rise of corporate planning departments and five-year formal plans	Diversification Multidivisional structures Quest for global market share	Greater industry and market selectivity Industry restructuring Active asset management	Corporate restructuring and business process re-engineering Refocusing and outsourcing	The virtual organization The knowledge-based firm Alliances and networks The quest for critical mass

Source: based on R. Grant (1998: 18).

relevant industries and markets, and, later, the structures and resources of the firm that could underpin the quest for competitive advantage. In the 1990s a more radical move occurred. Strategic management was forced to confront the unprecedented features of the reinvention of entire industries and markets by the innovative application of digital technology. In addition, new virtual organizational forms appeared. Finally, the search for sources of innovation and the knowledge that is required were pre-eminent concerns. As Ronald E. Purser's chapter in this volume shows, the implications for conventional frameworks of the temporal ordering of organizations are immense.

If the disruption to the subject matter of strategic management during this progression has become acute, then the effects on the interpretative schema of academics have been no less marked. The corporate strategy and planning tradition, with its heavy reliance on linear, quantifiable notions of time, has been sustained. The paradigm of neo-classical economics and its Newtonian assumptions dominates there. Yet, since the 1960s, a steady flow of revisionist and new approaches have appeared. Whilst the authors in question have not made time a separate object of their study, nevertheless the insights that they have offered add up to a formidable catalogue. Well-known examples include the work of March and Olsen (1976), who revealed the irrational behaviour of managers and the haphazard implementation of strategic programmes and the implicit temporal maelstrom within organizations. Mintzberg (1978, 1994) has offered a sustained critique of the hygienic accounts of strategic management, presenting direct challenges to the undue rationality of the succession of models that are charted in Table 1.1. He and others have emphasized that the formation and implementation of strategic decisions are difficult processes in their own right, informed by competing imperatives and multiple logics. During the 1970s and 1980s, work on the political and cultural aspects of such processes produced detailed accounts that laid out an array of inherent temporal features (Pettigrew 1977; Hickson *et al.* 1986). These included the complex cycles of decision making and the subtle aspects of timing and sequencing. (For accounts in this volume that address these issues, see the chapters by Tom Keenoy *et al.* and Ida Sabelis.)

In due course such work reached its fullest expression in the sub-specialism of strategic change (for a summary, see Whipp 2002). Whilst most of these scholars did not formally use the conceptual frameworks or vocabulary of the time specialists from sociology, the temporal implications of the sub-field accumulated. In the 1990s, some working in the area made the first attempts to link the two in a formal way (see Whipp 1996; Noss, this volume). Wilson's summary (1992) of the strategic change area is notable for the way it draws attention to the different types of change processes through a taxonomy that is built on the recognition of the plurality of time and the distinctions between continuity, evolution, and transformation (1992: 20). It is in this spirit that this volume wishes to move forward and to extend the brokering effort more fully.

Contemporary Opportunities

Today, any attempt to reinforce the potential links between the body of work on time theory and those interested in time within management (not to mention those who deal indirectly but productively with the temporal aspects of management) is supported by an advantageous institutional academic setting. It was highly symbolic and certainly instructive that the US Academy of Management conference for 2000 chose the theme of 'A New Time'. Even a cursory glance at the programme (AoM 2000) points to the way management researchers could relate to the problem of time in both the subject matter of their projects ('web businesses and time', 'speeding up work and time' (B7)) and at the abstract level ('culture and perspectives on time' (B8), 'time and multilevel research (B10)). The brokering project at the heart of this collection of essays is assisted by such events as well as by the following conducive features of the current management field: the creative adoption of time theory by certain management researchers; the spontaneous discovery of the plurality of time within the new economy; and the parallel development of a non-Newtonian science. The following gives a suggestion of some of the opportunities available from these three activities.

In its recent growth the management field contains notable examples of writers who fall into the first category in the way they exploit the theoretical literature on time in their work. At an abstract level, van den Bosch (2001) explores some of the core models of strategic management armed with a clear appreciation of the distinctions between the objective/physical dimensions of time and the subjective aspects of 'temporally related beliefs, values and behaviours' rooted in human perception (2001: 72; see also Mosakowski and Earley 2000). He also interrogates those who employ classic theories such as the resource-based theory of the firm or the punctuated equilibrium model in order to show how 'key concepts in strategy are time based' (van den Bosch 2001: 71). Meanwhile Collins (1998: 134–5), in ranging across contrasting specialisms in management, raises the issues of 'temporal interconnectedness' and 'temporal embeddedness' in relation to change within organizations. By doing so he is able to signal the limits of managerial action and identify how, for example, previous actions 'constrain the present and future trajectories of the organization' (see also Gersick 1991; Chia 1997; S. Cummings forthcoming). At the empirical level, others have taken the opportunity to base their detailed investigations of individual firms and sectors on key temporal concepts from outside their subject. Vreiling's work (1998) on the steel sector, for example, is founded on his observation that: 'Apart from functioning in time (i.e. continuity) phenomena also change over time. To admit that strategy formation is functioning in time remains rather static without admitting that strategy formation is changing through time. This marks a move from a synchronic (simultaneous) process towards a diachronic (historical) process.' (Vreiling 1998: 6). The chapters in

Part One of this volume by Laurids Hedaa and Jan-Åke Törnroos, Christian Noss, Pamela Odih and David Knights, and Alf Rehn are examples from this tradition of a time-sensitive management literature.

The second occurrence, which has placed time at the centre of management writers' thinking, is the diffusion of new technology. The majority of mainstream accounts of management discussed in the previous section were and are constructed against the dominance of the corporate form. Such structures are in the process of disintegrating in the face of microelectronics and communications technologies. Staff and the suppliers of services and resources who have been accustomed to relating to a single, divisional-based company may now be dispersed in loose federal or project-based network structures, made possible by appropriate software.

Conventional corporate calendars no longer apply. Start-up ventures in the computing industry, for example, change form more than a dozen times within the first year of their existence. Furthermore, the rules and bases of competition have also been the subject of extreme disruption. The phenomenon of 'hyper-competition' (Ilinitch *et al.* 1998) refers to the way existing markets are entered and their established operations dislocated by fast-moving firms that rely on rapid product or service innovation and the creation of new bundles of competences that enable them to adopt aggressive pricing policies. The new form of competition also feeds off the demand by consumers for higher quality and choice informed by the use of new technology, such as the Internet. The accepted temporal strategies of management, such as long-term planning, break down. They have been replaced by the problems of simultaneity and electronic interaction in all areas of business; these extend from computer-aided design and production to the electronic structuring of supply chains and the reworking of markets due to e-commerce. For both those who work in such organizations, and those who research them, the temporal issues are at the heart of these new challenges. The chapters in Part Two of this volume by Ida Sabelis, Nishimoto Ikuko, Emma Bell and Alan Tuckman, Heijin Lee and Jonathan Liebenau, and Paul Sergius Koku explore adaptive and responsive management practices in the context of far-reaching changes in technology and market conditions.

A third opportunity for the fusion of the management and time domains comes from further afield in the shape of what is sometimes called the 'new science'. At the risk of oversimplification, a small number of social scientists have taken seriously the questioning of the seventeenth-century foundations of the natural sciences and their reliance in turn on the machine imagery of Newton and Descartes. Instead they have turned to the theories of evolution and chaos that have arisen across the disciplines of physics, biology, and chemistry (Kauffman 1995). Alternatively, they have drawn on non-Newtonian metaphors such as the hologram to guide their work towards an elaboration of complexity (Keenoy 1999). The emphasis in the new approaches is not so much on the study of parts to understand a whole but on comprehending complete systems and the relationships within such networks (Wheatley 1999: 10). Whilst the elaboration of the new approach is still in its infancy outside the natural sciences, attempts are being made to adapt and apply its ideas to social systems and organizations (Marion 1999). Some believe the proposition of complexity theory, that order in the universe emerges naturally out of chaos, could in due course be applied to explaining the operation of phenomena such as the World Wide Web. Others have used the metaphor on organizations (Stacey 1992). Attention has been given to the way that small actions can be sources of complex patterns of change. Localized adjustments may have implications for a business as a whole. The examples of the stock market and the 'zero-tolerance' policy on petty crime in New York and its subsequent effect on all criminal behaviour in the city are frequently cited in this context.

These ideas are yet to be widely adopted in management studies, but they have attracted the attention of those who address time and change processes. Brown and Eisenhardt (1998), for example, take the lack of predictability in current environments as the reason for organizations to adjust continuously their orientation between order and chaos. At the heart of their argument is the need for organizations to identify the natural rhythms and temporal pacing of their organizational environments and to respond to the timing cues that result. The chapters in Part Three of this volume by Ronald E. Purser, Dirk Bunzel, and Tom Keenoy *et al.* are examples of the insights to be gained by employing such alternative constructs.

Overall, the contemporary setting is a positive one for a rapprochement between time specialists and management studies. In the context of such strong possibilities, what help can the time specialists provide both to understanding the role of time in relation to management and to advancing this joint project forward? In the next part of this introductory chapter we explore the temporal canvas from which and against which the field of management has developed. This involves us in detailing the specific temporal colour patterns of industrialization as well as showing their location within the broader outlines of socio-cultural activity. The themes and scope are deliberately wide-ranging. While the work detailed in the previous sections of this chapter came mainly from within the field of management, what follows is based on research in time studies and seeks to build connecting bridges from that direction.

TIME THEORY FOR THE FIELD OF MANAGEMENT

Every society embodies the temporal relations of its past and present members and institutions. This is so because all cultures ancient and modern have established collective ways of relating to the past and future, of synchronizing their activities, of coming to terms with finitude, and these still constitute an integral part of our present today: to have a relationship to time and finitude is a mark of human culture. *How* we extend ourselves into the past and future, *how* we pursue immortality, and *how* we temporally manage, organize, and regulate our social affairs, however, have provided a key to cultural differences from prehistory to the present.

Nature and culture, it is traditionally argued, have different means for overcoming transience and finitude. In nature, continuity is achieved through regeneration and reproduction. Cultural permanence, in contrast, is created through art, writing, all forms of record keeping, and the development of institutions. In addition, control over time itself has been accomplished by re-creating time in artefactual form—that is, in calendars, clocks, and standardized world time. This culturally constructed time could then be used to reform social practices so as to suit econo-political purposes. Each historical epoch with its new forms of socioeconomic expression, therefore, simultaneously restructures its social relations of time. Thus, we can say that cultural expression is inextricably bound to the social relations of time.[1]

This long history of cultural transcendence of the times of nature has lessened some of the human dependence on but not overcome our rootedness in the rhythmicity of the cosmos, the seasons, and the times of the body. The movement of earth, moon, and sun continues to affect all life on earth and, irrespective of calendars and clocks, time zones, and one standardized world time, our lives continue to be bounded by birth and death, growth and decay, night and day. This embodied time is lived and experienced alongside, despite, and in conflict with the culturally constituted social relations of time. In our daily lives we weave in and out of these different kinds of time without giving much thought to the matter. While space, place, and boundaries are tangible, time is lived and experienced as the invisible other. It is embodied knowledge, lived rather than theorized. 'We take our time values for granted,' proposes Rifkin (1987: 1), 'never stopping to consider the critical role they play in defining social order.' When thinking about management from a temporal perspective, it is therefore important to understand not only the contemporary condition but also some of the background forces and the processes that gave rise to its present forms.

As part of the deep structure of taken-for-granted, unquestioned assumptions, time shapes not only everyday understanding but also the theories that social scientists develop to explain their world. Up until the early 1990s, the explication of social time was considered to be a fringe activity of social science. At the beginning of the twenty-first century, this is no longer so. The interest in social time is burgeoning. Major conferences are devoted to time and a significant number of key social theorists have made it a central feature of their current work.[2]

---

[1] There are numerous fascinating books on the subject of time and culture. Reference to a small selection of these is therefore inevitably arbitrary. The following nevertheless are reasonably representative examples: Eliade (1949/1954); Dunne (1973); Bourdieu (1979); Le Goff (1980); Kern (1983).

[2] For example, Serres (1982/1995), Virilio (1991*a*, 1995*a*), Castells (1996), Melucci (1996), and Bauman (1998) have incorporated chapters on time in some of their current publications. This

In this part of the introductory chapter we want to make explicit the temporal underpinnings of modernity and management in industrial society. We want to show modernity with reference to its very unique social relations, structures, and institutions of time. As a result, we discuss modernity with reference to four Cs: the creation of time to human design (C1), the commodification of time (C2), the control of time (C3), and the colonization with and of time (C4).

C1. Creation of Time to Human Design

To understand the contemporary role of time in management requires that we appreciate some of the backcloth against which it has developed. Our first task is to consider the change from social life embedded in the earth's rhythmicity to social organization around the human creation of clock time, the shift from time in things and processes to a decontextualized time where one hour is the same irrespective of whether it is summer or winter in Los Angeles, Reykjavik, or Cape Town. This means focusing on abstraction, decontextualization, and rationalization as processes that underpin the project of modernization.

Clock time has a number of features that are fundamentally different from the temporal processes of nature: where nature's rhythmic cycles are marked by variance, the hourly cycle of the clock is invariable and precise. Where each rhythmic return in and of nature is simultaneously a context-dependent renewal, the return of the same hour of clock time is independent from context and content. Where animals and plants have time encoded in their being/becoming, the time expressed by the clock is external to and abstracted from the processes it measures. This means that the kind of time that is encoded in the clock is very different from the cosmic, planetary, and terrestrial times upon which it is based and which it is to measure.

Difficulties clearly arise when the invariable measure is imposed as the norm on highly context-dependent, rhythmic, and variable situations and processes. Thus, for example, we know that not all working time is the same: night-time is different from daytime, weekends and festive days are different from weekdays. The idea of working 'unsocial hours' acknowledges that there are significant differences in the apparently neutral working hours, and many a strike and labour dispute has arisen over this issue: while all hours are the same for machines, this is not the case for people. Furthermore, the length of working

literature is growing fast across the full range of social-science disciplines. Social theorists who have taken an earlier lead include: Moore (1963); Sorokin (1964); Hägerstrand (1975); Carlstein *et al.* (1978); Giddens (1979, 1981); Zerubavel (1979*a*, 1981, 1985); Thrift (1981, 1988); Clark (1982); Jaques (1982); Kern (1983); Ingold (1986); Melbin (1987); Rifkin (1987); Young (1988); Young and Schuller (1988); Harvey (1989); Nowotny (1989/1994); Adam (1990, 1995); Hassard (1990); Elias (1992); Lash and Urry (1994); Urry (1995, 2000). Their work in turn is rooted in the classical contributions by the founders of the major social-science perspectives: Marx (1857/1973, 1867/1976); Weber (1904–5/1989); Durkheim (1915); Mead (1932/1980); Schutz (1971).

day matters, because our bodies are rhythmically organized and dependent on periods of rest and recuperation.[3] Like other organisms, we are tuned to the diurnal and seasonal rhythms of our earth. These rhythms constitute the silent pulse of earthly being.

There is widespread agreement amongst social scientists[4] that the partitioning and structuring of the day into decontextualized segments and stretches of time were first introduced and perfected in the numerous monasteries of medieval Europe. Weber (1904–5) elaborated the link in *The Protestant Ethic and the Spirit of Capitalism*, where he made the connection to a range of monastic orders, including the Benedictines, the monks of Cluny, the Cistercians, and the Jesuits. He argued (1904–5/1989: 118, 154) that the purpose of such rationalized conduct was to overcome the natural state: the strict time discipline was to free monks from their dependence on impulses and the world of nature. It trained them objectively as workers in the service of God and with it ensured the salvation of their souls. Gradually, Weber suggested, this concern for rational action and proper time keeping spilled over into the countryside and the marketplace, until, by the end of the fourteenth century, it became a duty, an integral part of Protestant righteous conduct. The negative time discipline of preventing any 'waste of time' was fused with the more active one of intensifying efforts—that is, with the move towards maximum speed and efficiency (Foucault 1979: 154).

Western and Westernized societies have adopted this reified, abstracted time and its rationalized control as a social, economic, and educational strategy. In the sixth century, when the Benedictine monks first introduced fixed and preset times for each of their activities, this was a revolutionary practice. Today it is neither questioned as a practice nor doubted as a principle: it is simply taken for granted. It has become the 'natural state' for the Western way of life and its organizations. As such, it forms part of the deep structure from which management theory and practice have arisen.

Clock time had been gradually adopted worldwide, but not until the end of the nineteenth century was it imposed across the globe as standard time. Standard time brought to an end the myriad of local times and dates used by the peoples of the world. During the early part of the nineteenth century travellers moving from the east to the west coast of the United States, for example, encountered different local times in every town they went through until, after a lengthy and complex process, in 1883 the US railroads inaugurated a uniform time (Bartky 2000). By 1884 Greenwich was installed as the zero meridian and the earth divided into twenty-four equal zones, each one hour apart. Though it took many years for this standard time to be adopted worldwide, its establishment constituted the beginning of the *global day*, a day made up of the same disembedded twelve hours irrespective of context and number of daylight hours.

---

[3] Summaries of the extensive research on shift work, fatigue, and accidents are cited in Luce (1973) and Moore-Ede (1993).

[4] From Weber (1904–5/1989) to Mumford (1934/1955), Foucault (1979), Le Goff (1980), and Zerubavel (1981).

Closely associated with the globalization of the day is the development of world time, a globally synchronized, unified time. At 10.00 a.m., 1 July 1913, the Eiffel Tower transmitted the first time signal across the globe. Wireless signals travelling at the speed of light displaced local times and established one time for all people on this earth. The year 1913 marked the beginning of *world time* (Luhmann 1982: 289–324; Kern 1983). The institution of world time became an essential material precondition for the global network of trade, finance, transport, and communication. Today, it underpins the daily operations, cooperations, transactions, and management of local businesses, global organizations, and transnational corporations.

This global structuring with the aid of a time created to human design has to be differentiated from the globalization of industrial time and its associated economic values as an unquestioned norm. In the latter case it is the time values and the social relations of industrial time that are being *imposed* as well as *adopted* on a worldwide basis. To be 'modern' and 'progressive' means to embrace the industrial approach to time. Towards the latter part of the nineteenth century, for example, Japan (Nishimoto 1997) and Russia (Bauman 1998) proceeded to 'Westernize' their social relations of time. The political leaders of both societies considered this to be a prerequisite to becoming fully-fledged industrial nations. They realized that there was a heavy economic and political price to be paid for any deviance from the industrial norm.

The fact that clock time, world time, standard time, and time zones have become predominant vastly increases the difficulty of recognizing the role this created time plays in everyday life. Other temporal principles fade into the background. They become invisible. Clock time acts as a lens through which social relations and structures are refracted. It affects how industrial societies define and regulate the temporal structures of socio-economic life. It influences how businesses, organizations, and transnational corporations are managed.

C2. Commodification of Time

Time is money. This unquestioned assumption permeates contemporary Westernized economic activity and its management. For this belief to be internalized as a central economic fact of management, two preconditions had to be fulfilled: the sin of usury had to be transformed into a positive economic principle and production had to shift from use value to abstract exchange value.

In his book *Time, Work and Culture in the Middle Ages* (1980) Le Goff writes on the problem of usury and time. He quotes a text from the twelfth century that lays out clearly the Christian position on trading with time.

The usurer acts in contravention to universal law, because he sells time, which is the common possession of all creatures. Augustine says that every creature is obliged to give of itself: the sun is obliged to give of itself in order to shine; in the same way, the earth is obliged to give all that it can produce, as is the water. But nothing gives of itself in a way more in conformity with nature than time. Like it or not, everything has time. Since therefore the usurer sells what necessarily belongs to all creatures, he injures all creatures in general, even stones. Thus, even if men remain silent in the face of usurers, the stones would cry out if they could, and this is why the church prosecutes usury. This is why it was especially against the usurers that God said: 'When I take possession of time, when time is in my hands so that no usurer can sell it, then I will judge in accord with justice.' (G. d'Auxerre, 1160–1229, Summa aurea, III. 21; quoted in Le Goff 1980: 289–90 n. 2)

At the end of the thirteenth century the author of the *Tabula exemplorum* wrote: 'Since usurers sell nothing other than the hope of money, that is, time, they are selling the day and the night. But the day is the time of light and the night the time of rest. Therefore they are selling eternal light and rest.' (quoted in Le Goff 1980: 290 n. 2). From this Christian perspective, the trade in time was theft because it was trade in something that cannot belong to individuals, hence the charge of usury. As long as the notion of earnings on time was rejected outright, capitalism and the money economy could not develop (Le Goff 1980: 29–30). The commodification of time therefore relates to a shift from understanding the time–money relation as the sin of usury to viewing it as central to a virtuous, rational action in the service of God.

Interest and credit had been known and documented since 3,000 years BC in Babylonia and societies have taken a socio-moral and religious stance on the matter. Interest and credit, moreover, are always indicative of a specific relationship to time and the future. In 1311 the Council of Vienna still confirmed the taking of interest as a sin. Only in the late Middle Ages have historians identified a noticeable change of heart in the Church's position.[5] This, they suggest, opened the door for the huge banking systems of the merchants of the cities of northern Italy in which time as interest soon became a fact of economic life. With the religious acceptance of interest achieved by default, and the Protestants' ascetic pursuit of profit secularized, the transformation of time from sacred gift to secular object of trade was secured. Clock time, the created time to human design, was essential to this change in value and practice.

Equally important was the change from an emphasis on use value to the utilization of time as abstract exchange value. All the endlessly different products of work have different use values, which are always context and situation specific, as is clearly the case with, for example, the use value of a table, a coat, an operation, and a pension plan. However, when we want to exchange something for money, a third value has to be introduced to mediate between the two. Unlike the use value, which is context and situation specific, this mediating exchange value has to be context independent. The common, decontextualized value by which products, tasks, and services can be evaluated and exchanged is time. Not the variable time of seasons, ageing, growth and decay, joy and pain,

---

[5] See particularly the work of Le Goff (1980) and Wendorff (1980, 1991).

but the invariable, abstract time of the clock where one hour is the same irrespective of context and emotion. Only the quantitative, divisible time of the clock is translatable into money. Only in this decontextualized form, as Marx (1857/1973: 140–3) showed, can time become commodified, on the one hand, and an integral component of production, on the other. In Marx's analysis, therefore, clock time is the very expression of commodified time.[6] That is to say, the use of time as an abstract exchange value is possible only on the basis of 'empty time', a time separated from content and context, disembodied from events. Only as an abstract, standardized unit can time become a medium for exchange and a neutral value in the calculation of efficiency and profit.

Not all time in management, however, is of this kind. Beyond this specific human construction, time is marked by qualitative variation. It is lived and experienced in widely differing ways. Periods of high stress are different from times when routines dominate, times of economic growth are different from loss-making periods. Furthermore, unlike clock time, the time of life and social existence is temporal—that is, marked by change, transience, development. It is rooted in birth and death, growth and decay. It is the past and future gathered up in the present. It is origin and potential.

Money, however, has a cluster of characteristics that differentiate it from this social time. It is cumulative—money begets money. It is non-ageing and non-decaying. It is universally applicable and exchangeable. Despite the time-is-money equation, however, time is not like money. Time passes outside our control while money can be consumed at an intentional pace or it can be left to grow. For people the accumulation of days and years means ageing, growing older and therefore closer to death, while the accumulation of money means growth of wealth—that is, growth that potentially could continue indefinitely. As a constitutive dimension of our lives, time is lived, generated, and known. As a resource, it is used and allocated. As a commodity, it is exchanged for money on the labour market. Unlike money, however, time cannot be externally stored or accumulated. Whilst money stands in a direct quantitative relation to value—the more the better—this is clearly not the case with time, otherwise the time of prisoners would have to be accorded maximum value.

The economy is, however, traditionally conceived of in terms of an endless circular flow of money: from firm to workers to goods and services back to firms, with the accumulated surplus needing to be reinvested back into the system. This perpetual flow of money is the economic equivalent of Newtonian particles in motion: abstract, decontextualized, detemporalized. In both the Newtonian science and the economic perspective the physical environment is external to—that is, excluded from—the conception. While money may be endlessly circulating and growing, however, each transformation in the physical

[6] On the issue of commodified time, see also Giddens (1981: 118–20, 130–5), Harvey (1989), and Ingold (1995).

world involves a one-way direction of energy and information exchange, where, once transformed, the resources can no longer be used for the same work in the next round of exchanges: the petrol used for driving a car is dissipated into the environment as pollution; after their use, commodities end up as waste on the rubbish dump. Thus, the economic exchange of money may be conceived in abstraction but the economy operates in socio-natural environments. This means, management too is situated. It is always embedded and contextual, subject to entropy, unequal demands, relations of power, and econo-political (not just individual) interests at the social level. As a social activity, management operates with a complexity of different times and in multiple time frames where the context-specific timing and tempo of interactions and transactions matter. The move between those times is achieved without giving thought to the matter. The weaving in and out of different forms of time is an accomplishment that tends not to form part of the explicit repertoire of management tools. Instead it is sourced from a deeply sedimented stock of socially constituted, taken-for-granted knowledge.

Yet, despite the obvious diversity of time, the assumption that time is money underpins and dominates management theory and practice. From this economic perspective on time there arise for management a number of pertinent consequences: when time is money, then the faster something moves through the system the better it is for business. Accordingly, for management, efficiency and profitability are tied to speed. When time is money, time compression and rationalization schemes become management priorities. Taylorism, Fordism, flexibilization, and just-in-time production have been logical developments arising from this foundational premises. When time is money, any unused time is money wasted, hence the move towards non-stop production and shift work, first identified by Marx in 1867, and ultimately the 24/7 society (24 hours, 7 days a week). When time is money, any time that does not easily translate into money comes into conflict with the dominant relation to time—for example, family time, caring time, the intense periods of love and creativity, seasonal variations, differences in personal experience. Their discord in the time economy of money needs to be managed and minimized. Any time that is not exchangeable for money either falls outside the economic framework of evaluation or is filtered through that way of thinking about and evaluating the world.

Finally, 'time is money' means that capital has a built-in clock that is constantly ticking away. This inevitably leads to careful calculations with respect to the time that equipment is used, labour is paid for, materials spend in warehouses before they are used in the production process, and goods are stored and in transit and/or lie on shelves before they are sold. From such economic time calculations it is a short step to the need to control time as a managerial tool for the achievement of desired ends: economic, scientific, and political.

C3. Control of Time

With its commodification, time has become a scarce resource and its control a central task for management. This involves being faster than competitors, on the one hand, and shortening the time per operation and speeding up the turnover of resources, on the other. Times when nothing happens—breaks and pauses, waiting and rest periods—are considered unproductive, wasteful, lost opportunities that need to be eliminated or at least minimized. Time compression and intensification of processes are attractive means for management to increase efficiency.

This argument was first presented by Marx (1867) in '*Capital*', volume I, where he argued that, in a context of competition, commodified labour time as abstract exchange value had to be intensified in order for employers to stay competitive and profitable. Competition, he proposed, will compel employers to intensify the energy expended by workers.

It imposes on the worker an increased expenditure of labour within time which remains constant, a heightened tension of labour-power, a closer filling-up of the pores of the working day, i.e. a condensation of labour, to a degree which can only be attained within the limits of the shortened working day. This compression of the greater mass of labour into a given period now counts for what it really is, namely an increase in the quantity of labour. In addition, to the measure of its 'extensive magnitude', labour-time now acquires a measure of its intensity, or degree of density. The denser hour of the 10-hour working day contains more labour, i.e. expended labour power, than the more porous hour of the 12-hour working day.   (Marx 1867/1976: 540)

The means by which this intensification is to be achieved are manifold and can involve managerial approaches focused on the use of machinery, on the one hand, and the rationalization, mechanization, and reorganization of labour, on the other. All in turn are underpinned by a quantitative approach to time. One of the rationales for the industrial/izing societies' approach to time compression is thus to be sought in the quantification, decontextualization, rationalization, and commodification of time and in the calculation of time in relation to money, efficiency, competition, and profit.

The management of this speeding-up, as we show in this book, has been achieved by increasing activity within the same unit of time (introduction of machines and the intensification of labour—its compression) and/or by reorganizing the sequence and ordering of activities (Taylorism and Fordism). The control of time, however, is not exhausted by time compression. It includes in addition the slowing-down of processes, the rearrangement of past, present, and future, the reordering of sequence, the transformation of rhythmicity into a rationalized beat, the more effective use of peaks and troughs, and the elimination and externalization of all unproductive times from the process.[7]

---

[7] On the processes of time control, see Nishimoto (1999), as well as Noss, Nishimoto, and Bell and Tuckman, this volume.

Castells (1996: 439) therefore argues that time is not just compressed but processed. Clearly, both compression and processing are advances in the control of time.

Electronically constituted instantaneity is a logical extension of the modernist time project of creation, commodification, control, and colonization. It constitutes the holy grail of the quest for increasing speed: compression down to point zero. It brings with it powers that had previously been the preserve of god(s): the supernatural power to be everywhere at once and nowhere in particular.[8] The physical constraints of bodies in space are transcended by twentieth-century developments in transmission. Movement of information has been dematerialized. There is a paradox here that has been widely commented on: a precondition to mobility in cyberspace is the immobility of embodied beings: interaction can take place on a global level without participants having to leave their offices. Such structural relations and processes, which arise from the control of time, tend to be beyond the control of those involved, since the combination of instantaneity of communication with simultaneity of networked relations no longer functions to the principles of clock time and mechanical interaction. 'The new level of interconnectivity', as Poster (1990: 3) points out, 'heightens the fragility of social networks'. This means, in a context of globally networked electronic communication, that the increase in mastery is accompanied by a decrease in control and the intensification of the temporal logic has paradoxical consequences.[9] Thus the temporal complexity involved needs to be negotiated. This requires additional managerial competencies. At the very least, handling the temporal complexity involves the following: the electronically networked temporality (instantaneity, simultaneity, immediacy, real-time interactions, non-sequential and non-linear discontinuous processes), which is combined with clock time (externalized, invariable, decontextualized, spatial, quantitative, linear, and sequential), which, in turn, is superimposed on the time of living and social processes (embodied, system specific, contextual, irreversible). While some logics and aspects take priority over others, none is completely negated in its displacement. All are mutually implicating at the same time as their meaning and importance are altered.

This extreme speed coupled with multiple, simultaneous, reflexive connections poses management problems at the level of perception, understanding, expectation, and action: it constitutes at all these levels a largely unconquered reality. Social scientists have an important role to play here, elaborating the time connections, showing how the control of time can lead to loss of control, and identifying access points for alternative action. It is here that the sociological problematization of time is highly pertinent to management whose undisputed aim, as we noted above, is to control time.

---

[8] See also Virilio (1991a, 1995a) and Purser, this volume.
[9] For extended arguments on the contradictory logics, see Adam (1990, 1995, 1998) and Castells (1996).

C4. Colonization with and of Time: Past, Present, and Future

There are two sides to the colonization of time: the global imposition of a particular kind of time, on the one hand, and the incursion into the hours of darkness and the time of successors and predecessors, on the other. In the first case, Western clock time and commodified time have been exported across the globe and imposed as the unquestioned and unquestionable standard. This is colonization *with* time, which has been discussed above already. In the second case, night-time and the future are brought under human control. This is colonization *of* time, of which we want to outline some examples here.

First, with the establishment of gas and electricity towards the latter part of the eighteenth century, the night could be colonized, the period of daylight artificially extended to twenty-four hours.[10] Darkness was no longer a barrier to around-the-clock, machine-based production. Night work, shift work, and non-stop consumption are changes in the organization of social time that follow in the wake of these technologies being established. In combination with global electronically networked communications, the subsequent colonization of the night has fundamentally altered the management context: what happens during the hours of the night, in another's working day, in another part of the world, inescapably features in the daily management of transnational corporations and more local companies with global business networks.

Secondly, from its very inception the industrial economy was focused on the future. The future is understood with reference to the threat or benefit it holds for the present. The economy therefore operates in the sphere between present and future with a view to use the future to secure the present. To achieve that task, it borrows from the future to finance the present or it hedges against potential future disasters through saving and insurance. Thus, Giddens suggested in his Reith Lectures that 'Modern capitalism embeds itself into the future by calculating future profit and loss, and thereby risk, as a continuous process' (Giddens 1999: 2). The future is drawn into the activities of the present. Nowotny (1989/1994) conceptualizes those temporal incursions as the 'extended present', as a future that is organized, regulated, tamed, safeguarded, and foreclosed *now*. The following examples can serve to illustrate the argument.

Since the sixteenth century the insurance system has redistributed risk. It makes projections about the future on the basis of a known past and promises to compensate financially future loss in exchange for payments in the present. Whether this economic engagement with the future operates at the private, commercial, or (welfare) state level, it is based on the belief that the future is amenable to human regulation and design in the present. Insurance forms part of the unquestioned context of contemporary management.

---

[10] See the definitive text on this matter by Melbin (1987).

Today most money is made on the speculative market that trades not with goods but with futures and the volatility of small differences between currencies. Financial trading in stocks, futures, and derivatives relies heavily on electronic communication. In combination with its relationship to the future, this exercise in temporal control has extensive effects on companies that largely elude management control. Futures markets trade not in goods but in time alone (Boden 2000). They are bets on future prices of the stock market, currency prices, interest rates, even on the entire stock market indices. The trade in time, which was estimated at $18 trillion for 1999, equals the entire stock of productive fixed capital of the world. There is, however, an important difference between the two kinds of trade—the trade with goods and the trade with futures. While the trade with goods requires economic and financial stability to flourish, the speculation on, and trade with, time requires volatility. The higher the volatility, the greater the quick extractive returns. The difference spells trouble for management irrespective of its precise subject area. While the futures market creates wealth on the basis of volatility, the task for management (whether of goods and services) is the creation of stability.

Thus, we can see how management is actively engaged with the future through a number of economic strategies. In all cases a radical present orientation makes parasitic use of the future. However, in a context of networked instantaneity, the increase in mastery is once more accompanied by loss of control. This loss is due to the massively increased speed, instantaneity, and networked connections. Instantaneity involves real-time processes across the globe coupled with the elimination of linear cause-and-effect relations. This means not only volatility and with it a massive reduction in security, stability, and predictability but also loss of time to reflect and act in the intervening period between cause and effect. 'Throughout the modern era', writes Bauman (1998: 57), we have grown used to the idea that order is tantamount to 'being in control'. Today, he suggests, 'no one seems to be in control. Worse still—it is not clear what "being in control" could, under the circumstances, be like' (Bauman 1998: 58). Unintended consequences create a no man's land beyond design and action with far-reaching consequences for management practice. In a context where control is the undisputed objective, networked instantaneity poses huge challenges. For management, this changed context therefore means new orientations, theories, and practices. Time is at the centre of this change and therefore needs to feature explicitly in the re-vision.

On the basis of the four Cs of industrial time—creation, commodification, control, and colonization—it has been possible to identify some principles and processes of change with their accompanying paradoxes. We have been able to show how the system of temporal coordinates is changing. First, clock time as the dominant, naturalized temporal perspective is undermined by the results of its own logic. The problems of instantaneity, simultaneity, networked connections, and temporal volatility have been superimposed on the linearity of clock time. And clock time in turn, we need to remember, had been overlain on the variable and contextual times of life and nature. The resulting amalgam of contradictory temporal principles constitutes the present temporal context of management.

Secondly, the level of (*a*) time control and (*b*) temporal reach is changing. Again this is not about one system replacing another. Rather, it is about inter-penetration and mutual implication. All the historically established forms of temporal control and reach continue to exist and coexist with the new increased and intensified levels in an often conflictual and paradoxical relation. Thirdly, with transmission technologies operating at the speed of light, speeding up is no longer an option and economic advantage has to be achieved by other means. In other words, being faster than competitors is one economic principle for profit creation that comes to grief when communications technologies reach the speed of light. New means of time control for profit include flexibilization and the creation of simultaneity. There is a need, therefore, to understand the temporality of processes and developments as well as to grasp the implications of those changes. This, however, is not an easy task given that the temporal is largely taken for granted and its complexity does not fit the rationalist eco-nomic paradigm. Once one takes account in management theory and practice of these characteristics, and recognizes the multiple temporalities of both the phenomena and their contexts, the results are unsettling for the management tradition. In so doing, one has changed both the problems and the potential for solutions.

A NOTE ON APPROACHES TO TIME-SENSITIVE RESEARCH IN THE FIELD OF MANAGEMENT

Providing a response to the challenges posed in the previous sections cannot be achieved by narrow specialization. The contributors to this volume, accord-ingly, come from a wide range of academic disciplines that span from business and organization studies, industrial anthropology, industrial relations, history, marketing, and philosophy to sociology. Their research specialisms extend from change management to financial services, human-resource management, marketing, organization theory, strategic management, and social theory. Some authors have published extensively on the subject of time (Adam, Lee and Liebenau, Odih and Knights, Purser, Whipp), others have discovered time as a means to provide novel access to their respective areas of expertise (Bunzel, Hedaa and Törnroos, Keenoy, Koku, Tuckman), while for a number it has been a central feature of their Ph.D. research—currently and in the more distant past (Adam, Bell, Lee, Nishimoto, Odih, Sabelis, Rehn). Despite their considerable academic diversity, however, the contributors to *Making Time* are united in their broad orientation to the subject matter. The cohesion arises from an openness to transdisciplinary exploration, a particular time sensitivity, and a serious engagement with the temporal complexity of social relations and institutional processes.

The origins of this volume reflect these characteristics of diversity and cohesion. Most of the contributors were involved in three academic meetings in 2000 on time and management and two of the three editors were involved in each event: the third 'Time and Management' conference in Palermo hosted by the Istituto Superiore per Imprenditori e Dirigenti di Azienda (ISIDA) (co-organized by Morello, Adam, and Sabelis), the working group on 'Organization, Management and Time' at the European Group for Organization Studies (EGOS) conference in Helsinki (convened by Whipp), and the all-academy symposium on 'Timescapes in Management' at the US Academy of Management conference in Toronto (involving Adam, Purser, and Whipp). It became clear that all the eventual contributors to this volume were trying to do justice to the richness of the temporal features of contemporary organizations and management and seeking to share a more developed language of time. It was their overlapping concerns yet multilateral thinking that provided the impetus for this volume.

The field of management has always drawn on a wide range of disciplinary sources. It is therefore no stranger to transdisciplinary research. Taking time seriously similarly involves an openness to bodies of knowledge in allied academic disciplines and further afield. Since time permeates the entirety of existence, every conceivable discipline has studied the temporal relations appropriate to its sphere of expertise. Given that humans are also living organisms and subject to the rhythms of our planetary system, the time theories of most other disciplines, as we have indicated earlier, are of relevance for understanding the time of institutions, economic activity, and social relations. It is not surprising, therefore, that management scholars concerned with the temporal aspects of their subject matter share an openness towards crossing disciplinary boundaries. This in turn facilitates reflexivity and a more self-conscious approach to one's own disciplinary traditions. Hedaa and Törnroos, for example, bring together the world of myth and the realm of management. In the process they gain an expanded appreciation of mythology, a new perspective on their own sphere of expertise, and a novel explanatory device for managerial processes.

To develop a sensitivity for the temporal dimension of organizational life and social relations means being attentive to what tends to be taken for granted. It means seeing what is normally disattended, what is just below the surface of socio-economic interaction and somewhat opaque. Such sensitivity is extended not only to the subject matter of research but also to theory and method. It is a deeply reflexive process that involves constant checking across domains: observations against theory and underlying assumptions, theory against experience, practice against models. Given the enormous scope for this sensitivity to be developed, it is not surprising that it can take many forms. The chapters by Dirk Bunzel and Tom Keenoy and colleagues are just two of a number of examples that could be cited. As a consultant to the Seaside Hotel, Bunzel almost 'by accident' came across the underlying rhythm of the organization when he was looking for an explanation for what to him, as an outsider, seemed inexplicable. Keenoy and colleagues, in contrast, keep coming at their data from different temporal vantage points, enmeshing their subject matter in a web of encoded and decoded pasts, presents, and futures until the temporal multilayeredness of collective decision making becomes palpable. Wherever and in whichever form it is applied, time sensitivity expands and deepens the analysis.

Finally, the contributors to this volume are united in their engagement with temporal complexity. An explicit focus on time forces us to conceive of management in a much more complex, contextual, and interdependent way than tends to be the case when the temporal dimensions are ignored or merely translated into the x axis on a graph. This is so because time is a multilevel dimension of our lives and a concentration on any one aspect implicates all the others. At the structural level we are concerned with: time frame and point in time; temporality, which encompasses all change processes; tempo, which covers speed and pace; timing and synchronization; duration and its other, which is instantaneity; sequence and its other, which is simultaneity; rhythmicity and past, present, and future. All can be regarded as the interdependent, mutually implicating aspects of time. This temporal complexity is conceptualized by Adam (1998) as a timescape. It encompasses not merely the complexity of temporal features but the inseparable unity of time, space, and matter, and it acknowledges the centrality of context and reflexivity with regard to the researcher's position in the research process. The key structural features of the temporal complexity can be summarized as shown in Box 1.1. This timescape is to be understood as a heuristic, a conceptual schema to aid engagement with temporal complexity. In addition to the multiple structural features, the complexity of time encompasses the historically constituted social diversity, parts of which we have begun to outline above. The contributions to this volume show how this complexity in relation to management is played out and negotiated in the individual and institutional spheres, the private and public sectors, and the socio-cultural, economic, and political levels.

Taking account of the temporal complexity in management has knock-on effects. It suggests the need for changes not only in management practice but also in the social sciences' theoretical and empirical research traditions. Unlike earlier approaches to the study of time in management where quality superseded quantity and social time was considered more appropriate than clock time, the contributors to *Making Time* recognize and embrace the multi-layeredness of organizational time and associated temporal relations. They acknowledge and appreciate the pioneering work that shifted the balance towards a more qualitative understanding. They build on that work but then go beyond it. They understand the multiple structural and social aspects of time in management not as alternatives, not as either/or choices, but in relation to each

Box 1.1. Temporal features of timescape

Time frame	Past	Duration—Instantaneity
Time point	Present	Sequence—Simultaneity
Temporality	Future	Repetition ⇔ Rhythm ⇔ Beat
Tempo		Cause ⇔ Effect ⇔ Time lag
Timing		

other, and they grasp any one in the context of the others. Clearly, not every contributor reconceptualizes his or her field of expertise in its entirety. Taken together, however, the contributions to this volume complement each other. As such, *Making Time* is a re-visionary project that speaks to the field of management as a whole. The following overview outlines how the contributors approach this task.

OVERVIEW OF THE CHAPTERS

Part One offers a variety of theoretical perspectives on the timescapes of management and draws on empirical data to illustrate the theoretical arguments. Under the heading 'Masking Time, Making Time: Rethinking Basic Assumptions', the contributors target conceptual matters and taken-for-granted assumptions and explore their effects on social practices and structures.

In 'Towards a Theory of Timing: Kairology in Business Networks', Laurids Hedaa and Jan-Åke Törnroos argue that managerial thinking fundamentally alters when times and timing, rather than the dominant fixed clock time, are taken into account. Through the distinction between Chronos and Kairos they view managerial processes as 'streams of events' and argue that a new approach to time is needed to develop an eye for the unexpected. Such temporal sensitivity, they argue, is a pertinent management strategy for company survival.

Christian Noss focuses on the time dimension in change management. In his chapter 'Taking Time Seriously: Organizational Change, Flexibility, and the Present', Noss suggests that the challenges faced by contemporary management are primarily phenomena of the present, while the strategies for dealing with them are past and future oriented, thus incapable of dealing with crises, surprises, and discontinuities. Accordingly, the author argues the need for a shift in managerial emphasis from the past and future to the dynamic present.

Pamela Odih and David Knights locate temporal perspectives in current marketing theory and argue for an approach to time that transcends the dominant linear perspective. In 'Now's the Time! Consumption and Time (Space) Disruptions in Postmodern Virtual Worlds' the authors work with a multilayered view of time, linking the management world of consumption and distribution to processes of power, identity, and knowledge.

'Time and Management as a Morality Tale, or "What's Wrong with Linear Time, Damn It?"' offers a philosophical perspective on contemporary approaches to time in management. In this chapter Alf Rehn identifies the implicit moral project that underpins much of the time-based research in the management field. While Rehn himself may be chasing a chimera—'the possibility of an epistemology without an ethics'—his chapter gives much food for thought when he argues the need for researchers to make their disposition known instead of masking their analysis as dispassionate, objective study.

In Part Two the relationship between theory and practice is reversed. Here the empirical data are foregrounded against the backcloth of theory. Emphasis is on 'Temporal Strategies in a Rapidly Changing World'. Information and communications technologies feature heavily, but by no means exclusively in these chapters.

Ida Sabelis heads off this section with a report on research conducted in the Netherlands on top managers' time strategies. In 'Hidden Causes for Unknown Losses: Time Compression in Management' the author addresses the issue of temporal compression. In this chapter Sabelis is concerned to produce a layered view on 'what is happening' in organizations when time becomes the explicit focus of attention. Typically this chapter shows how 'compression' (only thinkable from a rational view on time) causes paradoxical effects: enhancing efficiency ('saving time'), on the one hand, *and* acceleration ('producing pressure and stress'), on the other.

With the next chapter we move from individual managers' strategies to Nishimoto Ikuko's discussion of an entire industry's temporal strategy in the pursuit of increasing profits. Nishimoto's historical analysis focuses on the Japanese automotive industry and shows that the just-in-time (JIT) system of production has not arisen from something deep in the Japanese character but has to be understood, instead, as an explicit economic strategy in which time plays a central role. In 'Cooperation Engineered: Efficiency in the "Just-in-Time" System' the author argues for a more complex understanding of the socio-economic and sociocultural processes involved in the development of corporate strategies in an economic context of global competition.

While information and communications technologies play a crucial role in the individual and corporate strategies discussed in the first two chapters of this part, they become the primary focus of attention in the chapters that follow. In 'Hanging on the Telephone: Temporal Flexibility and the Accessible Worker', Emma Bell and Alan Tuckman take time to the heart of organization theory and show how social time affects the definition of the employment relationship. Using data from ethnographic research in the UK chemical industry, they describe the consequences of temporal irregularity, as organizations demand increased flexibility from employees. They argue that technology does not liberate human labour from clock time but instead enables management to overcome spatial boundaries and achieve more effective surveillance and control.

The literature on time compression and rationalization in work and production processes forms the backcloth against which Heijin Lee and Jonathan Liebenau develop their analysis of management in the context of new information and communication technologies (ICTs). In their chapter entitled 'A New Time Discipline: Managing Virtual Work Environments' the authors show how ICT has enabled new working patterns such as teleworking, virtual teams, and virtual organizations and they address the time discipline, control, and flexibility, on the one hand, and the important issue of trust, on the other.

In 'The Use of Time by Management and Consumers: An Analysis of the Computer Industry' Paul Sergius Koku explores organizational marketing strategies around announcing and pre-announcing new products and their effects. The chapter is concerned with the issue of timing as a means of gaining a strategic marketing advantage for the company. The research shows that timing of pre/announcements affects consumers and competitors in different ways. Timing, Koku argues, therefore needs to become an explicit dimension of any effective marketing strategy.

The contributors to Part Three, 'The Temporal Implications of Alternative Approaches to Management', are each in quite different ways breaking the boundaries of social-science conventions, using time to find alternative ways of doing management research. Here it is not just the subject matter that gets more complex; these authors allow their respective subject matters to penetrate deep into the ways they do and write their theoretical and empirical research.

Ronald E. Purser explores and critically evaluates the so-called 'real-time' perspective associated with the new media of instantaneous digital communications. Drawing on the work of French postmodernist theorist Paul Virilio, the chapter examines, as well as makes speculations about, the cultural implications of digital technologies. In 'Contested Presents: Critical Perspectives on "Real Time" Management' Purser criticizes the now popularized notion of 'real-time' technology management for its narrow technological determinism and instrumental disregard for lived time and considers alternative topographies of time that involve the development of a participatory consciousness.

Drawing on an ethnographic account of an Australian hotel, Dirk Bunzel demonstrates how, under conditions of a coexistence of multiple temporal frames, members of the organization symbolically create a shared sense of simultaneity. In 'The Rhythm of the Organization: Simultaneity, Identity, and Discipline in an Australian Coastal Hotel', Bunzel shows how the rhythm of the organization represents a fundamental aspect of organizational identity. On the basis of his findings he concludes that the concept of rhythmicity can centrally inform future research in the intra- and inter-organizational domain.

Tom Keenoy, Cliff Oswick, Peter Anthony, David Grant, and Iain Mangham, finally, investigate the role of emotion in seemingly rational processes of decision making in a UK university context. Against the background of the decision-making literature, 'Interpretative Times: The Timescape of Decision Making' illustrates the concept of timescapes by showing how, over time, irrational aspects of the decision-making process are rationalized through processes of reconstruction of 'what really happened'. Giving us various aspects and perspectives on the discursive strategies involved, the authors show how the reconstructed past in the rationalized present is influenced by several layers of mutually implicating time experience.

The overall aim of this collection is a creative one: to bring together scholars of management and time in a joint venture. Consequently, this chapter has been at pains to recognize both the mutual implications of time and management and the largely separate previous efforts made by students from each domain. Building on work from each tradition, we argue that to understand management in temporal terms calls for the recognition not only of the historical forces that gave rise to it but equally of the culturally rooted character of time and management. The opportunity arises, therefore, for all concerned not to take time for granted but to question our in-built assumptions about time within management. By taking seriously the diversity of social relations and institutions of time and management we can move beyond a preoccupation with binary notions of clock and social time. Furthermore, addressing the range of temporal forms found in management may be a vital step towards coping with time in an era of technological interconnection. The authors of the following chapters supply some initial examples of how to carry forward this approach to the subject of time and management.

MASKING TIME, MAKING TIME: RETHINKING BASIC ASSUMPTIONS

Towards a Theory of Timing: Kairology in Business Networks

Laurids Hedaa and Jan-Åke Törnroos

INTRODUCTION

The concept of Kairology is derived from the ancient Greek, but largely unknown, god Kairos, who was assumed to be in control of the right moment, or god of the more contemporary notion of Timing. This chapter is an essay about new avenues for the basis of managerial thinking and theories with a temporal focus. The chapter looks specifically at the role of time and timing through event analysis in management theory. First, the impact of change and stability on models and theories in management are developed. Secondly, the role of temporality, change aspects, and timing related to the contemporary business environment is highlighted. Thirdly, a perspective of new directions of managerial thinking with a temporal focus is developed. Fourthly, proposals are made for a new research strategy and managerial practice. *Kairology* is a term denoting the theory of appropriate timing for action in differentiated managerial situations and contexts. Traditional management theory deals with autonomous actors working in a world of organizational routines. A novel perspective should be concerned with *heteronomous* actors in a world of complexity and surprises embedded in a network of interdependencies. If this is the case, we need a new management theory. Managers do in fact react to surprises as new opportunities or threats. They never do this alone; they always discuss, negotiate, or experiment with new variations of actions within relevant time space through interaction. Interaction moves from heteronomy, not to full autonomy, but rather to a state of *homonomy* (a neologism for the middle between autonomy and heteronomy, where relevant partners through interaction have arrived to a sort of common understanding for acceptable behaviour—that is, shared rules or norms). We can say that events control man, not the other way around, as general managerial thinking seems to propose. The essence of *timing* deals with this fact. When managers are timing correctly, they can handle or understand events and event trajectories. But appropriate timing may not be understood a priori, but only recognized a posteriori. Event analysis and timing of acts in a stream of events can be used as a possible strategy for partial control of company destiny (a predetermined course of events often held to be an irresistible power or agency).

It is almost trivial to point to the fact of increasing turbulence in our time. Turbulence within the environment is increasing, both because of the growing pace of technological, social, and other developments, and because of the growing interdependence of organizations across sectors, the positive feedback from whose actions can generate instability (Child and Kieser 1981). It is a characteristic of industrial, mature societies, that differentiation and, hence, interdependence increase. It is increasingly meaningless to talk about individual, autonomous actors who decide and act as passive recipients. Rather we should realize that actors are dependent or interdependent, limited or stimulated by other actors in networks creating opportunities and impediments for action. 'Actors are not fully in control of the activities that can satisfy their interests, but find some of those activities partially or wholly under the control of other actors' (Coleman 1990). To produce even a simple final good requires the participation of numerous organizations throughout the value chain, or, more precisely, the value net—each contributing with a decreasing fraction of the value-creating process, as increasing differentiation and specialization, emphasizing core competencies, continue to take place. We witness:

- a small world getting smaller as enabling technologies reduce the friction of time and space;
- national and industrial deregulation breaking down protective walls;
- globalization leading to increasing competition;
- the emergence of new regional markets;
- new demands for ever higher quality, lower prices, and faster deliveries;
- shorter product life cycles and faster time to market;
- radical changes—discontinuities—surprises.

(See e.g. Ohmae 1995; Castells 1996; Dicken 1998.)

In response to these new environmental forces affecting the business firm, new objectives and focuses of attention have emerged, for example:

- shareholder value;
- stakeholder value;
- human capital utilization;
- intellectual capital measurements and management;
- network capital creation;
- social responsibilities and ethics;
- environmental concerns.

And a plethora of new management fads, buzzwords, and three-letter acronyms swarm the business world: TQM, QFD, BPR, TBM, TPM, KSF, EVA, SCM, KAM, CRM, PPM, HRM, JIT, ABC, SBU, MBO, USP, TBC...

New and more environmental complexities, new and more managerial concerns, new and more management technologies, and faster pace contribute to managers' loss of control. Increasingly they lose autonomy and become heteronomous actors, and increasingly success becomes a function of good luck and timing when managers decide for and act in an unpredictable and fast-moving future. Or, in the words of Toffler (1970): there are many possible futures. Based on the foregoing, the role of time and timing in management and marketing in business networks forms the contextual perspective in this chapter. It is divided into the following sections.

First, we look into the environment where firms operate and relate this as an exposition into the frames of reference in management theory. The second section deals with the time concept and especially timing from a network perspective. Actor networks and especially the notion of event networks and the role of timing are presented in this section. The third section presents a managerial model, which treats timing and outcomes from both a chronological and an intentional time perspective. The model frames the discussion about time, event networks, and timing into a theoretical whole. The fourth section of the chapter summarizes the discussion and presents possible research strategies and practical managerial implications using timing and event networks as points of departure.

TIME, STABILITY, AND CHANGE IN EVENT NETWORKS

Time-based competition (TBC) is a buzzword in management aiming at creating competitive advantages through the shortening of lead times. Time is viewed from this perspective mainly as being chronological or absolute. Another view is the intentional or kairological view of time, which may also inform strategy and become a time-based competitive tool (see Box 2.1). Chung exemplifies this with the Honda–Yamaha war and how Honda was the winner through better commitment and performance of its labour force. He states that:

There are two dimensions of time: Succession and Intention. Issues in lead-time reduction mainly deal with the measurement of time and therefore belong to the dimension of succession. While it is important to reduce lead-times, it is equally (if not more) important to address the intentional dimension of time. After all, a strong winning desire and an unyielding fighting spirit are what it takes to compete successfully.   (Chung 1999: 300)

Time is also always related to space. What takes place in time is having a spatial implication (existence in real world or in the mindsets of humans). What is existing in space is also affecting and relating to time and temporal processes.

Box 2.1. Chronos and Kairos

The ancient Greeks recognized two concepts of time, symbolized by the two gods: Chronos and Kairos. Chronos was father of the Horae and of the mighty god Zeus. He represents linear, quantitative, and all-consuming time. He is in control of the past, present, and future. He ensures the orderly experience of life, and the appearance of things, making them look newer or older. From Chronos comes chronology, defined as the science that deals with measuring time by regular divisions and that assigns to events their proper dates.

Kairos was the youngest son of Zeus (Kelman 1969). He was young, with winged feet, and, most distinctly, has a long forelock in the midst of shorter hair. This forelock was symbolic of the 'right time' that must be seized before it 'flew' away. The Greeks used the word to give sense of a decisive point or place in time. It informed the 'best choice' of a particular time (Montesano 1995: 169). Kairos points to the significance of both time and the particular place in which an event occurs—the chronotype, the intersection of time and place. Kairotic moments potentially destabilize our belief system (Bakhtin 1981).

Richard Onians (1951/1973) has mentioned that besides 'the right time' or 'timeliness', Kairos also carries a spatial metaphor, that of a critical opening. The earliest Greek uses of the term, in both archery and weaving, referred to a 'a penetrable opening, an aperture', through which an arrow or a shuttle must pass. Dale L. Sullivan (1992) refers to this as a window of opportunity. The kind of truth that comes through this 'window' is that which is 'unveiled' or revealed, not one that lends itself easily to analysis and study. Or, as Paul Tillich (1963) notes, the 'right time' cannot be predicted: 'The holy spirit blows where it will.'

According to Carolyn Miller (1994), Kairos tells us to look for the particular opportunity in a given moment, to find—or construct—an opening in the here and now, in order to achieve something there and then. Pointing as it does to the ways that situations change over time, to relationships between past and future, to the ways that one moment differs from the next, Kairos seems to be a natural tool for examining discourse that emphasizes change, development, progress. Chronos splits time into past–present–future, whereas Kairos is positioned between 'not yet' and 'never more'.

'Space and time should be simultaneously considered in developing and implementing any competitive strategy' (Chung 1999: 307).

Time also relates to different *time scales* (Zaheer *et al.* 1999). The term strategy usually means to look ahead and towards a changing competitive position in time–space of a company. Corporate strategy is intentional in this sense. *Time lag* takes the perspective of cause–effect dimensions looking at time as separating two connected events in a specific social setting. Reaction time or 'latent periods' are other connotations of time lags. This can be understood by using Clark's notion that time-lag-oriented research has 'the intention to discover the ways in which effects emerge at some time after the initial intervention' (Clark 1985: 39). In event-network terms, the events affecting networks can materialize and become real after a time lag from where a prior connected event has been created. Defining and understanding the 'root cause' are often triggering acts.

Business networks are also influenced by time lags because of the existence of reaction times of different kinds (delays in decision making and deliveries of goods and information, political decisions, and regulations). *Waiting costs* for network actors, caused by delayed solutions, are the consequence. In business-networks research, this materializes, for example, in the form of so-called black holes (Hedaa 1999). Black holes are found where willing and able actors cannot act because of unfavourable opportunity structures in a network.

In this chapter we deal with another time-based issue, which is *timing*. One definition of timing is 'selection or the ability to select for maximum effect of the precise moment for beginning or doing something' (*Webster's* 1993). Timing is a situational time concept, which relates to a discernible event in a stream of other events in time–space in order to achieve intentional outcomes (for example, profits in the future). In a network context, timing is defined by us as *confluent event trajectories in a network of interrelated events*. Timing can have both chronological and intentional contents (or more precisely a continuum with both absolute and intentional meanings) (Chung 1999). We base our view of time as events appearing in time–space (Hedaa and Törnroos 1997). The event concept is used here as a way to look at time as event streams in business networks. The contextual element is framing the way temporality, and spatiality, come to terms in this setting (Hedaa and Törnroos 1997; Chung 1999).

Business networks are defined as sets of connected exchange relationships between (more than two) business actors. Both stability and change characterize business networks (Ford 1990; Möller and Wilson 1995). In business markets firms are developing business relationships with specific actors in the upstream as well as the downstream of activities in the value chain or net. Business relationships are often of long-term nature. This does not mean that they are everlasting or do not change. Mutual adaptations and investments in relationships occur continuously. Interdependence creates a need for individual network partners (or actors) to change and adapt in relation to other partners. Actors, activities, and resources are involved in exchange from an actor-network perspective (Håkansson and Snehota 1995).

We have defined events as 'an outcome of acts or changes caused by man or nature' (Hedaa and Törnroos 1997: 6). Events are temporally specific outcomes of performed acts. *Event networks* are time-based connected event relationships. Event networks (EvNs) have the following characteristics.

- The smallest unit of analysis is an event dyad (two interrelated events).
- An event is always an outcome of human acts or caused by nature.
- Actors (or nature) are mediators of events.
- Events are always contingent on the existence of some antecedent events.
- Objectively, event networks have no beginnings and no endings.

- Seemingly similar events are differentiated by their position in time and space and through their loadedness.
- Events may be loaded by the past or the future, and/or by the source or the affected objects (e.g. actor loaded).

EvNs may appear as streams of interconnected events (event trajectories). Intentional timing is about matching the firm's position for emergent event trajectories in intelligent competition with other firms. In the industrial-network approach, the firm is basing its existence and market relationships on doing business with other firms in the form of actor networks. Occasional, accidental, and random processes are also at play in the intertwined, global economy, where firms with limited network horizons act in networks of relationships with other firms, suppliers, customers, and competitors.

How does management theory address these issues? In this chapter we try to pinpoint some time-related issues in order to look at more process-oriented aspects of management theory.

STABILITY AND CHANGE IN MANAGEMENT THEORY

The essential driver of management is performance, to achieve objectives, to get results through and with other people. Usually, people's capabilities and motivation to do a certain job explain performance. The means to get the right quality of workers for a task are recruitment, training, and appropriate deployment of sanctions. In a stable and therefore predictable world, it is possible for management to establish routines and control that the workers follow instructions. The task is solved by the coordination and integration of differentiated specializations of constituent human and physical performative elements. By repeating activities, workers and management move down the learning curve and increase effectiveness and efficiency in performance—that is, increasing output consistency and quality at decreasing costs. The opportunity structure is static and well defined, and timing is obtained through planning, scheduling, and organization.

People obtain procedural knowledge—canonical and non-canonical practice (Brown and Duguid 1991)—and they are involved in relationship learning, where incremental changes in roles, authority, communications channels, information technologies, standard operational procedures, and shared vocabularies take place (March *et al.* 1996). Deviations from standard or performance expectations drive the people-to-task relationship towards equilibrium, steady states (Bertalanffy 1950), and homeostasis (Katz and Kahn 1966) through negative feedback. This is the world of Chronos, where ex-ante prescriptions and normative theories thrive.

This closed-system approach to organization and management comes under attack when a system opens up to the environment and gets involved with external interaction processes to obtain input to the system and to dispose of its output. The stable and controllable opportunity structure becomes dynamic and partly unpredictable. Organizations confront non-routine events and experience surprises. Resource dependency (Pfeffer and Salancik 1978) represents particular problems for organizations in high velocity environments, where 'changes in demand, competition and technology are so rapid and discontinuous that information is often inaccurate, unavailable, or obsolete' (Eisenhardt and Bourgeois 1988: 816). The opportunity structure obtains dynamic network properties rather than hierarchical characteristics. This is the world of Kairos, where ex-post explanations and descriptive theories prevail.

Kairology denotes a theory of timing (coinciding events) under conditions of uncertainty (for the Kairology concept, see Kirkeby 2000). If the wrong events coincide, it is bad timing or bad luck. If the right events coincide, it is good timing or good luck. The problem is, of course, that we are only partly in control of the appropriate event constellation. Business networks may be defined as connected dyads of firms, where a dyad is two firms and the relationship between them. Dyads of firms are connected in the sense that what happens (events) in one dyad conditions or are conditioned by what happens (events) in another dyad (Cook and Emerson 1978). Events also form networks in connected event dyads (Hedaa and Törnroos 1997).

The model presented in Fig. 2.1 attempts to elucidate relationships between two different ways of seeing the business world. One triangle collapses traditional thinking (individual, autonomous actors creating routines). Predominant business thinking and textbooks usually take the perspective of the individual actor—that is, manager or company—and build analysis and prescriptions on

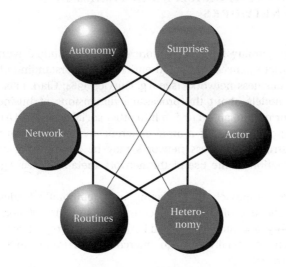

Fig. 2.1. Two triangles relating to management theory and practice

Source: Hedaa (1997).

the assumption that individual actors are autonomous. Also performing a situation analysis—that is, industry and company analysis—is aiming at building new or re-engineering old routines to create a better fit between the internal and the external world of the company. Hence, volatility and dynamism are dealt with as abrupt, infrequent adaptive changes in order to create periods of stability, as dealt with in Greiner's seminal *HBR* article (1972): 'Evolution and Revolution as Organizations Grow'.

The other triangle takes departure from the antonyms of the traditional approach, identifying a system where actors are heteronomously embedded in networks and acting on or enacting surprises. One wonders if this model of the business world fits reality better than the former triangle. If so, we need a new management theory. Managers do in fact react to surprises as new opportunities or threats. They never do this alone; always they discuss, negotiate, or experiment with new variations of actions within perceived relevant time–space. When they act, it is always a function of some prior interaction. Interaction is to move from heteronomy not to full autonomy, but rather to a state of homonomy (a neologism for the middle between autonomy and heteronomy, where relevant partners through interaction have arrived at a sort of common understanding for acceptable behaviour and shared rules or norms).

The latter part of the overlapping triangle model may help us in understanding how companies interact and why it is important for arriving at a better-situated and contextualized set of actions from which one may choose specific interactions (Hedaa 1997).

A MODEL OF TEMPORALITY AND TIMING IN BUSINESS NETWORKS

Time and temporality have been more extensively studied within sociology and other social sciences that could enrich the understanding of change and evolution of business networks (see e.g. Gurvich 1964; Clark 1985; Adam 1995). Developing models about the processual dimensions of business networks require, to our notion, an excursion into other social sciences. Using ideas and theories as springboards for a more coherent understanding of these mainly socially constructed business networks may be a promising avenue (for a closer examination of the use of the network metaphor, see e.g. Araujo and Easton 1996).

The network approach to marketing uses temporally loaded terms and vocabulary. The use of theoretical constructs and the relation to practical research, theory, and models is raised here with the perspective taken on time, on timing, and especially through interconnected events in understanding business networks.

When people explain their present favourable situation or position, they often refer to antecedent circumstantial luck: 'Well, I happened to be at the right place at the right time with the right kind of solution.' They admit that they exist under situational constraints beyond their own control. Situational constraints that regulate action either by supporting a certain set of activities or by impeding certain other activity sets may be referred to as opportunity. In a world of change, time becomes tim*ing* when an opportunity and an individual readiness to seize it coincide.

The processual approach to marketing and management deals with temporal and spatial change. When using events as temporal entities, the term process denotes how things change over time in the form of event trajectories. In context, timing is seen here as the situational act in the form of a discernible event, which is made in a certain resource constellation with other actors (individuals, departments, and firms). These actors directly or indirectly contribute to the value net and influence competitors and other actors in the markets.

The model (see Fig. 2.2) highlights the core perspectives concerning timing in business networks. At one end of the model we have the world of Chronos and order, at the other end unpredictability and the world of Kairos. Performance has two dimensions as well. The role of motivation and capability as a factor together with the opposite, but related force, of timing/luck and the prevailing opportunity structure. Order and routines can be found in the Chronos world (reducing lead times, syncronizing deliveries, JIT-management practices, and so on between network actors).

Timing requires the ability to sense trends, tastes, and combinations of new relationships and change in present network constellations. Finding new ways of combining former relationships (upstream or downstream) or connecting and investing into new relationships belongs to the world of Kairos. Both dimensions

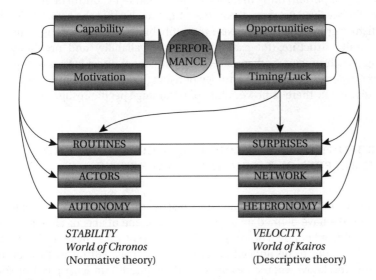

Fig. 2.2. Performance criteria in a two-dimensional time–space

should be considered. The four upper boxes in the model relate to performance in the time–space of Chronos versus Kairos (stability versus velocity). Capability and motivation relate more closely to the actor (firms, departments, individuals) in firms. Opportunity structure and timing relate more to the favourable moment and timing of new actions as prerequisites for success in the forthcoming future event trajectories. The notion of both stability and change of business networks falls well into this type of modelling, where both aspects should be considered.

'LET'S GO FISHING'

In an event network, perspective timing may be defined as *confluent event trajectories*. To illustrate this definition, let's go fishing. The fisherman and the fish exist in two independent streams of events. In order for the fisherman to catch the fish (good timing or good luck) and the fish to be caught (bad timing or bad luck) a number of compatibility conditions and acts must coincide. First of all, a favourable locational opportunity structure for fishing is water rather than soil. Secondly, the fisherman must use some kind of technology to get access to the fish world (fishing equipment, traps, or bait). Thirdly, the fisher-man may or may not have experience of good places to fish, or he may have knowledge as to how to recognize a favourable biotope and time (deep or low water, spring or autumn, morning or night). The more relevant knowledge and experience the fisherman possesses, the more likely it is that fish will be caught. But fish may have experience as well, so they can recognize what traps or bait to avoid. The important thing to notice is the limitation in control of events by any one of the involved actors in the interaction. But also that the actors (fisherman and fish) can increase or decrease the probability of catch through choice of opportunity structure (for example, mutual availability and proximity) and timing (synchronicity), rather than through the more direct factors of capability and motivation. Hence, the Kairology of fishing may impact on the probability of outcome but there is no certainty of obtaining specific results.

KAIROLOGY IN THE DYADIC EVENT CONFIGURATION WITH REFERENCE TO BUSINESS MARKETING

Let us now move on to a more abstract discussion of interaction at the level of the dyad. We have defined an event as 'an outcome of acts or changes caused by nature' (Hedaa and Törnroos 1997: 6). An event must have an informative content in order to be noticed (sensed). Weick (1995: 86) raises the question: 'How do you know when an event should be ignored (to let it pass) or something to pursue?' And he adds: 'The same uncertainty occurs when people

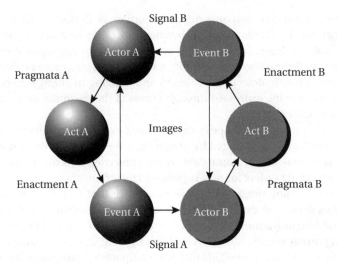

Fig. 2.3. Dyadic event configuration

notice salient, novel, unusual and unexpected cues. Occasionally those cues are pursued. Usually they are not.' The information in an event must be sufficient to overcome a certain threshold to be perceived and become a stimulus for an actor, whether that actor is the creator of the event or some other actor. A threshold may be defined as either (1) the amount of time and input necessary for sensing an event or (2) that intensity of stimulus from an event below which there is no response. Some events are noticed only by the actor who created the event, some are sensed only by others, and some are noticed by both the event creator and some other actors (see Fig. 2.3).

We notice events through a system of receptors. A receptor is that part of an organism that, in cooperation with the nervous system, detects what goes on (that is, receives stimuli from) outside or inside the organism. Receptors are highly differentiated to specific stimuli to allow perception processes like touching, hearing, seeing, tasting, and smelling. Receptors specialized to sense events emanating in the external world are named exteroceptors. Some of these, proprioceptors, are specialized in detecting position and movements of objects/ events. Organisms also include internal oriented receptors, introceptors, aiming at detecting stimuli arising inside the body, such as pain or hunger, and probably ambitions.

We interpret the existence of these receptors in organisms as a proposition— namely, that actors and associated acts (pragmata) are a function of (response to) events. Why else should we be equipped with our senses? This is also mirrored in the fact that a loss of one or more receptor functions is classified as disability, because reduced function of receptors impedes detection of events and thus invalidates our action repertoire.

The new normative response to globalization is flexibility. Organizations must react fast to events in global business. In order to react, organizations must be able to detect what is going on and select an appropriate response. Being close to the customer (availability and proximity) may also be interpreted as a means of timely detecting (visibility) and reacting to changes in customer needs (synchronicity, expressed through events at the customer or in supplier–customer relationship).

In an event perspective we posit that business events are connected, and that these connections are mediated by pragmata and enactment. We cannot think of any event that is not connected to an antecedent event, in one way or another. Incoming orders for new supplies do not come out of the blue. Neither can we think of any pragmata or enactments without connections to experienced prior events, or expected future events. In a sense all organizations are event-based organizations. It becomes especially clear when thinking of news media (reporting events), hospitals and fire-fighting service (repairing events), legal courts (settling events), insurance companies (compensating events), security firms (preventing events), advertising agencies (creating events). From these examples it can be seen that some firms tend to specialize according to type of events they deal with (event composites).

Also intra-organizational differentiation takes place based on event specialization, and on event composites, determining roles and role relationships. Most organization diagrams with incumbents and roles implicitly illustrate composite events by design. Actors are selected, instructed, and trained to notice and react to specific events, and to ignore most other events. If they go outside their assigned receptors' realm and action space, employees may be told 'to mind their own business'. If relevant and important events take place outside the organization that have no corresponding exteroceptors in the organization, then a crisis is likely to occur, sooner or later. Application of new technologies has hampered or even wiped out whole national industries. Contemporary business marketing ideologies of concentrating on existing customers and customer retention, and particularly attending to key accounts, at the cost of getting new customers, may exclude access to important informative events for addressing demands of the future markets.

Composite events also configure themselves through evolution (event variation (natural), event selection, and event retention). Each period of time may be seen as a latent period for a number of different and mutually excluding future event trajectories (that is, cumulative sequences of linked events). It is like snowballs collecting events on their way down the slope of time. Only at the end of the slope will it be possible to determine which one of the snowballs at the beginning accumulated most events on the way down, or if the initial events caused an avalanche. Alfred Marshall's, and later Arthur Brian's, theory of increasing returns may be an appropriate parallel exemplified by an account of why the VHS variety of VCRs was selected over BetaMax and System 2000 in consumer preference (VHS positive externalities, or events supporting VHS, sympathetic to this specific variety, increased its attractiveness for consumers, suppliers, and providers of auxiliary services, despite a technology claimed inferior to BetaMax).

Much of our learning takes place through observing the outcome of our own acts. If we sense that our acts concur with our intentions in the resulting events, we tend to repeat these acts whenever we want the event to occur. If the resulting event disconfirms our intentions, we tend to adjust our acts in new trials. Learning is a lot easier if the event occurs immediately after the act, and if we can observe and hence experience the relationship between act and event. Delays in feedback often create ambiguity about enactments and pragmata, which means that actors need many more trials in order to establish proper relationships between acts and events. The effect of human skin's contact with poison ivy appears twenty-four hours after the touch. This delay makes it difficult for man to identify the exact source among many possible causes of skin eruption, especially if one does not know the length of the incubation period. Even more difficult, the mushroom *Paxillus involutus* is edible only about ten times, after which it destroys your kidneys for good. The combined length of reaction time and cumulative potentiation of the mushroom was discovered only a generation ago.

In the dyadic event configuration learning becomes even more complicated. In Fig. 2.3 we combine two actor–act–event cycles, A and B. The relationship between events and actors is denoted 'images'. There are four images in a dyadic event configuration: AA, AB, BB, and BA, of which only two are accessible for any one of the two actors involved. Actor A can, within limitations, sense Event A (image AA) and Event B (image BA), but can only guess about how Actor B, also in a limited way, senses Event A (image AB) and Event B (image BB). Here again, time lag and additive effect of separate event stimuli complicate learning and, hence, complicate timing. Furthermore, separation by space and cultural distance disturbs image congruencies and gets in the way for Kairos. Because our receptors have limited reach in dyadic event configuration, we spend a lot of time in trying to make sense of fragmented and often puzzling contradictory images.

In undisturbed, stable dyadic relationships, experience and experience exchange and transfer through generations may disclose patterns and event trajectories concurrent with refined expectations. But when dyadic relationships expand into wider networks of many actor–act–event cycles, our requisite variety of receptors and mental faculties becomes insufficient. Nobody today will deny that business firms exist in a global maelstrom or vortex of events, some of which have global reach and impact all business firms one way or another. We have spent aeons figuring out what goes on in the mind of human beings, we have been occupied for generations with understanding how people decide and behave, but very little has been done to understand Kairos, how events are connected. Research has been focused on actors, pragmata, acts, and enactments. They are much less observable than are events. Hence, much of our understanding is based on speculation, which of course is not wrong *per se*. However, management fads seem to replace each other at an increasing speed (recently for example: total quality management, bench marking, just in time, business process engineering, learning organizations, team development, empowerment, and relationship marketing). Most of these fads are tool based rather than based on understanding of the underlying phenomena the tools should deal with. They deal more with pragmata and enactment than with events and images. The fads also respond to managers' need for being in control. Evolution of tool applications (variation, selection, retention) and the short duration of fads may indicate that control mechanisms and methods are based on illusionary notions of autonomy and independence, where notions of heteronomy and (inter)dependence may be a more realistic foundation for management and marketing theory.

OUTLINE FOR A RESEARCH STRATEGY AND MANAGERIAL PRACTICE

Research Strategy

We have looked at temporality as a continuum of both Chrono-time and Kairos temporality in time–space. Event networks and actor networks both affect the outcome regarding the timing of events in the form of relational time (that is, contextual elements embedded in the flow of events from the past to the present and to the future) (Halinen and Törnroos 1995). Both normative and descriptive theories relate to business marketing strategy in networks (see Fig. 2.2). The normative ones have been dominating the world of Chronos. The contemporary turbulent environment of business creates disorder and unpredictability. Timing is a key word to find a match between possible favourable outcomes of acts between event trajectories coinciding in time–space. A research strategy, based on the foregoing discussion, should take a holistic perspective on time and timing in framing the world of actors as being heteronomous, rapidly changing, loaded with surprises, and increasingly networked. Luck and surprises are usually not included as a part of managerial strategy. Managers think they should know how to make decisions under uncertainty and try to predict the coming future. We feel that it is important to address and realize the existence of non-controllable and unpredictable realities and make 'sense' of it as a part of the networked environment where firms operate. Having the ability to read cues and make sense of changes and possibilities is a part of a research strategy when noting that the world consists of heteronomous actors, is networked, and is filled with surprises (cf. Weick 1995).

Managerial Practice

From a managerial point of view, noting temporality and timing forms a core competitive tool in marketing and management in networks in the turbulent global economy. The presented triangle with heteronomy, surprises, and networks of actors could be a way to expand managers' understanding of reality in time space (Fig. 2.1). Chung (1999)—in a similar manner—notes the role of extending temporal realities from chronological, absolute time notions to include time-based, intended, social time constructs as a strategy. Management buzzwords and managerial tools developed for obtaining more efficient market strategies have, so far, predominantly used managerial routines in order to find more efficient time use in decreasing lead times, time-to-market models, and JIT management practices in the value net. Timing is the art of sensing and reacting to environmental changes as intended and unintended cues and signals for coming events. From a network perspective relationships with other firms are in focus. Network management has mainly the following objectives to consider (1) establishing new relationships, (2) developing existing relationships, or (3) dissolving non-profitable relationships. New combinations of relationships form resource constellations (network capital) to meet corporate objectives. New investments and changes in existing business networks can create resource constellations to prepare for a new and unpredictable future. Kairology is a theory of timing in a stream of coinciding event networks and the random, accidental, and potentially favourable upcoming event networks in the future. Sensing and making sense of cues extracted from imagination about the coming time and requirements may be an important prerequisite for success—whether understood a priori or a posteriori.

Performance relates both to the Chronos part of time and to the Kairos part. Seeing the future possibilities and the impact of surprises as an opportunity structure for corporate performance leads to a focus on flexibility and rapid reaction rather than focus on being big and powerful. When firms position themselves in a network with other actors, they can reduce uncertainty and create common structures to meet environmental turbulence.

3

Taking Time Seriously: Organizational Change, Flexibility, and the Present Time in a New Perspective

Christian Noss

INTRODUCTION

Despite the fact that time is underlying any change processes, in general, conventional organizational discourse still depicts the problem of change mainly from a 'content' view. If time plays a role at all, it is rendered to be of inferior conceptual importance. It will be argued that the dominant time perspectives that are implied in contemporary managerial thinking prove to be a retarding element as far as an enriched perspective on change and a conceptual consideration and integration of organizational flexibility are concerned. In particular, the fact that today's organizations have to deal with an emergent environment, which is increasingly hard to determine and never stands still, underlines the need to reformulate the organization–environment relationship as a relationship-in-time. Therefore, a new conceptual outline of flexible and 'movable' organizations in a relentlessly changing environment is suggested. Modern systems theory and a social-phenomenological conception of the present time serve as the conceptual points of departure. Implications for a new change management are addressed.

THE TIME DIMENSION IN CHANGE MANAGEMENT CONCEPTS

During the second half of the twentieth century, numerous approaches were developed in the field of change management, all of which provided substantial strategies to master change requirements. Prominent examples are concepts of planned change (for example, strategic planning, strategic management, organizational development), concepts of transition management (for example, managerial implications of life-cycle approaches), and/or concepts depicting change as a transformation project (for example, punctuated equilibrium models).

Focusing primarily on these content-oriented aspects, the second important dimension that is constitutive for any change in general is underrepresented in management and organization thinking—that is, the dynamic basis of change processes and, closely connected, the conception of time. It is the first thesis of this contribution that the predominant change management concepts rest on a simplistic view of the time dimension in general and the 'movement' of organizations 'in time' in particular. To be more precise, most contemporary concepts of organizational change reveal at least two severe time deficits.

First, whereas every organization is confronted with its own history, present developments, and the coming future, in so far as it has to deal with (all) three time dimensions, contemporary management thinking focuses at best on only one time dimension as the relevant time implication. Some concepts are solely future oriented, others rely on an exclusive orientation towards the past. So far, no concept integrates all three time horizons.

Secondly, the time dimension of the present in particular remains largely unconsidered. It is still a blind spot in management thinking about change and development. From a temporal point of view this is problematic because—empirically—organizations are faced with an emergent (or contingent) environmental context. This basic emergence is structurally related to the present time. For the management of organizations this implies the need for special competencies in institutional flexibility—that is, special capabilities that help to handle emergent developments as they currently unfold.

Future or Past as Dominant Time Implications

If we take a closer look at contemporary change management thinking, two basic conceptions of time become obvious that remind us of Gould's differentiation (1987) between 'time's arrow' and 'time's cycle'.

'Time's arrow' stands for the notion of time as a relatively homogeneous and linear sequence of events with the future as the ultimate point of reference. Concepts explicitly based on this time perspective are, for instance, all planning-oriented approaches (Ansoff and MacDonnell 1990), as well as all kinds of change-project models—of organization development, for instance (Cummings and Worley 1993). Within those concepts only planning is able to give reason to any kind of managerial action. The underlying assumption is about the following: because the world is complex, environmental and organizational developments are uncertain and ambiguous in nature; a 'good' management works on this uncertainty and tries to solve the resulting problems in advance. In order to do so, managers need a, potentially, total overview of the conditions and constellations of future aspects, events, and developments.

The basic vehicle to obtain this perfect overview is planning. Planning informs management—via the results of comprehensive analyses—about environmental complexity of the future already in the present and enables management to design 'reasonable' action steps, which are codified in the form of plans (Brews and Hunt 1999). While undertaking action steps and implementing these plans, management 'moves' the whole organization towards the formerly analysed future, disrupted only by (contingent) environmental disturbances or the inter-mediated results of control. In such cases, revisions of the once formulated plan might become necessary, as it is also the case when future projections or basic preferences of management change for any other reason.

In this scenario, time seems to be a linear and homogeneous medium, an interval between a present state and the future. By this, time appears divisible into phases and intervals of any scope. Long-range, medium, and short time frames can be differentiated by management at will (Weihrich and Koontz 1993: 134). Time itself has no real quality or meaning, beside the fact that, for pure logical reasons, it is needed to combine intentions and actions. The (artificial) time frames make it possible for all activities to be projected and rationally organized—through more detailed plans, milestones, and the like. At the same time, if the future is covered with a net or grid of projected connections of times and actions (plans), then the future itself becomes 'controllable'; complexity, thus, becomes manageable. From this point of view, the future is seen as the ultimate point of reference for any managerial action. It is regarded as the controllable extension of the present state of affairs, both being integrated through the quality-less medium of time (Wildavsky 1973).

'Time's cycle' interprets the flow of time as a repetition of similar activities, events, or trajectories. The primacy lies in the past, which is—because of the inherent assumption of similarity of events over time—understood as the basic 'container' of present and future states of the world. The notion of time as a cycle underlies—in a more implicit but, nevertheless, strongly influential way— the punctuated equilibrium approaches (Gersick 1991) and, as the name already indicates, the life-cycle concepts on organizational change (Quinn and Cameron 1983).

Life-cycle models depict the development and change of institutions in strong analogy to biological processes of growth and maturity (van de Ven and Poole 1995). The basic argument is that the unfolding change of an organization follows an inner logic or inherent programme that regulates the succession of events and evolutionary phases. In this line of thinking, birth, growth, maturity, decline, death, or renewal form the basic development of an institution in which each stage is seen as a necessary precursor of the succeeding stage or phase. Thus, the core features of change lie in the basic programme, which—once an organization's development is 'under way'—is embedded in the organization's history. In this perspective, the cause–effect relationships are assumed to be stable and prefixed over time. The organization's development is encoded in the initial basic programme, which, for instance, becomes obvious when the change trajectory is repeated as the result of an organizational renewal.

Punctuated equilibrium models reveal a somewhat similar line of thinking in so far as—once again—a deterministic succession of phases is assumed, which unfold due to a past driven logic. The Punctuated Equilibrium Paradigm conceptualizes organizational change as an alternation between long periods of organizational stability and relatively short eruptions of transition and dramatic shifts (Romanelli and Tushman 1994; Sastry 1997). In phases of stability, which are conceived of as equilibrium periods, organizations establish basic orientation patterns and systems design. By and large these basic features stay the same for a long time, accidentally modified by minor adjustments and/or incremental variations.

The reason for this continuity is to be seen in a phenomenon to which Gersick (1991) refers as 'deep structure'. Deep structures are established during an organization's past development. They encompass certain core features, as, for instance, basic beliefs, power distribution, and organizational design. Stemming from the past, deep structures largely determine a system's actual behaviour. Thus, they lead an institution towards a quasi-natural inertia, which represents a relatively stable state of affairs. In other words, the behaviour of systems in convergence (equilibrium) periods becomes nearly predictable. Compared to the enriched repertoire of possible actions, which characterizes organizations in an initial state of their development, deep structures simplify and narrow the frame of action (D. Miller 1993). Under these conditions organizational change is possible only in the form of an institutional revolution—a more or less sudden punctuation of (artificially) normalized processes, which bring about confusion and disarray in an organization's life (Schreyögg and Noss 2000).

Because of the equilibrium logic, all organizations' problems, which finally evoke change processes, are clearly to be located in the past evolution of the institution. Thus, organizational history, materialized in the form of deep structures, becomes the ultimate reservoir of all problematic developments. At the same time this logic delivers the very reason why in transformation phases the old deep structures must crumble and finally become substituted by new patterns, which in turn serve as the foundation for the next deep structures (and so on).

The Forgotten Present

Since either future or past is accentuated as the primary time reference in contemporary management thinking, the concept and time horizon of the present are trivialized or completely neglected (Mosakowski and Earley 2000: 802).

For logical reasons, the planning-oriented management approaches treat the present as a homogeneous and undifferentiated point on a linear time axis that is of concern only because it is the necessary starting point of all planning endeavour. The present is the initial point of the distinguished period or interval during which the formulated plan is valid. It is the logical enabler of the plan to get started. From the point of view of an imaginary time axis starting at t_0 and moving over t_{+1}, t_{+2}, t_{+3}, and so forth until t_{+n}, the present basically equals the point t_0 (Weihrich and Koontz 1993). The same present-less conditions hold true for the cyclical and equilibrium models of change. In those concepts the present as a time horizon is principally dispensable because the evolution of an organization is encoded either in the basic programme of the life cycle or in the alternation logic of the equilibrium perspective. Although the specific development of a social entity might not be foreseeable in every detail, nevertheless, those models assume the *logic* of the change processes to be well known. Therefore, the present is a logical result of the succession of stages or phases of past developments. The actual time horizon itself is not considered to be a source of organizational problems in its own right. So the present might be there, but it can appear only as a symptom of any problematic situation and never as its reason.

To sum up, the present situation, which every organization has to face every day, is not represented as a problematic time horizon conceptually. Empirically, however, all organizations operate and thus change during or in the present, which implies that the present time represents the basis for the simultaneity of existing organizations. In reality, this present time is far from being unproblematic: because of the complexity of multiple environmental developments and interdependencies that evolve and co-evolve simultaneously (Starbuck 1976: 1106), the present time is the ultimate horizon for the emergence of all expected and unexpected events and contingencies.

In addition, the present time is hard to recognize within the daily activities and operations. Under normal conditions no person or organization is aware of the fact that acting is possible only in the present. And, moreover, it is even hard to see or name what the present exactly is (Shackle 1972: 278). Is it the minute that is just going to disappear—or ten minutes, or one hour? One way to get notice of the deceptive present time is to turn attention to extraordinary events, when normal developments and operations are disrupted—when the ongoing moment makes the difference (Heirich 1964: 390).

Prominent (empirical) findings demonstrate the problems of a sudden burst in the daily operations of an organization. In these cases, disturbances of the normal functions and conditions in organizations take place as sudden surprises. In particular, enquiries into crises have shown the dramatic effect of such emergent events. Prominent cases, for example, the Bhopal or Challenger catastrophes are expressing the dangers for organizations and environments in a clear voice (Shrivastava 1987; Starbuck and Milliken 1988). They make sense of the fact that it is possible for the actual situation or the 'present time' of an organization to be suddenly transformed in an unforeseen manner, irreversibly disrupting the normal flow of events and redefining organizational history and future from one moment to another.

With respect to the problems of flexibility and adaptability, an enriched time perspective, which encompasses the present time, is indispensable. Flexible systems are those that have specific capacities to master a great many of the problems mentioned, even if these are new in their basic character and, thus, unpredictable. That means flexible and in this sense adaptive systems reveal special competencies in managing the contingency (or emergence) of phenomena that no plan can foresee and no cyclic perspective can represent in advance.

In order to develop a realistic perspective on change in general and organizational flexibility in particular, a new conceptual frame is needed—a theoretical frame that incorporates an enriched, in a way more complex view of organizations and environment, their simultaneous operating and co-processing, and the nature and relevance that time plays in such a constellation. The new concept should incorporate the time dimension in a very basic sense and should be able to offer a new way of reformulating managerial action systematically as action-in-time. Therefore, it has to be built from a completely dynamic and time-centred paradigm.

In the following the new conceptual basis is built in two steps. First, central insights of the work of E. Husserl and G. H. Mead will serve as the initial starting point, focusing on their conceptualization of (social) time and emergence. Since the management of organizations is the main subject of this contribution and since neither Husserl nor Mead was concerned with organized systems, in a second step the focus will be extended to the field of modern systems theory (MST)—strictly speaking, to the work of N. Luhmann. With respect to the so far trivialized time perspective, the proposed reformulation will offer a conceptual way of integrating all three time dimensions, locating social entities in the empirical relevant time of the present, and relating all phenomena of past and future systematically to the present time horizon.

TOWARDS A PRESENT-BASED CONCEPTION OF SOCIAL TIME

The Time Constitution of Individuals and Social Situations

In his well-known phenomenological enquiries, Edmund Husserl (1928/1964) focused on the different ways in which human consciousness works and operates. He found out that the basic mechanism is a relentless reproduction of ongoing 'nows'. That means that, in the human consciousness, the world is

intentionally represented through an endless flow of impressions. Human consciousness differentiates between an inner and an outer perspective, between
the world and the representation of its phenomena. This is accomplished by
being aware of itself and the inner processing, on the one hand, and the ongoing
world outside, on the other. Thus, human consciousness draws a boundary
between inner and outer processes recognizing that both operate simultaneously in time.

According to Husserl's insights, the basic operation of human consciousness
takes place during the actual present, constituted by the always new emerging
flow of impressions, which (finally) disappear through an ongoing transformation and modification into retentions. Moreover, this basic processing of the
actual here and now is transcended on the basis of reproductions of past
experiences and anticipations into the future. By this the human consciousness
is able to reflect itself and go beyond the actual moment of impressional
operating. In summary, human consciousness is bound to operate during the
present time, but within this operating it is basically able to create remote time
perspectives and, therefore, extend the present during the present time.

George Herbert Mead (1932/1980) elaborated a basic conception of human
agents acting in time that is quite similar to Husserl's position as far as the
importance of the present time is concerned. According to Mead, the world is
composed, exists, and operates as a succession of objective events that are
happening in the present. 'We live in a visible world, within which what is seen
is existent at the moment at which it is seen. Every distant object is at present
existent' (Mead 1963: 517). In order to exist, this implies the necessity of the
objects to be permanently reconstituted. Objects of the world are, therefore,
objects of *becoming*; their basic mode of being takes the form of events. For
Mead 'objects' are of all kinds, such as individuals, organisms, or physical artefacts. These are not 'once and for all time' invariantly given, but—with reference
to Whitehead's view (1929)—(individual) processes of spatio-temporal intersectings, which means that all events (of the becoming objects) have specific
perspectives and locations in space and time.

It is far beyond the scope of this contribution to elaborate on Mead's—
admittedly abstract—thinking in more detail. The point to be made here is the
temporal constitution of the world and its relevance for social situations. In *The
Philosophy of the Act* (1938/1950) Mead transferred central insights of his theory
of temporality to the social context, redefining social situations as taking place
in the present and identifying human acts as the constituting events.

Central to Mead's conception of temporalized intersubjectivity are the phases
of the act. Generally speaking, Mead (1938/1950: 3) conceptualizes individuals to
be engaged in a permanent process of (selective) readiness to respond to any
external (environmental) stimuli. For Mead, the 'normal way' of organisms and
humans acting is to process in a direct 'behaviouristic' way, without any dis-
turbance from 'impulse' or stimulus to response. Therefore, each act is conceptualized as an elementary event and as such it is irrevocably bound to time.

Each act involves a spatio-temporal perspective of its own and happens in the actual or, in Mead's words, the 'specious' present.

With respect to time the most intriguing problem arises when the act is disrupted and cannot find its completion in the 'phase of consummation'. In such cases an inhibition of the act follows that calls for reflection and finally for overcoming the inhibition (Mead 1938/1950: 24). During the inhibited act, the individual reflects on the (present) situation and, moreover, the factors and developments that—stemming from the past—have finally led to the actual situation as well as possibilities for further continuing. In other words, while the concrete act is inhibited, the individual is preoccupied with reflexive processes and the conscious mind of the individual shapes or creates time and the time horizons of history and future that are exclusively related to the inhibited act in the actual situation. Thus, a unique system of time is created by the acting individual with time references that are at his or her disposal.

Finally, these theoretical components are constitutive for Mead's conception of the social reality. Because each socially engaged individual realizes his or her specific time perspective (aspects of present-now, history, and future) in communicative acts, Mead (1932/1980: 47) conceptualizes the social world as a simultaneous and ongoing interchange of perspective intersectings of time and space. Sociality, this becomes clear, is a purely temporal phenomenon by its very nature foreseeable to a limited degree only. Moreover, as being bound to the co-presence of different actors, it is principally a complex human endeavour (Schutz 1967; Adam 1995: 80). According to Mead's thinking, social interaction takes place in an enriched, temporally extended present, potentially establishing new time references within the passage of time (Tillman 1970). In a modern language one could interpret this to come close to the notion of 'social construction of time' (R. Butler 1995), providing the very reason why in reality a plurality of time systems is operating simultaneously.

The Time Constitution of Social Systems

In this contribution organized social systems are the systems of major concern, which modern systems theory (MST) depicts as communications systems (Luhmann 1990, 1995). This means that they 'consist' of communication; their basic elements are self-reflexive communicative acts (Luhmann 1982: 69). Faced with environmental complexity, social systems have to be selective and partly ignorant in order to handle that complex environment. In other words, organizations are not able to deal with the environmental world as a whole; they, therefore, have to reduce environmental complexity to a workable level so that their members can act upon it. By doing this, systems inevitably establish a difference, a systems boundary between themselves and the environment. As a result, each system itself remains complex, but it is always less complex than its environment. The continuing existence of the system is secured by permanently maintaining the systems boundary (Luhmann 1995).

The systems boundary is a boundary of meaning—not every incident that occurs in the environment is meaningful for every system—but, with respect to time, it is also a time boundary, since not every event in the environment necessarily implies a corresponding system's event or (re)action. Although MST is based upon the observation that systems and environment (co)operate and, thus, (co-)evolve simultaneously during the present (Luhmann 1995: 185), the existence of the systems boundary points to the fact that (self-reflexive) social systems are able to operate on the basis of their own arrangement of event and process times or their own *time-reckoning system* (Clark 1990).

Empirically, this provides the very reason why (different) social systems can act and/or react instantaneously or with a delay, perform specific programmes very fast or with reduced velocity, synchronize their actions in a rather complicated way, or operate on the basis of relatively simple sequences of steps (Luhmann 1995: 41). Moreover, by means of self-reference, these systems establish their own perspectives of past and future in a higher-level present; an extended one, in which communication about past and future incidences is possible without the immediate disappearance of the *meaning* of the communicated events (Luhmann 1982: 289). These higher-level time references are based on the usage of time-bridging 'mechanisms' like systems experiences (for example, collective memory, organizational culture, and so on) and/or behavioural expectations (for example, structural dispositions, and so on).

To conclude, their special mode of time constitution enables social systems to integrate references of past and future simultaneously within an extended and enduring present, synchronous to the actual present in which communicative events are emerging and disappearing. In consonance with similar insights from other social theorists (Gurvitch 1964; Lewis and Weigert 1981; Adam 1990), in MST time is understood as a *social quality* in its own right, which is created and perceived systems-specifically in many different ways.

ORGANIZATIONS IN A TEMPORALIZED CONTEXT: IMPLICATIONS FOR MANAGEMENT

The main insight we can learn from the process theories is that organizations are permanently operating in a temporalized world—they are, basically, *entities of becoming* (Chia 1997). Within the temporalized world, organizations are bound to the present. As a whole, the present is constituted by emerging events, which are the results of the unfolding actions and interactions of the participating systems. In this view, all organizations evolve and operate simultaneously, which at the same time implies that the next emerging events are foreseeable to a limited degree only. In a temporalized world, one situation emerges out of the selections of its predecessors. Principally, each organization has a surplus of possibilities for action, which explains why the environmental conditions are complex and the specific constellation of the 'next' emerging situation finally remains underdetermined and opaque in many respects.

In taking this temporalized context seriously as the conceptual point of departure, MST and Husserl's and Mead's concept reveal the fact that reflexive social entities (human consciousness, interacting individuals, and organizations) are operating on the basis of at least two presents, the actual 'now' (in the following referred to as 'time layer I') and an extended present (in the following referred to as 'time layer II'). Both time layers are simultaneously 'used' by all social entities as a time frame for action formation, but both are totally different in nature. Fig. 3.1 summarizes them and provides an integrative overview.

If the analysis so far is accurate, the two time layers do not only comprise the general contextual features for human acting, they also provide the basic frame of reference for management from a temporal point of view. Thus, each time layer implies specific starting points for a temporally enriched management concept. It will be argued that each one reveals qualities of its own and in this sense unique possibilities and restrictions for organizational management in general and the management of change and flexibility in particular.

Management and Time Layer II: Reflexive Planning

Opposed to the management approaches mentioned at the beginning of this contribution, the reformulated concept reveals a *primacy of the present*, at least with respect to the ongoing operating-in-time of the social entities. However, as far as reflexive managerial action is concerned, it also has to accept the special relevance of the *future* (Mintzberg 1994: 291). For logical reasons, the intended shaping and development of an organization are possible only with respect to

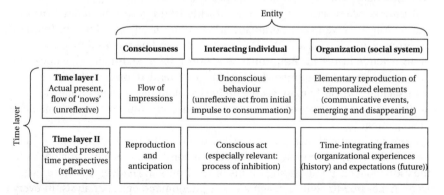

	Consciousness	Interacting individual	Organization (social system)
Time layer I Actual present, flow of 'nows' (unreflexive)	Flow of impressions	Unconscious behaviour (unreflexive act from initial impulse to consummation)	Elementary reproduction of temporalized elements (communicative events, emerging and disappearing)
Time layer II Extended present, time perspectives (reflexive)	Reproduction and anticipation	Conscious act (especially relevant: process of inhibition)	Time-integrating frames (organizational experiences (history) and expectations (future))

Fig. 3.1. The time layers of social entities

the future, although they may be motivated by *past* experiences (Walsh and Ungson 1991) and—as concrete and actual action steps—can take place only in the time horizon of the present.

But, in contrast to the planning-oriented concepts, the reformulated perspective depicts future, not as a frame of factors, which is easily to be stabilized and (simply) reached at a later point in time, but as a permanently moving horizon, which can never really be approached. In this sense, 'a horizon is a boundary which moves back as we move toward it' (Taschdjian 1977: 41). According to the concept of a temporalized world, the future—as well as the past—emerges as a perspective of an operating entity during the present. Being in a fundamental way both the projection of the present, on the one hand, and an important factor that influences and defines the present, on the other hand, the future is a reflection of the present and changes as the (emergent) present changes! In this perspective, the future has to be seen as an open horizon for the existing present, which has room for several mutually exclusive future presents (Luhmann 1976: 140). So, future and present are interrelated by their very nature and both are permanently moving (Luhmann 1982: 302; 1995: 89).

As the future is a moving boundary, a horizon for reflection, projections and expectations can be only preliminary (Das 1991). Thus planning activity has to be fundamentally reformulated. It should now be seen as a self-observing (reflexive) activity, which tries not to forecast future states of the world but to provide orientation to the daily activities of the organization and evaluate the possible range of corresponding actions and re-actions of the environmental forces (or perhaps better: the other organizations in the environment). In the reformulated perspective, planning has the task of minimizing the distance between the design process of a system's intentions and the developments of the world that are actually happening (Brown and Eisenhardt 1997). Therefore, within reflexive planning intended action steps are substantiated more explicitly on the basis of tentative and actual syntheses of the environment than on detailed and fine-grained analyses—as, for instance, strategic management has recommended since the 1980s (Schendel and Hofer 1979).

If time is taken seriously, the image of the future as a well-defined project can no longer serve as the dominant orientation for organizations. In (partial) accordance to what Nowotny (1989) argues, it has to be replaced by the notion of an extended present. But, unlike Nowotny's basic argument, this does not necessarily imply that organizations in an extended present become fully controllable and easily manageable. Reflexive planning does not finally lead to an infinite time compression and in this sense an unproblematic 'real time management'.

From an organization's point of view, the present-based extension itself is first of all a cognitive and not a technical phenomenon. It is more analogous to the individual or 'Being' caring for his or her future in Heidegger's sense (1926/1962). According to central insights of his phenomenological analysis, in every moment of existence the Being is engaged in drawing a temporally extended picture of him or herself ('temporal ecstasis'), which—because of the fact of existential care—at any time feeds back to the actual and ongoing present of being (Sköldberg 1998). Therefore, with respect to intentional acting (as far as individuals are concerned) or management (as far as organizations are concerned), the actual being-in-time of a reflexive entity has to be understood as an ongoing processing of a cognitive future/present tension during the present.

Reflexive planning is no longer preoccupied with formulating completely finished and, thus, 'valid' plans but with creating 'steering impulses' for the ongoing interaction and co-processing of organization and environment. For this reason it is much more focused on the use of real-time information (Eisenhardt 1989), which is continuously communicated throughout the organization. Reflexive planning, therefore, opens the perspective towards a permanently ongoing learning endeavour (Schreyögg and Noss 2000).

Moreover, with respect to the environmental conditions, reflexive planning has to face a world of temporalized complexity (Luhmann 1978; Noss 1998). As is the case with any planning activity, (even) reflexive planning is necessarily selective in its effort to reduce this environmental complexity. Because of the empirical fact that all selective acting is confronted with the risk of failure, the operative selectivity of (reflexive) planning has to be compensated by overarching processes of environmental 'scanning'. These scanning operations take the character of a 'second-order observation' of the ongoing system–environment interaction (von Foerster 1981; Schreyögg and Steinmann 1987). In principal, they have to proceed synchronously to the planning activities and extend the actual reflecting and manœuvring process of an organization in time, focusing on far more remote futures and providing information and experiences that stem from the organization's history (Luhmann 1982: 304).

Management and Time Layer I: Instantaneous (Re)organizing

By contrast, management and management problems in time layer I are totally different in character and origin. As mentioned, the time on time layer I indicates the incessant emergence of new 'nows'. Thus, time layer I comprises the elementary time of the actual world, in which events are occurring and, after a limited span of becoming, finally disappearing. This actual time gives reason to problems as sudden surprises or crises that no reflection can foresee and in which all expectations finally have to fail (Shackle 1972).

As the conception of a temporalized context revealed, the actual (present) time implies a surplus of possibilities for further continuation (that is, 'temporalized complexity'). Within the moment of occurrence the elements enlarge or narrow the possibilities for the following ones to take a specific form (or in the social world 'meaning'). Therefore, the occurrence of concrete events is emergent in nature and, thus, foreseeable or expectable to a very limited degree only. Consequently, any concept of intentional (change) management has to acknowledge that the conjunction of time and events on the basic time layer is finally *not controllable* (Luhmann 1997).

The circumstances of time layer I resist any efforts of direct control or steering in a fundamental way. For logical reasons, managerial acting is dependent on the existence of an (at least minimal) extended time horizon in which temporal remote events and actions can be integrated. On the basis of this integration—which all meaning-operating social systems typically form during reflection—intentions and expectations can be generated, which in turn are the preconditions for any managerial activity. The central problem is, however, that reflection always takes (at least some) time into account, whereas in the basic time layer, time and events are fundamentally coupled and emerge together (or simultaneously).

Moreover, this points to the related problem that something always happens during or simultaneously with any reflection process of individuals or planning process of organizations (Mintzberg 1994: 239). Under conditions of simultaneity, cause–effect relationships are largely suspended; a great deal of what happens simultaneously with reflexive managerial processes (like planning) cannot be influenced by the same reflexive managerial operations (Luhmann 1997: 45). Therefore, organizations need special managerial capacities to deal with the problems of the actual and emerging flow of 'nows'. A managerial concept that wants to take time seriously into consideration has to consider these special problems and at least has to provide a perspective for a solution.

Up until now the classical answer to the problems of the actual present is contingency planning, still the most central ingredient of all kinds of preparation for crisis and/or other unforeseen events. But, with respect to the concept of a temporalized context, this special form of planning can help to a very limited degree only (Quarantelli 1988: 374). The actual moment when events finally amount to a critical situation is a transformation of a potential of possibilities into facts to which an organization has to react. The intention to be prepared for all possibilities is finally not realizable, since all planning (including contingency planning) is necessarily selective in nature, and in the world of time not only all possible constellations of the emerging events but all possible changes of the constellations must be ex-ante imaginable or observable to planning in order to be successful.

Thus, institutions have to take other managerial potentials into account— that is, management capacities, which have to be generally held in store and are able to act immediately the problematic situation unfolds. Research findings indicate that the most promising candidate for such a task is to be located in the management capacity of organizing. Serving as a generator of immediate actions, an organization's configuration comes into the foreground (Ilinitch *et al.* 1996). Special capacities for absorbing environmental stimuli, information, and/ or knowledge as well as specific capabilities for coordinating and dispersing them internally are starting points that emphasize the unique problem-solving potential of organizations' functioning. This finally opens the perspective to the more recently discussed 'flexible forms', which no longer treat reflection and action as two (totally) separate spheres but help to approximate or integrate them in an institutional context (Volberda 1998).

Most important in this respect is the structural capacity of ubiquitous communication—that is, the possibility of an organization's members organizing their relevant communicative arena according to the actual emergence of the problematic situation. The concluding point of such a line of thinking is the organization, in which communicative structure and leadership are able to change corresponding to the environmental conditions and where new impulses are immediately transformed into systems operations and/or structural dispositions. So far, such 'instantaneous' organized forms have been much discussed with reference to the capability of organizational improvisation (Weick 1987; Moorman and Miner 1998) and are particularly to be found in specific branches of arts. Formations of modern jazz orchestras or theatre groups are organized social systems and, as such, they operate on the basis of a diversity of structures (social, musical, dramaturgical, for example), rely on a division of labour, and are basically engaged in performing or producing something (Bastien and Hostager 1988).

But they proceed in a totally different way from other organizations. They integrate their operations without pre-fixed programmes; by improvising they are looking for the next possibilities for action; and, while communicating and acting, the members decide which are the next steps to be carried out. Apparently, for those kinds of organizations real surprises do not exist, because the structure itself has a high degree of ('built-in') emergence and, therefore, every new emerging event is absorbed or integrated into the operations instantaneously.

The 'organization structure', if one wants to label it in the traditional way, is underspecified itself and there is—so to speak—a necessity for emerging events to be pulled into the ongoing processes in order for systems' operations (reproduction) to carry on. In this state of affairs flexibility has become a general competency of such organizations. It is no extraordinary feature that has to be added artificially.

CONCLUSION

This contribution explores the relationship of organizations and environment from a temporal point of view, focusing on possibilities for managing flexibility and change. It is argued that, in the world of time—no artificial world but the world in which we live—it is short-sighted to understand management either as exclusively planning and thus future oriented, or as pre-programmed and a past-driven set of activities. With the subject matter reformulated, the specific

character of management has changed fundamentally. The main features of the
new conceptual outline are as follows.

- Organization(s), environment, and management are conceived of as
  processing in parallel and simultaneously during the moving horizon of
  the present time.
- The reformulation of the primary time conception is not only an important
  issue for the elaborated perspective but the view of different managerial
  capacities in combination with their time implication. As indicated,
  management should be seen as a basic systems operation in the present
  time. As such it is conceptualized as an orchestrated endeavour with
  specific focal points, which clearly differentiate temporal requirements
  and managerial competencies.
- In this respect, reflexive planning (and processes of higher-order
  observation) could be identified to manage the extended present and
  provide revisionable expectations and rationalizations of past experiences.
  In addition, a 'fluid' mode of organizing helps with the problems on the
  ultimate actual time layer and keeps the system flexible and open for even
  instantaneous change. For this reason the reworked concept is composed
  of *functional equivalents*, in which one of them takes the leading part
  according to the problems to be solved.

So far, the elaborated perspective consists mainly of conceptual considerations. It surely needs additional clarifying how specific time-based management approaches could be further developed in order to meet the requirements
of each time layer in a more practical sense. Furthermore, empirical insights
are needed concentrating on the possible ways in which the two time layers and
the corresponding managerial competencies should be combined and/or
synchronized in an institutionalized context.

4

Now's the Time! Consumption and Time–Space Disruptions in Postmodern Virtual Worlds

Pamela Odih and David Knights

INTRODUCTION

Linear, irreversible, measurable, predictable time is being shattered in the network society, in a movement of extraordinary historical significance. But we are not just witnessing a relativisation of time...The transformation is more profound; it is the mixing of tenses to create a forever universe, not self-expanding but self-maintaining, not cyclical but random, not recursive but inclusive; timeless time, using technology to escape the context of its existence, and to appropriate selectively any value each context could offer to the ever-present.   (Castells 1996: 433)

There is little doubt that virtual reality and advances in global electronic communication involve a more intense compression of time and space than we have previously experienced. In the microelectronic world of virtual communication, time has to be seen much more as tied to the social context of its use rather than as an unproblematic medium whose neutrality permits comparison and communication across diverse boundaries. These very boundaries are in disarray as we begin to realize that every communication is a prosthesis or projection of a unique identity. Instantaneous communication and consumption mean that we no longer experience a common time 'in' which we all live in more or less mutual relevance, but, on the contrary, events in cyberspace are simultaneously global and local, representing a unique and unrepeatable period of time (Adam 1990; Ermarth 1992). Global communications through the Internet make possible a new kind of relationship between place and space; in effect, 'through their capacity to transgress frontiers and subvert territories, they are implicated in a complex interplay of deterritorialisation and reterritorialisation'

(Morley and Robins 1995: 75). Places are no longer rationally defined and ordered by their boundaries and frontiers. Instead of demarcating places, the boundary becomes 'permeable, an "osmotic membrane", through which information and communication flow' (Morley and Robins 1995: 75). Consequently, previously distant time and space relativities now form part of the daily interaction of global communities, financial markets, business corporations, academic institutions, and so on.

As a comparatively new discipline, marketing has aspired ever since its early development to emulate the positive sciences, and, in particular, economics and psychology (Sheth and Garrett 1986). Departing from this tradition we extend Foucault's early epistemological analysis of biology, linguistics, and economics (1973b) to adopt a genealogical analysis of marketing in modern and postmodern time–space. More specifically, in this chapter, we move from representation to discourse in an attempt to resist the 'closure of meaning' (Derrida 1978) around time–space. In this sense, deconstruction uncovers the sociohistorical and political assumptions that sustain representational discourses of time–space. However, it is not just the discursive meandering of intellectual postmodernists that is affecting our conceptions of time. At a practical level, current material transformations in microelectronic communications and cyberspace relations are producing a compression of space and time that is incompatible with distribution and marketing practices that seem caught in a representational time warp.

The concern of this chapter is to argue that, despite the theoretical and empirical disruptions to linear and universalist conceptions of time and space, marketing discourses of consumption are reluctant to abandon representational time–space in favour of more contextually grounded understandings. This is unsurprising in the sense that marketing is a discourse that seeks to control, predict, or manage the consumer. The indexical character of social life where meaning is tied to the social context of its expression and use (Garfinkel 1967) can only leave marketing 'throwing its arms in the air' in despair. It could be argued, then, that this chapter anticipates the possible demise of marketing. Unless it relinquishes its mission of control over the consumer, it will remain out of sync with the way people live their lives. Yet, if it reflects the diverse and context-dependent character of time and space, marketing loses its claim to technical expertise in the control and prediction of consumer behaviour.

The chapter begins by identifying the representational roots of marketing conceptions of time and its power effects. It prepares the epistemological ground for a discussion in the second section of the three dominant representational approaches to time within the literature on distribution and consumption in marketing. The 'objectivist', 'subjectivist', and 'social' approaches to time are critically examined respectively, before, in the final section, we address the implications for consumption and distribution of both microelectronic technology and postmodern sensibilities on conceptions of time and space.

REPRESENTING TIME–SPACE AND
CONSUMER SUBJECTIVITY

Although there are a variety of frameworks for understanding what constitutes marketing knowledge, a central feature is its unproblematic allegiance to positivist methods within an empiricist epistemology. In its fervour to be recognized as a scientific discipline, there is an almost universal claim to objective neutrality within the discourse of marketing (Hunt 1983). Science is, above all else, an empirical activity embedded in objective observation devoid of judgement, interpretation, and other forms of subjective mental operations. In an attempt to emulate the success and prestige of scientific practice, marketing treats the objects of its investigation as coterminous with the objects of nature. This is the positivist turn that discounts any ontological discontinuity between social phenomena and the world of nature (J. D. Douglas 1970). Marketing thereby reduces the complexity of its subject matter to a set of quantifiable independent and dependent variables that are amenable to causal analysis through comparative study and/or statistical manipulation. The social world that is the 'raw material' of marketing is assumed to exist independently of the observer, although made knowable only through sense perception and thereby representations of actions and events. It can be thought of as a stable, predictable structure composed of a network of determinate relationships between constituent parts. Reality is to be found in the concrete behaviour and relationships between these parts. Alongside other representational epistemologies, marketing subscribes to a correspondence theory of knowledge, where the truth or accuracy of statements is seen to reside in some direct correspondence with the reality they describe. Within marketing, there is little epistemological questioning of the 'reality' of representation for language is seen unproblematically to mirror reality and in so doing to provide the means of 'uncovering' the essential structures and dynamics of the social world.

In the same way that knowledge and 'control' of the 'natural' world have been made possible through scientific methods and engineering technologies, so it is thought that society can be measured and 'controlled' once the 'correct' techniques of analysis are devised and developed. Within this technical-rational view of knowledge consumers are knowable, limited entities, the characteristics of which can be captured in the same way as can any natural object of science. Thus, for example, in order to be able to generate representations of markets that facilitate profitable distribution for corporations, it is necessary to objectify the consumer, the effect of which is to 'normalize' consumption.

This objectification of the consumer was unproblematic in pre-marketing days when there was a shortage of productive goods such that effective demand exceeded supply. Anyone with surplus income or wealth was a consumer and would seek out the supplier without the latter having to make the kind of effort that is today seen as marketing, sales, and distribution. Mass production began to change all that, but again, in its early days, consumers were seen as an aggregated mass and consumption simply about consumers having the effective means (that is, money) to purchase products. The famous Ford declaration that 'you can have any colour as long as it is black' reflected the fact that simply buying a car was sufficiently distinctive not to have to be bothered about its colour. Efficient production and growing affluence meant that mass consumption began to reach points of saturation and there was the potential danger of supply exceeding demand. Bartels (1986) claims that 'interest in advertising increased around 1900 ... as buyers' markets began to replace sellers' markets ...' (1986: 192). This appears to have been the turning point for marketing and advertising, although it was not until the second decade of the century that basic concepts in marketing 'emerged and were crystallised' (1986: 193) and until around 1940 that 'mere description was subordinated to a management viewpoint' (1986: 204). Interestingly at a more conceptual level, Sheth and Gardner (1986: 212) argued that early developments perceived marketing as exclusively about 'economic exchange' and therefore not about other kinds of human behaviour and emphasized the power of the marketer to influence or control consumer behaviour. Axiomatic to this concept of economic exchange is a notion of transactions as 'one-time exchanges of values between two parties who have no prior or subsequent interaction' (Easton and Araujo 1994: 74). The identities of parties are of limited significance as 'transactions are assumed to be perfectly replaceable across parties with similar utility functions' (Easton and Araujo 1994: 74). Discursively, the 'pure transaction' seductively contrives to detach the exchange relationship from its embeddedness in a plethora of densely woven temporal conditions. Transactions have no historical context as the 'history of past relations is immaterial and all elements of exchange are contained in sharply defined time frames' (Easton and Araujo 1994: 74). Rather, timeless agents are represented as engaging in a zero-sum game of self-seeking opportunism. We have elsewhere (Odih and Knights 2000) described this discourse of time as 'objectivist'.

The assumption that both underlies but also legitimizes the 'objectivist' approach is a utilitarian belief in the utility of time as a unit that is readily given a monetary value (Becker and Michael 1973; Berry 1979). So, for example, time can be used to price products in relation to the labour cost of their production or simply to measure the opportunity cost of time spent on consumption. When abstracted from its context, it is no surprise to find the 'clockwork precision' of this objective notion of time applied to a wide variety of instances and issues. So time is conceptualized as, for example, a controllable scarce resource (Becker 1965) and a 'pressure' in decision making (Engel et al. 1990; Dhar and Nowlis 1999). In each of these examples, it is clear that time (and space) are like commodities—that we accumulate, possess, exchange, lose, save, or waste (Knights forthcoming).

Although objectivist studies have time as their focus, they fail to problematize either its conceptualization or its use. Time is not an 'emergent' concept in these studies; rather, it is predefined in advance of whatever is being studied (Adam 1990). Moreover, in treating time as objective, external, and invariant, a position of neutrality is assumed producing a consciousness that is capable of being everywhere and nowhere in particular, 'a consciousness at once immobile and omnipresent' (Ingold 1993: 155). The objectivist position presents an untenable reality, an independence from the specific, contextual vantage point of observation.

Time–Space Cognition

The epistemological conditions conducive to objectivist discourses of time–space were radically questioned in the 1960s as the ensuing focus on exchange of values admitted other non-economic aspects of behaviour to be included in the remit of marketing. It also returned to a traditional economist view of the consumer as sovereign, and therefore to a concentration on the psychology and motivation behind buyer behaviour. This was a time when a simple objectification of the consumer became problematic.[1] Objectifications had to become more sophisticated and involve the segmenting of the market into a range of types of consumer. At first, segmentation appeared to be no more than a managerial response to an external (market) environment (Knights and Sturdy 1997). However, the intensification of competition, flexible production technologies, and increased consumer sophistication and/or heterogeneity began to play their part in promoting new ways of understanding the market or what might be seen as a heightened marketing orientation (W. R. Smith 1956). Fully confirming the role that Foucault (1973b) saw the human sciences fulfilling, segmentation practices within marketing soon began to draw on the assistance of the science of psychology to provide more precise and evidence-based constructions of different subjects. It is as though the objectification of groups in time–space required a series of subjectifying methods and procedures to interpret their underlying meaning, albeit in the guise of 'needs', values, and desires.

While not rejecting the positivist paradigm, cognitive subjective approaches recognize that time does not exist as the exclusive property of an external object. Instead it is said to reside in the mind of the subject that experiences time. Subjective notions of time focus, therefore, on the cognitive, perceptual

[1] We are talking in very generalized or grand narrative terms here simply to provide some sense of the developments that were occurring. Clearly, there are numerous exceptions that could be understood only through detailed investigations of the specific and localized contexts. Competition is the major stimulant for a company to engage in marketing and distribution strategies and this will occur differentially according to a range of circumstances. Prior to mass production, this would occur particularly when limited income meant that consumers had to be persuaded to buy goods and from one source rather than another.

apparatus by which individuals comprehend time (Hirschman 1987; Gibbs 1993). Because consciousness, the mind, or reason precede all human experience, time is presumed to represent a synoptic view that the subject has of events (Elias 1992). As the repository of time, the mind is objectified as a physical property of the brain in exactly the same way objectivists treat time as a property of external objects. While seemingly existing in the subject rather than the object, not surprisingly, time remains unilinear and fixed rather than polymorphous and fragmented. Indeed, a cognitive conception of the subject is equally objectivist, so that the distance between the two perspectives is one of degree rather than kind. An example to illustrate the parallel between the two perspectives can be seen in consumer decision-making models (Engel *et al.* 1968; Howard and Sheth 1969; Bettman 1979), where the 'memory construct' plays a pivotal role. Represented as an objective observable entity, this memory is presumed to store semantic information (Bettman 1979: 57), which then leaves what is called a *memory trace* that is activated by consciousness at appropriate points in time.

This physical conception of mind perceives memory in a machine-like fashion such that a spark or energy input can release the past from the raw, physical matter where it is believed to reside. In short, it is assumed that the past is carried forward in time by the brain's physicality (Arcaya 1992: 303). The account of memory that underlies this understanding of consumption has been heavily criticized (e.g. Strauss 1966; Zimbardo *et al.* 1971; Arcaya 1992), particularly in relation to its disembodied perspective of time and space. As numerous phenomenologists (e.g. Husserl 1928/1964; Merleau-Ponty 1945; Heidegger 1971) argue, memory is (re)constructed in and through time–space events. Any reinvocation of the past from physical fragments (for example, the recognition that an existing product is in need of replacing) or intangible influences (for example, an advertisement for a more advanced version of a product) in the present requires the individual to engage in a 'bi-temporal' (Strauss 1966) splitting of consciousness. Subjectivist accounts fail to recognize how subjects do not simply restore the past from memory when buying products but often reconstruct themselves as they reinterpret the past to coincide with anticipated or desirable senses of the present or the future (see Keenoy *et al.*, this volume). Individuals are capable of uniting the literal with the virtual and linking one temporal order (the present) with others (the past and future). Within a phenomenological frame of reference, time is inextricably bound up with places, spaces, and the body. For people 'do not so much think real time but actually live it sensuously, qualitatively' (Urry 1995: 6).

Indications of a paradigmatic shift are, however, evident in the anti-positivistic research (Arndt 1985; Foxall 1986, 1987, 1990; P. F. Anderson 1989; Hirschman and Holbrook 1992). Arndt (1985), for example, argues that marketing has for too long been dominated by a highly reductionist structural-functional approach (as evident in the *memory construct*). He contrasts this with a 'subjective world paradigm' drawn from social constructivism and symbolic interactionism. This 'interpretivist' approach has, in recent years, gained a considerable following in consumer behaviour (see Hirschman and Holbrook 1992; Brownlie *et al.* 1994). The increasing popularity of 'interpretivist' and 'interactionist' perspectives has resulted in the emergence of radical alternatives to linear discourses of time and consumer behaviour.

Shopping for Subjectivity in Social Time–Space

A social approach draws largely on an interactionist perspective where the meaning of anything, including time, is seen as profoundly to do with language considered as a medium and outcome of social interaction. Material objects are seen to embody a system of meanings, through which we express ourselves and communicate with each other. In their capacity as consumers, individuals engage with a proliferating multitude of goods for the purposes of 'fashion[ing]' (Bauman 1988: 808) a distinct and differentiated subjectivity at the level either of the individual or of the group and subculture (for example, youth). Indeed, consumerism has meant that consumption has become a way of life and one of the most important sources of identity, perhaps displacing the preeminence of work and occupation in the late twentieth century. Identity in this formulation does not relate to fixed attributes of personality or self, still less to certain fixed forms of behaviour. Instead, as Giddens (1990: 54) argues, identity lies now 'in the capacity to keep a particular narrative going'. What this signifies is that every person is only as 'good' as his or her last 'claim' to a particular identity. In premodern societies where identities were primarily ascribed at birth through kinship and blood lineage or acquired through affinal ties of marriage, this precarious and unending process of achieving and sustaining one's identity through social activity was unknown. However, in modern society, identity becomes ever more absorbing as it is precarious and it begins to be the measure of life—a fluid reflexive process instantiated through the time–space events, which it also serves to constitute (Mort 1988; Giddens 1990; Lefèbvre 1991).

There is a wide range of social approaches to time within consumer research. Some merely replace the objectification of time and/or the subject with equally reified structural or cultural conditions or causes of their production. Within such discourses (e.g. Nicosia and Myer 1976; R. Graham 1981; Gronomo 1989; G. Davies 1994), consumer subjectivity is constituted as an emergent property of specific structurally determinant tempo-spatial processes. A more active subject is to be found in the 'experiential' temporal models of Hirschman and Holbrook (1992) and Bergadaa (1992), and the 'relativity' temporal model of Gibbs (1993). Here time and space are conceptualized not as standing outside the self and its cultural, stratified, or gendered contexts to determine the subject of consumption. Rather, identity is embedded in, and constituted through, time–space 'events' that are themselves in continuous flux and reformation as the self-reflexive monitoring of action and interaction unfolds.

However, few of these researchers theorize the power and knowledge relations that serve to constitute linear time. They, therefore, are unable to appreciate the social processes through which alternative conceptions of time are subjugated or obscured by the dominance of linear time. Moreover, by failing to engage theoretically with the discursively constituted existence of linear time, social approaches contribute to many of the everyday assumptions of linear time—that is, they take it for granted as a given and inevitable part of our social existence. Despite problematizing social conceptions of time, these approaches continue to reinforce the hegemony of linear time, and thereby inadvertently contribute to marginalizing their own discourse. That is to say, the intimate and irreducible tie between time and social life is remaindered as we are seen to busy ourselves with meeting the routines and rituals of linear time as imposed on us by a masculine and institutional pragmatics. Yet a simple reflection on everyday life would reveal to us that subjectivity is not stable, continuous, and consistent as and between distinct linear time frames. Rather, it is historically and culturally contingent, discontinuous, potentially fractured, and multiple (Knights and Odih 1995, 1997). In order to reflect further on these problems, it is helpful to embark on a deconstruction of linear time. This can be conducted not just at a theoretical level of analysing power–knowledge relations but also at the practical level of observing the power effects of what might be seen as a cyberspace revolution in communication and distribution.

MARKETING IN POSTMODERN TIMES

Abstraction today is no longer that of the map, the double, the mirror or the concept. Simulation is no longer that of territory, a referential being or a substance. It is the generation of models of a real without origin or reality; a hyper-real. The territory no longer precedes the map nor survives it. Henceforth, it is the map that precedes the territory—PRECESSION OF SIMULACRA—it is the map that engenders.   (Baudrillard 1983: 2).

The postmodern condition suggests that we are experiencing an intense phase of time–space compression and their fragmentation both globally and locally (Harvey 1991). Unparalleled advances in communications technology have intensified, fragmented, and dramatically delineated complex value chains inducing a 'systemic perturbation in the sequential' ordering of time–space (Castells 1996: 464). One might suggest this intense time–space compression is simply an intensification of the dilemmas that have, from time to time, beset capitalist procedures and their demand for a constant revolution of the forces of production. Whilst the economic, cultural, and political responses may not be exactly new, the range of these responses differs in certain important respects from those that have occurred before. The intensity of time–space compression in Western capitalism since the 1960s with all of its emergent features of excessive ephemerality and fragmentation in the political and private, as well as in the social, realm does seem to indicate an experiential context that makes the condition of postmodernity somewhat distinctive (Harvey 1991).

Consider the fate of location dependent concepts such as market segmentation, in the light of instantaneous global communication. Castells (1996: 428) describes how the technological infrastructure of a globally networked society defines a new space of financial markets and communication, glacial in its dimensions as it imposes 'its logic over scattered, segmented places'. The new 'space of flows' is about technologically facilitated connection rather than our material places. New media precipitate a disconnection of localities from their cultural, historical, geographic meaning and a reintegration 'into functional networks, or into image collages, inducing a space of flows that substitutes for the space of places' (Castells 1996: 375).

Consider also the cyclical rhythms of business processes and consumer markets (Morgan 1997). Innovations in communication, production, and distribution have radically developed our relationship with these temporal cycles, resulting in their becoming compressed and relational (Adam 1990; Papows 1999). There are no longer common times and spaces 'in' which we all live in more or less mutual relevance. On the contrary, time and space are constituted as a local definition, a dimension of an event, a unique and unrepeatable location or period (Adam 1990; Ermarth 1992). In the writings of Castells (1996: 467) the 'space of flows' is seen to engulf time by dissolving the sequential ordering of past, present, and future 'making them simultaneous thus installing society in eternal ephemerality' and precipitating a 'timeless time'. There is clearly intensity and tension (Cooper and Law 1995) around postmodern temporal–spatial relations that were perhaps not so evident within representational regimes where the boundaries between one time and another or different spaces were more clear-cut.

Whilst appearing to embrace the marketing possibilities of postmodernity, consumer research reflects tensions around postmodern time–space in its reluctance to relinquish an epistemological allegiance to representational linear time. Rapidly developing information technology is often seen as enabling 'mass customization', 'one-to-one marketing', and the development of long-term 'marketing relationships' (Sheth and Sisodia 1997; Ahola 2000: 2). Wigand (1996) describes e-commerce, as enabling unique opportunities for personalized interactivity and spontaneous 'marketspace' accessibility. Clear inferences are made, here and elsewhere (Sheth and Sisodia 1997; Venkatesh et al. 1998; Elliot 1999), to the differentiated instantaneous, fragmented times and spaces of postmodern consumer culture. However, on closer inspection the rhetoric of 'customer-centric', 'fluid-marketing', and 'empowered consumers' (Elliot 1999: 120) often conceals a specific notion of the subject, self, and subjectivity—one that we intend to reveal as discursively aligning with linear time's *Cartesian Cogito*.

The 'Subject' of Marketing in Postmodern Time–Space

Venkatesh, Meamber, and Firat (1998: 303), in a fascinating and enlightened article, describe the new marketing frontier that is cyberspace as follows:

...there are some features of cyberspace not found in the real space. Virtual environments are both marginal (in the sense that they are not accorded equal status with real life) environments and simulated environments. They do not need physical referents and individuals can experience virtual conditions not encountered in the real world. People can construct virtual objects in cyberspace and interact with them both as real and imaginary objects.

Cyberspace as a 'marketspace' (Papows 1999), eliminates the physical restrictions between buyer and seller, thus enhancing the exchange value of this interaction (Venkatesh *et al.* 1998; Papows 1999). Cyberspaces as vehicles for interactivity are 'not only cognitive spaces but behavioural spaces and experiential spaces' (Venkatesh *et al.* 1998: 306). Cyberspaces permit 'considerable exploration of the kind unattainable in the real world' (Venkatesh *et al.* 1998: 306). But cyberspaces, according to this and many similar discourses (e.g. Papows 1999; Ahola 2000), are not 'real' spaces. Thus, for example, when exploring the construction of identities online, Venkatesh *et al.* (1998: 318) state that 'the individual is able to protect his/her real identity and revert to it without having to surrender his/her entire persona to strangers'. But surely this is the self of objectivist and subjectivist linear temporal models? For, if the self is recognized as embedded in and through time–space 'events', so as to reflect and reproduce them in its own image, then cyberspace will provide for a context in, and through, which to construct a sense of self. Thus there can be no 'real' extra-discursive time–space in which the self might retreat. Moreover, the dualistic opposition between 'real' and 'unreal' clearly partakes of a modernist epistemology.

   Modernity, amongst other things, is about the creation of truth, the universality of reason, the disciplining of the soul, mastery and control (Foucault 1973*b*). Venkatesh *et al.* (1998) partake of a modernist discourse in so much as they identify a temporal origin—a 'real' self unaffected by its encounter with cyberspace—that is assumed to authenticate the existence of a 'real'. This discourse appears, therefore, to reflect and reproduce a representational epistemology, which ascribes language the function of mirroring an 'objective reality'. Elsewhere we have argued that the meanings and values privileged by representational epistemologies naturalize pervasive forms of gender power–knowledge relations (Knights and Odih 1995, 1997; Odih 1999). It might suffice here to state that representational linear time is premised on the rational ordering and control of time–space and the denial of *différance*; it knows no Other. In their continuous and systematic references to a 'non-real' market-space, Venkatesh *et al.* (1998) serve to reproduce the discursive conditions of linear time and, in so doing, unintentionally partake in the subjugation of their alternative discourse (Knights and Odih 1995). The unintentionality of this discursive effect is particularly significant when one reflects on their enlight-ened description of 'Cyberspace as the Site of (Marketing) Control'. In this final section of their paper, Venkatesh *et al.* (1998: 319), describe how '80% of the Internet is now completely occupied by merchants of commerce'. Despite their astute sense of foreboding and concerns for the protection of civil liberties, this narrative of control continues to be informed by a discourse of time–space predicated on mastery and control. It is only when time–space is conceived as homogenous, empty, and representational that it can be associated with 'a desire to know what the social is in totality' (Game 1991: 26). In the following section we begin to explore an alternative discourse of marketing and consumer subjectivity in postmodern time–space.

Performativity, Self and Subjectivity in Postmodern Time–Space

Postmodern writers such as Baudrillard (1983) have identified contemporary consumer and multimedia culture to be producing a surfeit of images and signs that give rise to a world of simulations that efface the distinction between the real and the imaginary, a depth-less aestheticized hallucination of reality. Baudrillard (1975) describes how increasingly in postmodern consumption the commodity assumes its importance as a sign rather than something that is useful. In line with Saussurian semiotics, this understanding of representation goes beyond the reductive notion of the sign as a vehicle of meaning and sig-nification. Rather the relation between sign and referent is completely arbitrary 'determined by its [their] position in a self-referential system of [floating] sig-nifiers' (Featherstone 1991: 85). In this sense, signification means simply dif-ference and nothing else. For Baudrillard (1968/1996), the only meaning that signs retain is their difference from other signs. Signs are entirely self-referential, making no attempt at signification or classification, their only point being to make a temporary impact on our consciousness. It might help here to reflect on the countless times you have watched an advertisement and momentarily deliberated about its tenuous links to a recognizable object, product, or even experience. Similar reflections have lead Baudrillard (1983: 4) to state that 'it is no longer a question of imitation, nor of reduplication, nor even of parody. It is rather a question of substituting signs of the real for the real itself.'

This detached status of the code enables a bypassing of the 'real' and opens up what Baudrillard (1975) terms a 'hyper-reality', where the hype or simulation—the signifier of the signifier—is what is 'real' and the direct focus of consumption

(Rodaway 1995: 251). Often-cited examples of hyper-reality include Disney Land (Rodaway 1995), theme parks (O'Rourke 1990), and shopping arcades (Morse 1990; Rojek 1993). Collectively these authors describe how postmodern consumers in hyper-reality experience disorientation, confusion, and bewilderment as they become subject to an unceasing barrage of abstract images, sounds, and artefacts. Morse (1990: 193), for example, using the concept of 'distraction', describes the de-realized spaces of the 'shopping mall' as inducing a sensation of floating, 'a partial loss of touch with the here and now'. Completely separated from the outside world, shopping arcades constitute a non-space 'of both experience and representation, an elsewhere which inhabits the everyday' (Morse 1990: 195). They induce an 'attenuated fiction effect' (Morse 1990: 193), a liquid flow between levels of attention and different ontological states (Frow 1997). Liquidity in the sense that de-realized 'non-spaces' invite forms of *flanerie*. Resembling, vicariously participative aimless strolling 'as everyday shopping activities are foregrounded as if on a theatre stage' (Shields 1992: 6). Intriguingly, Morse's subjects (1990: 193) are conscious agents who know 'a representation is not real, but nevertheless momentarily closing off the here and now and sinking into another world'. Conversely, Baudrillard's world of simulacra (1983) displaces the coherent reflexive and responsible modernist self and in its place presents us with a fragmented, multivocal plethora of tempo-spatial 'event'-based subjectivities.

Central to Baudrillard's world of simulacra and hyper-reality (1983) is a loss of a sense of history and the fragmentation of time into a series of perpetual 'presents' where experiences of a multi-phrenic intensity break down any sense of permanency, stability, or unity regarding the self. Indeed, Baudrillard identifies hyper-reality as ensuing dramatic discontinuities in the contextual link between the subject and its specific world. In the 'third order of representation', technologies gain their own momentum, providing a simulacra of actual events effacing any access to a 'real', which itself is an effect of the code system (Sarup 1996: 111). Advertising provides an apt and particularly pertinent example here. Advertisers are constantly involved in complex processes of meaning transfer, whereby commodities come to be imbued with cultural meanings only arbitrarily linked to the referent that they originally signified (Firat 1994). Advertising in the current era lives on the playful and self-reflexive nature of postmodern culture. Advertisers 'attach signifiers to disparate objects and just as quickly detach them, all in the name of novelty and play' (Knights and Morgan 1993: 227). In the hyper-real world of postmodern advertising everything mutates into everything else, all is image, appearance, and simulation. Reflect on the indiscriminate pillaging of the past in the shape of rhetro-advertisements. And the more recent tendency to reincarnate Hollywood idols for the purpose of selling products the likes of which are, at best, arbitrarily associated with their lifetime. Time as a function of position, as a dimension of particular self-referential events, is fractured, multiple, and discontinuous in these postmodern advertising practices. Moreover, the search for an authentic, integrated self through identification is displaced, disrupted, and fragmented by the 'pure' sign that resides within a self-referential tempo-spatial context and almost coincidentally collides with 'products' (which are themselves mere signs).

In the absence of a coherent or unified subject, it is increasingly difficult to speak of temporality in terms of memory, narrative, and history (Homer 1994: 4). Rather, the 'I', ego, cogito of postmodern consumer subjectivity exists for a situationally specific duration then disappears or undergoes transformation into some new state of being (Ermarth 1992). Condemned to a perpetual present and the immediacy of seemingly random unconnected signifiers, we are subject not only to a multiplicity, but also to a continually shifting set, of identities. This suggests a radical break from the conditions of late modernity where 'identity is the creation of constancy over time, that very bringing of the past into conjunction with the future' (Giddens, as quoted in Clarke 2000: 219). For a notion of identity as a process, project relies upon an organizing future time sequentially linked to a past and present (Clarke 2000: 219). In the absence of this signifying chain, our sense of identity becomes increasingly tense and insecure, as meaning is perpetually deferred, constantly slipping beyond our reach. Jameson (1984) describes postmodern culture as characterized by stylistic diversity and heterogeneity, an overload of imagery and simulations that have lost any sense of a point of reference, or stable object of representation. Time and space have collapsed into a perpetual 'present' in which the past has been severed from its historical context 'in order to circulate anew in the present, devoid of its original meanings but contributing to the cluttered texture of our commodified surroundings' (Springer 1996: 40). The outcome, according to Jameson (1984), is historical amnesia, and, in its extreme pathological form, a schizophrenic inability to sustain a coherent identity (Springer 1996).

The fragmentation of time into a series of 'presents' violates any sense of signs and images linked by narrative sequences; there are only vivid immediate isolated affect-charged experiences of presentness of the world—of intensities (Jameson 1984). For us, the marketspace of the Internet provides an emblematic medium for which to demonstrate the provisionality of postmodern subjectivity. In the writings of Baudrillard (1988) and Sobchack (1991) the flat surface of the computer screen becomes an allegory for depthless selves. As Sobchack (1991: 257) explains, 'only superficial beings without "psyche" without depth can successfully manœuvre a space that exists solely to display'. In this discourse, the space of the Internet is no longer a context, providing for continuities between time, movement, and event (Sobchack 1991: 257). Rather, 'space is now more often a "text" than a "context"' (Sobchack 1991: 231–2). And electronic selves assume a seemingly limitless array of identities at the drop of a keystroke (Poster 1995; Turkle 1995; Springer 1996). In this discourse, the transient spaces and places of postmodern time(s) appear as seductive hosts to unique multifaceted forms of consumer subjectivity (Poster 1995; Turkle 1995). Fleeting transient performed selves (J. Butler 1990), vicariously meandering amongst virtual arcades are sampling infinite lifestyles seductive in their promises of new context-dependent personas.

Postmodern disruptions in our experiences of spatial and temporal contiguity have dramatically transformed identity construction such that identities have become 'eminently contingent and continually reproduced in specific discursive contexts' (Tribe 1993: 4). The fleeting presence of multivocal consumer subjectivities coupled with their incessant, unceasing performativity suggests the need for modes of representation that radically depart from all that went before.

Marketing in the modern world has been characterized by a belief that a relatively fixed system of human needs could be discovered for different segments of the consumer market. In its more sophisticated renditions and especially within innovative advertising, these needs are seen as socially constructed and thereby open to being formed and furnished by those seeking to sell their products and services. From this perspective, products and services can be seen as solutions looking for a problem to solve. Distributors that have moved this far within the framework of modernism have less difficulty in confronting the challenge of postmodern markets, where consumption involves the exchange of signs (Baudrillard 1975, 1983) that are 'free floating'—not tied to an object of signification but simply circulating in a space of signifiers. However, there are dangers in consumer research of the challenge to representational time and space simply involving its negation and replacement with the free-floating and self-referential significations of time.

Despite the postmodern tendencies for time to become contingent on and fragmented around local circumstances, there is no escape from the universality of linear time as constituted by the clock, schedules, timetables, and work routines (Adam 1995). While virtual reality is clearly beyond linearity and concreteness, our ways of relating to cyberspace technology readily takes a linear temporal sequence as we allow ourselves to be controlled by its routines feeling the ever demanding pressures to provide instant responses to messages. Indeed, non-linear temporal experiences seem easily caught up in the perceptions of time that are tied to more local, social, gendered, ethnic power relations (Kendall 1998). Consequently, no matter what is the level of disjunction and discrepancy, local socially constructed conceptions of time are mediated through a universally imposed linear time. Much of the reason for this is simply the practical one of a necessity that timetables and schedules be taken for granted, but it is important to realize that this conceals or obscures the power–knowledge relations in which the linear time and concrete space are embedded. This chapter has attempted to introduce linear time–space as existing in, and through, a plurality of discourses that are informed, and inform, particular types of knowledges that come into being through relations of power. Representational time–space is thus recognized as emerging through discursive formations and discursive practices that privilege specific regimes of truth while suppressing or subjugating discourses that do not conform to and concur with the regime of truth thereby established (Foucault 1982).

Because of their attachment to subjectivities that are a product of specific social categories such as gender, status, age, and so on, conventional marketing strategies are not well designed to make sense of, let alone advise on, distribution in the microelectronic and postmodern age. Cyberspace renders problematic the continued segmentation of markets using traditional categories and in accordance with objectified dimensions of time, space, and subjectivity. As e-commerce in retailing begins to expand, it has to be asked whether the products and services can remain as tied as at present to particular segments of the market. As soon as digital television sets are universal—a consumption trend that has already been guaranteed by the eventual withdrawal of non-digital services—it will not be possible to segment the market between the computer 'nerds' and 'the rest', let alone along categories of age, class, ethnicity, or gender. Internet usage will be as simple as changing channels on TV and the fascination of shopping in the comfort of one's own home will presumably appeal to almost everyone. But even the subsequent possibilities of mass customization may have difficulty in convincing the consumer, for, in general, it has simply sought to conceal the true character of the mass-produced commodity by embellishing it with an individually designed (that is, customized) service wrapper.

CONCLUSION

This chapter has been concerned to raise questions about time and transformations within the field of consumption and distribution, as we move beyond the mechanical age and the norms of modernity. Interestingly, time represents a taken-for-granted concept that remains largely unexplored and unquestioned even when it is the focus of social attention—for example, during the change to the new millennium. Where the issue is explored, all too often analysis is guided by an operational definition of time, which relates to its measurement. With a few limited exceptions, time is presupposed as an objective, quantifiable phenomenon divisible into discrete and disembodied units. This is reflected in linear time and its measurement through the mechanistic calculations of the clock. Hegemonic in its power effects on everyday life and science, linear time is represented as if it were time *per se*. Situationally embedded or specific contextually bound experiences of time and its diversity are, as a consequence, understood through the mediating filter of linear time. Firmly embedded in linear representations of time, qualitative variations that precede their quantified representation tend to be disregarded, as does also the vast experiential chasm that divides embedded times and their second-order constructs. Steeped in our dominant linear consciousness of clock time, we transcend the finitude of the event, 'flee in the face' of its *present* value, and accept the illusion of a stable identity despite an experience of continuous change and uncertainty. Deterministic in structure, 'reality' lends itself to accurate observation and measurement by appropriate research instruments. It is axiomatic to this form of knowledge that time (and space) should be conceptualized as abstract and fixed immutable units existing outside the human subject.

However, more recently fractures and fissures in the hegemony of time as a fixed object have increasingly surfaced. It cannot easily be established whether this is a result of the cultural impact of Einstein's theory of relativity or simply a product of contradictions and inconsistencies arising when time is so detached from the human subject of its ultimate embodiment. A response to these difficulties is the development of psychological discourses that offer alternative 'subjectivist' and social tempo-spatial models. In effect, these models provide different sources of the representation of time as existing respectively in mind and social interaction, but they remain wedded to time as being unilinear in form and having a fixed content of finite meaning. But, whether objective, subjective, or social conceptions prevail, 'now's the time' for deconstruction to uncover the socio-historical grounding and political role of representational knowledge about time. From what has been said about the masculine preoccupation with representing reality as an orderly structure within which identity is readily secured (Knights forthcoming), the link between a hegemony of linear time and gendered power–knowledge relations cannot be ignored (Knights and Odih 1995; Odih 1999).

It has been our intention within this chapter to identify marketing approaches to time as reinforcing, to various degrees, the hegemonic status of linear time. What we are hinting at here is that it is not so much feminist resistance that might have the greatest impact on puncturing the balloon of masculine discourses of linear time. Rather, linear time could be most threatened precisely by a masculine-driven interest in pursuing microelectronic communications and cyber relations. While this may be part of a continuing struggle to secure a range of identities through control of their content over the cyber waves, it may also mark the earliest signs of a disruption of hegemonic linear time as a significant condition and consequence of masculine discourses of mastery and manipulation. What is interesting, though highly speculative, is whether through the disruption of linear time we are witnessing the imminent demise of marketing.

5

Time and Management as a Morality Tale, or 'What's Wrong with Linear Time, Damn It?'

Alf Rehn

INTRODUCTION

Although it seems that time has been actively discussed in the social sciences ever since the sudden proliferation of 'seminal' books in the 1960s (Fraisse 1963; Moore 1963; De Grazia 1964; Gurvitch 1964; Sorokin 1964), the 1990s and onwards have quite clearly been a period with an abundant interest directed towards the temporal. It has also been a period when time studies have filtered into popular culture, with a number of books on time selling fairly well to the general public (e.g. Lightman 1993; Gleick 1999; Griffiths 1999). Time has become a 'topic', something you might even hear politicians ponder, and the multifaceted nature of time is no longer discussed merely in the halls of academia but in magazines and on 'Oprah'. And in all these arenas, just as in scholarly writing on the issue of time as a social phenomenon, the consensus is astounding. There is not merely one time, that rigid linear flow of clock time, but a veritable plethora of times and rhythms and flows and what not. In a sense, talking about social time has truly become part of the ongoing moralization that we call culture.

Alfred Gell, who in the general field of time studies is better known for his *The Anthropology of Time* (Gell 1996), has in an essay on barter and gift exchange ironically remarked that there exists a penchant conceptually to organize different ways of economic behaviour according to a simplified and moralistic principle (Gell 1992: 142): ' "Gift–reciprocity–Good/market–exchange–Bad" is a simple, easy-to-memorize formula.' Although he goes on to point out that this myopia is being addressed in modern economic anthropology, it is still interesting to note that the inherently critical project of analysing alternative economic systems can be summarized in such a simple manner. The positing of one aspect of the studied reality as Good and the other as Bad (or at least Worse) seems like the kind of trivial, non-reflexive methodological error an undergraduate would commit. Seasoned research professionals should be immuned to this kind of moralizing in their work, and, if they do choose to moralize for political reasons (as would be the case in, for example, works with an agenda of raising awareness), they supposedly will make their stand an explicit one. In reality, we know that this structure of objectivity/explicit subjectivity is untenable. For political reasons, research with an agenda needs to present itself as objective, whereas pure objectivity in research as a social endeavour might be a logical impossibility.

Turning to the field of time studies, and specifically to the question of time and management, a similar structure emerges. The origin of this chapter lies in my (later aborted) attempt to write a book on temporary organizing, and my later dilemma in trying to come to terms with my own prejudices regarding time. As any reasonably enlightened junior scholar would, I almost instantly became enamoured with the notion that the 'normal' way of viewing the temporal was insufficient and quite possibly a capitalist conspiracy. Somewhat later, though, I experienced what can best be described as an epistemo-existential crisis. I realized that I was capable of regurgitating the party line regarding the ills of linear time on cue, but I really did not know why linear time was bad. Unconsciously I seemed to have bought into the following, a version of Gell's 'easy-to-memorize formula':

Linear–homogeneous–capitalism–Bad/Circular–heterogeneous–critical–Good

The problem was, and still is, that I have no real proof that 'heterogeneous chronological codes' (Clark 1990) are superior in any way, pragmatic or epistemological, to the old-time religion of a linear and uniform time. Sure, quite a few excellent studies have been conducted where heterogeneous times have functioned as a perspective or variable (e.g. Whipp and Clark 1986; Das 1987; Dubinskas 1988). Sure, people will listen and frequently pay for lectures and consultations where the ways of a homogenous time culture are maligned. And, importantly enough for a junior scholar, it is far easier to get 'temporally sensitive' material published, making linearity-bashing a viable career move. But, even though these are excellent points, they do not address the issue. The fact that one can live a good life and have a fine career with/on the conviction that linear time is Bad does not say anything about linear time as such. I can easily find quite brilliant studies that care not a whit for the pluralistic nature of the temporal, and, although it is a logical tautology that a study of heterogeneous time codes must pay attention to time, there is nothing in the adoption of a perspective that proves that this perspective is superior to any other. Unless, of course, we can actually derive some sense of understanding, of 'Aha!'

(Koestler 1970), out of the mere mention and reference to time, which would make the issue a socio-psychological one.

This chapter will deal, therefore, with the issues of how linear time is approached in the study of time and management. I will argue that there is a general tendency towards moralization in these studies, and that linear time in effect stands in for the Villain in their narratives of time. I will further suggest that a more reflexive and less condemning view of 'clock time' would enhance the study of temporal processes in organizations. In a sense I am calling for a cultural turn, an appraisal of time studies as an academic culture. Thus, this chapter is itself a moral project, a political call for reflection.

TIME STUDIES AS VIRTUOUS TALES

In their views of time, it may be perhaps that ancient cultures were more sophisticated than we are today. For example, Minoan society upon the island of Crete developed a culture in which there was an aversion to the straight line.... The Minoans had an ethics of geometry (Lachterman, 1989) which reflected a belief in 'life after life' where the 'sleeping' dead were buried in the foetal position. Arguably, this shape is not unlike the coiled snake and its potent symbolism for another civilization. (Burrell 1992: 169)

The quote above is from Burrell's 'Back to the Future: Time and Organization', a text that is fairly often referenced in the field of time and management. Dealing with a wide range of issues related to the dimension of time in social theory, it has the Minoans as a recurring theme, and tries to make a strong case for anti-linearity. Instead, it argues for a 'spiral' conception of time, one that combines the direction of the linear with the recurrence of the cyclical. Burrell returns to this theme a few years later with 'Linearity, Control and Death' (1998), where linear time is equated with railroads, which in turn are equated with the movement of armies, war, and the Holocaust. In the first case, the Minoans are portrayed as sophisticated merely through their curious moral condemnation of straight lines, whereas in the second case the possibility to reach death effectively makes linearity a metaphorical evil *a priori*. In both cases, statements regarding the ills of linear time are presented as fact, with little or no argumentation. The ease with which time in general and linearity in particular can be presented as a universally moral issue makes for a speedy argument, and the reader is presented with views that are extremely difficult to disagree with or meet critically. In Burrell's texts, you are basically placed in a position where you feel you cannot be interested in linearity without becoming either uncultured or standing on the side of military aggression or worse. Looking at some other texts on time and social theory, this tendency seems widespread. There is a constant evoking of themes meant to stir up feelings. Burkhard Sievers (1990) in effect claims that the permanent nature of the modern corporation is synonymous with a lack of understanding with regards to death. In Adam (1995) the first line of the introduction is a quote from a 10-year-old boy: 'When I think about time I think that it won't be long before I am old and die.' Argue against either and you will immediately find yourself apologetic for being such an insensitive clod. Then there is the cultural turn. Levine (1997: pp. xii–xvi) extols the carefree attitudes of his Brazilian students, and seems ashamed of being punctual when others are not. Edward Hall repeatedly refers to Native Americans arguing for 'the other dimension of time' (the subtitle of his book), arguing less than subtly that the time reckoning of the Hopi is more natural than ours (Hall 1983: ch. 2). Argue against them and you might very well feel yourself instantly turning into a bigot and a racist. The reader is encouraged to find her own examples.

Of course, such dramatization might be inescapable in any form of writing. As, for example, Vladimir Propp (1958) and Kenneth Burke (1950) have gone some way towards showing, the act of telling a story, any story, by necessity introduces specific motifs and functions. In order to show that something is worth doing, a Villain and a Goal must be established, among other things. For time studies, being an interdisciplinary field, this brings in a twofold dynamic. In order to show that time studies is worthwhile *at all*, it is necessary to construct an opposition, those who 'take time for granted' (Lee and Liebenau 1999: 1035). In addition, one has to create a starting point internally within the field in order to construct a quest, something to combat, someone to vanquish:

The authors in this collection aim to challenge the linear, rationalist time logic which characterizes management discourses by adopting a contrary view. They emphasize the richness of the temporal dimensions involved and the wealth of competing attempts to order, regulate and control time in the act of managing.... The authors reveal how qualitative aspects of temporal relations and practices engage with the rational time economy of management.   (From the book proposal of this volume)

We 'challenge', we are 'contrary', and we 'reveal'. It is almost as if we time scholars were a band of guerillas in the mist, coming down upon the establishment like the wrath of God. But at the same time we situate ourselves at the very vertex of thinking, pondering the eternal questions and the foundations of ontology. We are deep thinkers, battling ignorance—a truly romantic tale. But such a tale requires a very specific bad guy. He cannot be too smart, but still powerful. He should at the same time be the Established and something we all know to be contingent. The Linear and his cohorts (the rationalists and the un-reflective) have thus been designated Villains. Such a starting point makes it possible quickly and deftly to create an argument for time as a necessary dimension of reflexivity, giving the scholar a solid foundation from which to continue an argument. Taking a contrary view to linearity might therefore be a necessary starting point for studies on time and management, but it is not an unproblematic one.

ON THE ETHICS OF TIME STUDIES

It is difficult to find fault with time studies as a field. Few disciplines contain quite as many and quite as varied good intentions. Helga Nowotny (1994) wants to emancipate the individual, helping her to achieve 'a time of one's own'. Furthermore, time studies can in her treatment be a way towards the subversive forms of experience that post-industrial man yearns for. Robert Levine (1997) wants to help bring forth a 'multitemporal society', one where different cultures can understand each other, continuing Hall's project (1983) to show that Western time notions are not superior and may be inferior. Roy (1960) makes a heartfelt case for the creation of meaning in tedious work, showing how 'banana time' can be an act of sedition against the heartless corporation. Simpson (1995) discusses how a more nuanced view of time is necessary in creating an ethics in this technological age. Importantly and timely, Adam (1998) wants to save the environment through a greater sensitivity to 'timescapes'. There is a plethora of work, particularly in the field of time and management, which at least in part tries to show that awareness of different ways to pattern the temporal will bring about greater understanding between men (e.g. Ebert and Piehl 1973; Schriber and Gutek 1987; Dubinskas 1988; R. Butler 1995). And, fittingly, in the literature on management and organization, time has repeatedly been referred to as an important aspect in organizational life, with the implication that enhanced knowledge of time will lead to improvements (e.g. Gersick 1988, 1989; Gherardi and Strati 1988; Blyton *et al.* 1989; Hassard 1991; Ramaprasad and Stone 1992; Das 1993). As can be seen, it is a wide range of (ethical) projects that can be fitted in under the auspices of time studies, fine and laudable attempts, united in trying to improve the (organizational) world through more attention to the temporal.

Now, when we study time and management, we are trying to say something either about how we think organizations should be *understood* or about how we think they should *be* (efficient, responsible, money-making, good). The problem is that with an epistemological category such as time it might not be possible to differentiate between the two. Ian Hacking (2000) has remarked that the notion of things being socially constructed—and I would wish to argue that the analysis of time in organizations and management falls within this category—is at the very least implicitly related to the idea that the thing being studied could be totally different. If time reckoning is 'socially constructed', it could be constructed differently, and an analysis of how we view time might be impossible to disentangle from normative prescriptions regarding how we should view time, and consequently that which is studied through this vantage point. Claiming that there are other temporal dimensions beside the linear time of management and planning is a call for taking these into consideration, a project of raising awareness with definite connections to altering practice. As the notion of time we hold does in fact structure the world around us in a specific way, the neutrally presented 'new' notion(s) must in fact logically be synonymous with the presentation of a new world. What seldom becomes very clear, though, is whether the authors and time scholars engaged in these projects see themselves as neutral observers just stating facts or participants with their own personal notions of how the world should be. In many cases, the fact that the presented 'new' conceptions of time are put forth in such a manner as to make the authors' wider agenda viable is presented not as a political move, but as statements of science. To present the 'linear time of management' as false or insufficient is synonymous with presenting an alternative, a way in which one thinks organizations should function. More succinctly put: if time structures our world, time studies might never be able to be fully neutral, but are in part an attempt to change the world. Within the field of management and organization theory this tendency becomes even more pronounced, owing to the empirical nature of the field. In addition, this field can itself be described as practical ethics, born out of moral philosophy and concentrating on doing well (ambiguity very much intended).

But is all this a problem? There might be no reason why a discipline could not be based upon an ethics and function mainly through its strive towards the good. From a postmodern viewpoint, it might even be a more excusable strive than the strive towards the truth (cf. Rorty 1979; Lyotard 1984). Within the scope of this chapter the problem is not that time studies functions through moralizations, but that it tries to hold up a front of objectivity in a position where it is clear that a choice of perspective must have at least a moral component. There can in this perspective be no fundamental way to state that linear time is better or worse than say cyclic time, as this by necessity is a moral choice. And, though a moral choice is absolute in the sense that it is by its holder thought to be logical and necessary, this does not mean that it can be held to be global. The research community can very well hold onto its prejudices, but cannot claim scientific objectivity to such claims.

In the case of management, the claim is that the 'normal' stance, where a strictly linear view of time is adhered to, is insufficient, because it hides among other things the lived rhythms of the individuals working under the regime of the clock (see e.g. Thompson 1967; Zerubavel 1981; Adam 1995: 84–106). But what is here meant by 'insufficient'? Logically, it would refer to a case where we cannot fully understand the phenomenon in question from the original perspective— that is, linear time. But what is the phenomenon in question? If it is an organization, the choice of perspective will by necessity alter the observed phenomenon (cf. Maturana and Varela 1980; Morgan 1986). An organization studied through the perspective of heterogeneous times is *not the same thing* as an organization observed with the belief that time is homogeneous. If we are discussing economy in general, the same point stands (Callon 1998). What we *can* say is either that we feel our knowledge to be better, making it a matter of taste, or that our new picture of the organization is better *for some other purpose*. Opposing linear time perspective could be a way to improve working conditions (Perlow 1999), improve the standing of women in the workplace (Forman and Sowton 1989), or just generally show support for the working man (Roy 1960). But in none of these cases is a clear theory of time necessary, were it not for the fact that it makes the greater argument seem more neutral. What arguments on time in processes of organizing do is that they implicitly make the claim that adopting more perspectives on a subject by necessity results in an improved picture, a statement that lends such adoption scientific credibility. The logic of this thinking is that time is so complex an issue that one cannot handle it with simple categories, and therefore one must want to replace the relatively straightforward idea of a linear time with something more multifaceted. Such an argumentation seems faultless, were it not for the one element missing: power. By redefining the basis of knowledge, time being *the* epistemological category, time studies tries to establish a power relation (cf. Foucault 1973*a*).

The risk is that, by becoming a discipline, one with its own journal (the admittedly excellent *Time and Society*) and more conferences than one can shake a moderately sized stick at, time studies are frightfully close to becoming Theory and, in this process, prescriptive. By presenting the 'time of management' as wrong *a priori* and 'attention to time' as the way to right this wrong, one easily falls into the trap of presenting dogma as research, preferences as science. Marx (1867/1976) needed to create a view of time in capitalist society that would make his thesis regarding the oppression of the proletariat feasible, and accordingly presented the case of working time under industrialism in the manner he did. Still, however pleasing we find the argument (I happen to find it tremendously attractive), it never does anything besides presenting *another* view of time. He does, naturally, argue that this is the *correct* view, but fails to notice that it is so only because it is in line with his ethics. The result: a cadre of devout believers who are unable to adapt the theory to contextual changes (cf. Guillet de Monthoux 1983). Likewise, at the moment at least, the prescription of time studies can be summarized in the simple formula I began with: Linear–homogeneous–capitalism–Bad/Circular–heterogeneous–critical–Good.   This is the Theory, and, if time studies cannot escape this, it will lose much of its own dynamic. It will become a Keeper of the Flame, and time studies might degenerate into mere jargon. As Walter Nash argues in *Jargon: Its Uses and Abuses*, theory can simultaneously be 'shop talk' whilst moving towards 'show talk', a way of impressing the notion of unassailable truth upon the uninitiated. If time studies can muster the same degree of reflexivity towards itself as it demands from other disciplines, much would be won.

What this would entail, though, is a certain humility on the part of the individual researcher. I started the writing of this from a simple question: 'Why does everybody hate the linear so?' The answer is: 'They don't.' But the moralizations inherent in the study of time and management create the field in such a way that certain prejudices become entrenched and certain discourses are taken as true *a priori*. Statements such as 'time is socially constructed' are part and parcel of this approach, discursive titbits that are rarely thought through since they correspond with the world view the community of time studies holds on to. This world view makes up a culture, and the possibility to analyse time unaffectedly is made impossible, and maybe moot, by the boundaries drawn up by such a culture. Still, to be a researcher takes a certain reflexivity towards ones own biases. To retain epistemology without abandoning the ethics would demand that researchers make their dispositions known, instead of treating (or worse, masking) the analysis of time and management as a field for objective and dispassionate study. Openness to the necessary ethical element of epistemology might enrich the study of time, and at the very least it would lessen the self-importance thereof.

As a further observation, if we were to take time wholly seriously as an objectively approachable issue in the writing of management and organization theory, we would in addition come up against a major problem: that the temporal does not respond well to theorizing. Any statements we make within the language game of theory automatically make our statements about time seem fixed and static, and therefore lack temporality in their reflection. This can be seen, for instance, in the history Hassard (1996) writes with its rigid ordering of metaphors. Also, any more plural approach is quickly subverted by the inherent linearity of writing, something that can be discerned in Burrell's texts where the argument for less linear perspectives are presented in a clear, coherent, and very linear way (although Burrell's *Pandemonium* can be read as a valiant attempt at perverting the linearity of argument). And, even if we were to pass these hurdles, the problems presented in the beginning of this chapter make themselves known. To think that the question 'What is time?' can be answered is a fallacy. To make statements beginning with 'Time is...' is a continuation of this fallacy. Time can never be approached in this fashion, simply because any and every attempt to define time leads us into a recursive and everlasting spiral of definitions and their definitions. This holds for typologies as well as matrixes, for plurivocalities as well as clear-cut attempts at definitions. Any and all of these are based on the idea of a thing-out-there as well as on the possibility to catch the temporal and fix it to a page. And this notion creates a foundation from which time studies can be projected as a scientific endeavour.

LINEAR APOLOGIES

So, why not instead take a step back, and assume that time, to a great degree, is just as it seems to be, a rather homogenous flow in one direction only, measurable by clocks and calendars? It seems that the hardest thing to do for a scholar is accepting that a thing sometimes might be just as it appears, or, in the harsher words of Ludwig Wittgenstein: 'Nothing is so difficult as not deceiving oneself.' In the *Blue Book*, Wittgenstein ponders this particular problem, how people try to study things like time by defining them and creating taxonomies. But, he says, most things cannot be contained in such devices. And thinking that the lack of clear meanings for words and concepts is a deficiency or a call for research is like saying that the light from my (Wittgenstein's) reading lamp is no real light at all, simply because it lacks clear boundaries. Similarly, I find little to be gained from saying that the notion of linear time— which, after all, we (also) live with and usually experience little difficulty in doing so—is faulty just because things get fuzzy at the edges.

We could infer that, on the whole, the field of time studies takes itself far too seriously, and that the epistemology of time studies could be enhanced by irony. Here I refer to the work of Richard Rorty (1989, 1998), who has repeatedly argued that, in order to develop a thinking that can handle the complex, ambiguous, and often paradoxical nature of human social existence, one needs to adopt a stance he has called *ironical*, the opposite of which in Rorty's par- lance is *metaphysics*. An ironical thinker never takes her set of basic beliefs as eternally true, but is able to question them simultaneously and work with them. In time studies there exists the implicit basic belief that their role as a discipline to a great degree is that of questioning and critiquing linear and homogeneous views of time. As reasonable as this sounds, particularly within the culture of time studies, it does not follow that this is the only possibility for developing theories of time. In the field of business studies, there is the implicit notion that the role of such studies lies in the improvement of organizations, by making them either more efficient or more humane. But, as reasonable as this also sounds, there is no logical reason why this should be the aim. It is only if we take the scholar's greater project into consideration that such steps become sensible. Choosing to do so we have accomplished and accepted the pragmatic turn, and can in the tradition of American pragmatism concentrate on devel- oping theory that accomplishes what we *want* to accomplish, creating theories that should be analysed through what they do instead of an assumed universal truthfulness. But this takes irony, for then we can no longer pose as neutral thinkers, merely stating facts. Neither can we then claim that linear time is a faulty way to view time, merely that it is insufficient for what we wish to do through time studies. Then linear time will finally be free.

I have at the beginning of this chapter put forth the argument that linear time has got a bad reputation, and that this well-meant bias may even have hindered time studies. But by this I do not mean to criticize the work done in the study of time and management. My aim is not to present a new dogma. Rather, I would like to exhort students of time to become aware of the multifaceted nature of their projects in the same manner they/we are trying to make other people aware of the multifaceted nature of time. When it comes to the studies I have referred to, in most if not all cases I admire and respect these. They are often brilliant, witty, and thoughtful. But they are never final, not in that they would be able to present a more *complete* picture of time. As Wittgenstein (1973) stated: 'It is not new facts about time that we wish to find. All the facts that concern us are out in the open. It is instead the use of the noun "time" that mystifies us.'

II

TEMPORAL STRATEGIES IN A RAPIDLY CHANGING WORLD

II

PART

6

Hidden Causes for Unknown Losses: Time Compression in Management

Ida Sabelis

> It's all a sort of relativity. The faster you live, the more time stretches out. To a nome, a year lasts as long as ten years do to a human. Remember it. Don't let it concern you. They don't. They don't even know.
>
> (Terry Pratchett, 'Introduction' to *Truckers*, 1998)[1]

INTRODUCTION

As a reaction to the instrumental way in which 'organizational culture' has been 'discovered' and used by practitioners and consultants since the 1980s, some anthropologists have entered the realm of organization studies to shed light on values, habits, and the taken-for-granted aspects in the world of organization and management. In a research project conducted from 1996 to 2000, Willem Koot and I studied the lives, views, and opinions of top managers[2] of big organizations and institutions in the Netherlands.[3] The main goal of the research was to find out how top managers *survive* amid the increasing 'complexity' of

---

[1] From Terry Pratchett, 'Introduction' to *Truckers*, in Pratchett (1998). 'Nome' is in the original version, referring to a type of gnomes. Of course, the use of this term should be regarded as one of the unparalleled wordplays of this author, who in my opinion should be read by every person interested in time—if only to render clock time relative.

[2] Involved were thirteen CEOs and two senior executives of 'big' firms and institutions (over 1,000 employees).

[3] The research was a project of Willem Koot and myself. It was published as *Over-Leven aan de Top: Topmanagers in Complexe Tijden* (*Surviving at the Top: TopManagers in Complex Times*). (Utrecht: Lemma 2000). We used several methods to 'share time' with the executives, entering via life stories and continuing with discussions over their views on contemporary

modern times.[4] My parallel goal was to discover how time(s) are involved in everyday management practice in order to make time dimensions explicit and demonstrate the multiplicity of times in a world that is usually considered to be dominated and inspired by singular, linear clock time. In this chapter I focus on one of the time themes, compression, to show how an explicit time perspective in management research helps to expose paradoxes in the everyday reality of management. Compression can be viewed as a theme in itself: the reduction or condensation of tasks within a time frame, the struggle over performance by doing more in less time, the dynamics arising when things are 'left out' in order to concentrate on what is considered a *core* task. Simultaneously, compression can be seen as a consequence of acceleration, paradoxically reinforcing its cause as compression leads to an increase of acceleration and a loss of 'quality' in managerial work.

MEANINGS OF COMPRESSION

The topic of compression emerged in several ways during the whole of my research. Initially it was addressed by one of the managers as a 'side topic', just mentioned in a story about current changes in management practice. When I was reflecting upon the interviews, the idea of compression as a time topic kept lingering in my head. It kept popping up: in remarks about how to deal with flows of information, in stories about managerial strategies, and in solutions for managerial problems that were presented as unquestionable matters of fact. Compression seemed to be one of the main strategies for survival in the managerial world, be it compression of information, of meeting times, of working hours in a week, or, on a more general level, of management as a profession and a process of work.

Before I can present compression from the research, I should like to start with a definition of the term. According to *Webster's Dictionary*, 'to compress' is defined as 'to reduce the volume, duration, etc. *of, by* or *as if* by pressure' (1991: 201; emphasis added). The synonyms are listed as: 'to condense, express concisely' (1991: 201). The use of the term is explained as: 'to make more dense or compact, to express in fewer words, to concentrate, increase the strength of',

---

society, managerial issues, and their personal ways of dealing with all this, their 'survival strategies'. Also, the research entailed observations (weeks) and analysis of documents.

[4] Complexity is a more or less common description for 'our times', addressing several phenomena as they emerge in contemporary (post)modern society. In the research we drew, for instance, on Latour (1991), Beck (1992), Handy (1994, 1998), Watson (1994)—and more recent literature, focused on 'management', by Pahl (1995), Knights and Willmott (1999), and Watson and Harris (1999). 'Complexity' emerges in relationship with ambiguity, risk, turbulence, and chaos.

leading to the definition of 'to reduce'. From a formal linguistic point of view, most of the layers of meaning found in the research are already present. The use of prepositions in the definition is particularly interesting. Three dimensions of time arise. 'To reduce duration *of* pressure' leads to a view of compression as a helpful phenomenon: if pressure can be reduced in time, it may help in finding or keeping balance—less time under pressure may seem a healthy way to gain ('free') time for other things. To reduce duration *by* pressure implies something different: the shortening of, for instance, a time frame available for performing a task either by putting pressure on the time frame itself (shorter time frames for meetings) or by compressing the contents of what has to happen in a given time frame. The preposition 'by' also presupposes the possibility of pressure from the outside, thereby reducing the free will or the individual choice of subjects under this kind of compression. In a general sense there is nothing wrong with having time frames tightened from the 'outside', as long as reduction through this pressure enables one to reach the desired goals or address management problems with the necessary time and attention. The *Eigenzeiten* of managerial processes are relevant in this context. Some problems just need 'ripening' or extensive communication for some time. Alternatively, problems need to be considered from several perspectives, which also takes time. Sometimes a fixed time frame is necessary to produce any outcomes at all. Yet the reduction of duration by pressure from the outside may increase the amount of experienced or perceived pressure and thereby cause unexpected or undesired effects. This may happen, for instance, when the reduction is experienced as unfair, which in turn may increase the perceived pressure. Finally, we have the definition 'to reduce duration *as if* by pressure'. The 'as if' asks for a critical review of compression that is experienced, compared with a supposed need for compressing. This sense of the word includes the political use of pressure, the strategic application of 'haste', the delegation of time-consuming tasks to others (who are supposed to 'have' more time), and a perceived understanding of what people may perform within time frames—that is, the status attached to 'haste' and 'being busy'. All of these will be addressed in the examples below.

The description of compression as 'concentration' combined with 'increasing strength' is interesting from a time perspective. The linguistic descriptions suggest that the definitions are applied to material objects; they have a different sense when applied to time or times. The concentration on time as duration suggests a concentration on temporality leading to a tighter time frame. Or, to put it another way, it might even lead to the experience of a shorter time frame with the aim of increasing productivity where this may very well not be the case. I shall return to this point when I present the empirical data. Another aspect to consider from the definition of compression is 'compression by condensation'. In physics, condensation is known as the transition of a substance from one state to the other—for instance, gasses into liquid form.

92   IDA SABELIS

An example is water condensing from the air on single-glazed windows when it is cold outside. Or we know how liquid condenses into a solid substance, usually through the use of a compressor—the principle by which, for instance, water is turned into ice for many Dutch skating rinks. Substances may even be transformed by this process on the molecular level: in chemistry condensation is used to describe a class of chemical reactions 'involving the union of two or more atoms or molecules... to form a usually more complex molecule' (*Webster's* 1991: 203). In the relationship between time(s) and the performance of tasks the suggestion could be made that, under pressure, tasks (molecules, atoms, or units) are condensed into different (merged) outcomes. Though this comparison may not be fully viable, it seems an interesting point of view: the possibility that tasks or performances could be completely transformed by the experience of compression in the condensation sense. The idea of the convergence or merger of different data, pieces of information, communication (saying more in less words), or even political strategies makes one wonder about the outcome of decisions made under pressure.

For a better understanding, it is also important to view compression as a term in everyday use. An anecdote may illustrate the point I want to make here. Increasingly, products are compressed to save transportation and storage space or as a service for customers. Last summer my daughter needed a new bed, so we went to one of the shops of a European-wide furniture chain. To transport the bed I had borrowed a van from a friend, expecting the transportation of a double-sized mattress would not be possible in my little car. We were supposed to wait for our order in the basement of the shop. We waited and waited, looking at the door of the storage rooms, expecting a huge mattress to arrive in its usual, rectangular size. After a time we noticed a woman shouting out a number—she was getting red with impatience because no one reacted. She was standing beside a little cart with a huge round pack on it—to our surprise this turned out to be the mattress we had been waiting for: fully compressed, taking up less than a quarter of its expected space. The van seemed rather superfluous and we were easily capable of carrying the thing, even up to my daughter's bedroom, which is reachable only by a typical Dutch, very narrow staircase. To make a long story short: it took the mattress several weeks to inflate and reach its desired size and the mattress is never ever going to be carried out of that room unless we find a way of compressing it again. This anecdote illustrates several characteristics of compression: compression serves some good, at least practical, purposes, depending on the context. However, it also illustrates the importance of *de*-compression: one must be aware of the full range of tasks implicit in a problem. And, once de-compressed, a huge effort is needed (including special equipment) to regain a possibly desired state of re-compression. In terms of time this suggests compression as a process of 'loops', disregarding the specific need for compression in relationship to certain tasks within various contexts. Without negating its advantages, sometimes the process of compression, de-compression, and re-compression enlarges (total) duration: the reduction of duration may be the desired outcome for some people, but it can produce more work for others.

The everyday use of the term compression is illustrative in other ways as well. There is a limit to which people, objects, time frames, or work processes can be compressed. Little creativity is needed to see the connection between physical objects that crack under too much pressure from compression and people under such conditions: if time pressure increases too much, people too can 'crack'. The societal and academic attention to topics such as burnout point to the relevance of recognizing huge pressures that can cause a great deal of pain. But, without neglecting the serious damage done to some people, that explanation is a little too facile for the exploration of compression in top management. The relationships are usually more complex and pressure changes over time—in top management the high pressure leading to crack-up is usually avoided, by 'delegating' (in terms of time: externalizing) pressure to others or by 'planning' periods of pressure to be alternated with relaxation. Let us take an example in which the outcome is not so evidently damaging. Imagine the pillow of a couch being compressed when I sit on it. As soon as someone else decides to sit next to me, the compression caused by the other person causes me to lift a bit, and, though this can make me feel uneasy, no harm is done. Yet the picture here is that compression at a certain point, or for a certain time, increases pressure elsewhere. Starting from compression as an aspect (or a consequence) of acceleration, this gives an idea of how compression can be diverted to others and to other contexts—inside or outside the organization.

Problems or events are coped with or dealt with at different levels and by other people. Two consequences of compression of this kind should be mentioned. First, compression can cause *re*pression elsewhere, deliberately or inadvertently. Secondly, if this is applied at random, the 'receiving' party cannot easily decide from where the pressure came. This is more or less the picture of a huge organizational pillow on which many people plop down and get up again, causing and lifting pressure all the time until everybody gets 'used to the rhythms' of constant pressure and lifting.

To sum up: compression implies pressure on and within time frames and other temporal aspects with implications both within and outside organizations. It thereby provokes a change in the actual duration of work processes. However, the process of compressing is often diffuse in the sense that causes and effects are hard to discriminate. Compression encompasses a cluster of phenomena, causing real or assumed pressure on people and their time(s), and change or transformation of tasks, and possibly also triggering a decrease in the most important way of communication, the expression and exchange of meaning(s) in words. Investigating processes of compression in the context of causes and effects and from the perspective of multiple time dimensions should therefore shed some light on underlying experiences and sometimes unexpected, maybe even unintended, effects.

COMPRESSION AND MANAGERIAL WORK

Various modes of compression need to be addressed in order to analyse the empirical data available in my research. First there is the question of what (task, process, strategy) is being compressed or reduced in time, for what reason(s), and with what outcomes and consequences. Then it is important to assess when compression is applied, both at an individual as well as at a more collective level (context, team, age, and habits of work). Finally it is essential to find out how this is brought about: by internal or individual desire or drive, by pressure from the situation of the individual (that is, including position, branch of business, and type of organization), by a perceived need (that is, fear of competition, ideas about globalization, striving for a unique position) or, most likely, by a combination of these factors. Taken as a whole, it seems important to assess when, how, in what time frames, and where compression occurs in order to draw conclusions about the effects of the process and the possible 'loops' in time that will, without doubt, have an impact of their own. For this purpose I should like to introduce some of the remarks made by top managers, which triggered my interest in the topic of compression in the first place.

The very first remark was by the vice president of a consultancy firm, Daniel Lievegoed.[5] In our final meeting (out of seven), I asked him to reflect upon some remarks he had made earlier about acceleration as one of the main societal changes over the previous twenty years. He answered:

> I have a strong feeling that practically everything I experienced can only be regarded as part of this acceleration.... There is something like 'building times'—Tom Peters calls it compression, not unrightfully so. Compression is not some kind of condensation, as we tend to think. Compression is putting more information into less memory by leaving out an excess of information. If you look at the latest technological developments, the art of leaving things out is called compression. Then what is left is the essence and this essence can again be compressed. You can transfer it with less time into less memory space. The idea of compression is not condensation, which would make things less manageable. It is a relief actually, leaving things aside or out—it is predominantly an answer to the wish or the perceived need that things have to happen faster...

Various aspects of the issues I have raised so far are illustrated in this quotation: the aspect of reduction—that is, of information—the rejection of condensation (and thereby of transformation), and relief about the possibility of dealing with 'the essence' of one's job. And very clearly the purpose of the exercise is

---

[5] The names of the participants have been changed, not only to protect their personal sphere, but also to enhance the quality of the analysis. For some it provided more 'openness' in the meetings, and, afterwards, it turned out to be important on a different level: it avoided readers being detracted from the analysis because of the images they already had of some of the well-known people in the research.

presented as a consequence of acceleration. Different aspects of the concept of compression are also apparent, whether of an intuitive or an associative nature. First Daniel expresses the idea of 'building times', which implies a rational and manageable view of work and task performance. This is also related to the principles of just in time as they are assumed to have been 'imported' during the 1980s from Japan (compare the critical remarks about JIT by Nishimoto, this volume). The idea of 'excess'—that is, including excess of information—is also mentioned. Thirdly, the culture of the new economy and the IT business (compare the chapters by Lee and Liebenau and by Koku for an elaboration of the assumptions in this 'culture') has an effect on his view of the process of compression and reduction, within a system that reduces information to bits and bytes, promising the (future) possibility of further reduction of the essence by compressing it again (and again, and again...?). Daniel's remarks suggest that he is equating compression with computerization. To find out more about this, it may be illustrative to elaborate further on Daniel's background and professional life below. I follow this with examples from other top managers to show how they deal with compression.

Compression and a Lack of Memory

Daniel Lievegoed is a very thoughtful, hard-working person. Born into a well-to-do family in the north-west of the Netherlands, with links to well-known industrial families, he followed a career path in which he worked for most of the big Dutch-based firms in the food and IT business. He insists that all his career moves 'came upon him'; he never really 'strove' for a career: 'It just came my way, I don't think I ever deliberately made strategic choices; they [the opportunities] just crossed my path. I was in a certain area and I did my best within that. I never felt the urge fundamentally to dig into things.'

In the 1960s he was one of the first Dutch students to take courses in the USA, which gave him an advantage, especially in the field of computerized MIT systems. In order to get some practice in business, his first job was in the corporate planning department of one of Holland's big food companies, working closely with the CEOs of the firm. This job was intended as a stepping stone for a 'real job'; yet they had to 'tap him on the shoulder' before he completed the formal application. Daniel recounts that he was rather nervous about the selection process and that when he got through and told his boss that he would leave the firm, the man burst into laughter, as he had known about it all the time. Afterwards he learned:

that was the way it was always done. Later I applied it myself! And it turned out to be a necessary experience for the job that followed. Yet, at the time, it just felt peculiar; it may have been a pre-designed path, but it didn't feel that way.... For me it was the first time I was in touch with real, hard life—... [later on, work became] a continuing process during which you learned to forget about hours...

When I ask him if he remembers how long the application procedure took, he does not remember. He does not remember a lot of things anyway. During the interviews a pattern emerges, both for the choices he has made during his career and for how he remembers situations and 'the way things went': 'I don't think I ever chose: it always happened to me, the invitation for a job, the circumstances...'. This is also expressed in his ways of dealing with problems, whether of a managerial or private nature:

IS. How did you deal with that [problem]?
DL. I don't remember. From that time up to very recently I have lived with tensions, problems at home, problems at work—it is no excuse for not doing both things right...
IS. So that's your way?
DL. Yes, to press ahead, to go on—and again....I don't look back...takes me half an hour to get over frustrations....
IS. What happens then, during that half-hour?
DL. I don't know, some kind of suppression I guess...

Suppression may be one of the important aspects of compression, as it is a way of 'leaving things aside or out'. If one can suppress the need to reflect upon, for instance, what causes frustration, or if one is capable of avoiding reflection about the longer-term consequences of a decision, life becomes a lot easier. But what effect does that have on the decisions taken and the strategies applied later? Does it enhance the quality of a decision and can it result in a situation where in the end the gains of the compression process are lost? If, in decision making, the process of information gathering is shortened by leaving relevant information aside, it may well be that this 'failure' comes back to the decision-maker later, resulting in longer time being spent on a topic than there would have been in the first place.

Reflection in top management is also influenced by other time frames. The duration of tenure in top management might be of importance here. Strikingly it was Daniel who pointed to the fast 'turnover' of top managers, citing how in big firms CEOs tend to have a three-year cycle—the first year to get used to the organization and to clean up some of the mess left by predecessors; the second year to develop 'new' ideas about how to put a personal stamp on the organization; and the third year for implementing the 'new ways' and to get out again before the disadvantages of the strategy became fully visible. Daniel tends to talk about this phenomenon in a joking manner; he himself left the rat race of industrial top managers some years ago, as he felt he lacked a good balance in his time, money, and social relationships. 'If you don't conform to their methods, you are not taken seriously anymore and then this little world loses all attraction.'

The overall picture of compression, according to Daniel Lievegoed, is a combination of being swept along (in his career), suppressing reflection during work, and a (selective) lack of memory, possibly caused by the speed with which he has learned to deal with tasks in his work. It seems that remembering is a time-consuming activity and not appreciated, or maybe not functional, in his type of business. As for context, he seems to have conformed to the speed and the superficiality of his surroundings: acceleration comes from the outside as a marker of 'how things are in business'. There seems to be only one choice, surrendering to it or leaving the business, as he has finally done. However, before we broaden the scope of compression, we should turn to how it is experienced by some of the other managers.

Juggling—but Sometimes a Bit Fuzzy

Pieter de Waard is President of the 'HBO-Raad' (Council for Institutes of Higher Education) and CEO of one of the institutes. He is a highly intelligent, careful, and conscientious man, who is clear about the strategic choices in his career ('business would just not be my world'). Yet this does not prevent him from being affected by compression. To illustrate the context of acceleration and compression in his daily practice and how he deals with it, I should like to present a large part of the conversation in which this topic came up:

PW. I never felt the pressure of things that were left undone. During university this changed...we were so busy with all kinds of things. Lots of weekend with...I remember having six weekends fully planned, being a board member of this and that—and still, looking back, it was a very relaxed period [laughs and sighs]. But that's what it is: looking back you remember being occupied and yet I think 'what did I do really?'...I think it has to do with efficiency. You can just do more, it accumulates. And you will be able to be active, working in a goal-orientated way for a longer period. Until you reach a limit—for me that is 60 [hours]. I can keep up with that for a long time...

IS. Do you ever have less?

PW. Oh, yes, I worked forty hours a week more often than sixty. But all right, sixty hours is reasonable. You may be busy with perhaps thirty different tasks. And you have a better performance because you do more things; you become more efficient under pressure. For me there is a link with being so busy that I stop planning. But then things go wrong. I can be so busy that I become less successful. And then I reach a point where I have to pull myself together and decelerate: stop, take time out and make choices...

IS. And you have to smooth away things? When does that happen?

PW. Well, if there are too many things at a time, by mail, by phone. But there is a pattern in that and I usually notice it quite early. Then I can handle it quite well and I skip things...in order to create peace for doing the things I really find important. Actually I can say that, paradoxically, peace has increased over the years...

IS. Peace has increased...

PW. Yes, in the sense of the things I do...even if it is too much and I cannot avoid it, I just compress things or perform a task less well. But that's a decision: I do it within the given time and that should be it. There are increasingly more tasks and responsibilities, but at the same time I don't feel that stress or pressure is increasing. On the contrary, I don't feel stressed.

IS. Let me just take one point out of this: you say that over time you improved in dealing with the workload, by thinking 'I just let it be'. Has it ever gone wrong?

PW. Oh, yes, it goes wrong from time to time...

IS. What happens then? I mean, have you ever been over the edge...

PW. Once—I don't know how to explain that well. I was mixed up with other things. I had flu—and I thought 'Hey, there is more to this...'—Then I dropped out for a couple of weeks. I was dealing with different topics from nowadays. I was President of the Free [Anthroposophist] School and I was expected to deal with finances all by myself. There was no financial system whatsoever, a real mess. It was like skating on thin ice...and I was responsible ...They have no idea about money, you are the only one and so what you say is right...well, I couldn't cope with that, I had no grip...That's the only memory of really—if I would have carried on there...Someone else would really find that a point for falling over the edge...

IS. Did it take a lot of time and concentration?

PW. Yes, from the point of worrying it took twenty hours too much. I couldn't cope with that at all....It's a matter of concentrating on the things I really have to do. It is not a question of perfectionism—if I have to do ten things, well, then I do them less thoroughly, in less time and I am perfectly happy with that, because it is a conscious decision.

In Pieter's account we find some similarities with Daniel's position: top management means that a lot of tasks, decisions, and things 'to handle' arrive on one's desk. Pressure increases, which is sometimes a healthy thing ('one becomes more efficient') and sometimes a bad thing ('I decide to be a bit more "sluggish"'). Surviving all that means 'leaving things out', but also finding a balance between what is still experienced as productive and where compression becomes 'edgy' in the sense that things get out of hand. The idea of doing things less well also derives from having to cope with multiple responsibilities. The main difference between Daniel and Pieter (apart from the difference in professional context) is that Pieter has a more philosophical attitude: he keeps 'looking back' (remembering) and trying to learn from former situations. He 'steps out' when he feels that the quality of his efforts is decreasing. He consciously tries to reflect upon his work in terms of 'balancing' and estimating where and when compression is still 'functional' or where risks may occur. He would never agree with Daniel Lievegoed that even the essence of things could be compressed again, as he is very much aware of the limits of compression—some tasks just need their 'own time'. At a certain point one is left with ten things to do, and these are all equally important—you juggle, though the balls may not be kept in the air all that elegantly. And he acknowledges 'rhythmicity' in the sense of accumulation of experiences as a factor, not just for efficiency, but also for effective performance.

We may conclude that, although Pieter does experience the risks of compression, he finds other ways of dealing with it—in being reflective, by taking a more holistic view of other aspects of life, and in accepting that sometimes tasks and responsibilities are dealt with in a less effective manner. Yet, even if this suggests that Pieter deals better with compression than Daniel, we should acknowledge that many of the problems, demands, and responsibilities in higher education deal with longer time frames than in business. However, if non-profit institutions continue to adopt the same methods and outlooks as profit-making businesses, will it not be just a question of time before Pieter is confronted with the same ambiguity as Daniel? Though the aim of my research is not a comparison of individual traits in order to gain a representative pattern of compression, it is interesting to look at the experiences and attitudes of a top manager positioned 'between' Daniel and Pieter, someone who views the topic from a different angle, in a different professional context: Dick van Roden.

Dealing with Flows of Information

Dick van Roden is Permanent Secretary of one of the Ministries in The Hague. As such he is, as a colleague to the Minister, the CEO of the organization. Ministers change every four years, but he is the 'constant factor'. In the context of top managers, he might be considered 'in between' administration and business, because he deals with both. For him the main compressing factor at the individual level is his position between politics and administration and between the demands from society and business. In addition, from his background as an (urban) planner, he has developed an explicit view on time and time-related topics, resulting in several brochures and reports by his organization, with a strong link to environmental policy and a call for deceleration. He can talk for hours about the more philosophical aspects of time(s), the importance of social time versus economic time, and the role of 'emotional time', a term that he himself claims to have coined and introduced into politics and his everyday practice of management. In dealing with questions about the daily practice of his work and his view on societal change over the previous decades, we discussed the topic of compression in relationship to the increasing flow of information, expressed by computerization in management practice and in society as a whole. Dick starts from a more abstract level, stating:

Computerization—that is a very important phenomenon in our society—but what is its basic trend? It is all hidden in the drive to 'want to know everything' in our life—and the fact that we want to know, to comprehend with our brains. If you consider that life is so limited and we have an average of, say, eighty years to 'have it all'...This all leads to our desire to participate in the flow of information. In fact this represents the realization of how limited we are in a lifetime. In that sense, yes, information is a problem. Computerization, however, is not—it is all about the selection of relevant information, choosing information. We seem to be incapable of doing that because of the huge availability of information we have nowadays. We cannot decide what is relevant. You have to know about this and that—and what about the rest?—Just leave it be! And the drive to think that we have to do it ever faster, the acceleration of it all, wanting to have and do everything within this life...it all has to be shortened and fast and accelerating. We are always in a hurry, always rushing.

But then, immediately, he turns to the practical level, saying:

And if I ask you something and you want to give me the right answer, you [researchers] just take a book or ten from the shelves and you think you have got it...we all try it that way. But, when I get a report that is longer than two or three pages, it cannot be well thought through. It is sent back because of its length. It has to be done within two pages—if you can't do that, you're doing a lousy job and you haven't taken the time to consider the essence of what you want to convey. It takes an enormous amount of time to produce relevant information. And we do not take enough time. So we give information a huge 'spin' and it just cannot all get through and it cannot all be relevant...

In the course of the interview Dick comes back to the nature of his responsibilities, his Ministry being one of the few dealing with long-term decision making (in his view), but his main point about compression is made in the above quote. Acceleration is there, flows of information are increasing, necessitating compression of information at the managerial level. This causes a somewhat tense, or even paradoxical relationship between a rather holistic view of time dimensions and at the same time the necessity of compressing important information into the 'maximum' of a two-page note. Though he realizes the importance of qualitative good information, you cannot 'dig yourself into a three hundred page report, where you can't find any orientation'. Two patterns emerge from his story. First, the fact that, as a top manager, you must rely on short reports in order to survive in the flow of information. Though this process appears logical, the 'essence' of the information, on which final decisions are made, may well lack breadth. Dick refers to criteria only in terms of 'density' and 'clarity'. Though he has definite ideas about time frames for decisions and the risks involved, he finds himself in a position between the speed of politics and his desire to be an intellectual.

The second pattern is the way in which increased flows of information and the parallel need for compression cause more work for other levels of the organization. A consequence of compression, in the sense of time saving for top management, is more work and time investment for other people. A report is sent back if it is not considered sufficiently 'dense'; others 'should have spent more time' and are asked to do it again in order to keep strictly to the essence of the contents. This means that, in order for decision making at the managerial level to be effective, more time has to be spent in the organization to 'have it all'. This can be done only if either more people are brought in, or the people already there learn how to process more information in less time. This again creates further responsibility for management: not how to manage information itself, but how to have the information managed elsewhere. The increasing warnings about burnout could point to the fact that this process also causes stress in the organization and that the need for distilled information contributes to the problem.[6]

Dick's case illustrates that compression of information has a direct effect on the speed of decision making, the depth of the matters considered ('you can't have it both ways'), and the effects of acceleration in politics. He definitely 'uses' compression as a coping strategy, though at the same time this gives him distance from some of his 'products': where he sees the losses of acceleration and compression, he backs out personally. If not, he would 'go mad'. This pattern of top managers being concerned about the possible risks of their work recurs throughout the research. Some of the managers back out of the conversation altogether if we reach this point in the conversation; others just say something like they are sorry 'but the problems will outlive me...'. Here another time aspect comes in: the dimension of taking into account the effects of compression over a longer period of time illustrates the emergence of 'loops in time'. Ultimately, compression may necessitate spending more time on a problem or a task because of the reflexive (that is, backfiring) nature of management processes. Whether it is the spending of tax money on unnecessary planning and projects or on the costs of burnout, sooner or later these factors have to be taken into account and they may well cause a greater loss over time than the short-term gains of compression.

CONCLUSION

Compression as a focus for investigating management processes reveals how acceleration affects the daily practice of processing information, juggling with

---

[6] 'Burnout' is reported to be increasing in the Netherlands: according to a recent survey approximately 4% of the Dutch population, a quarter of a million people, suffer from burnout in a more or less severe manner (*Volkskrant*, 25 Mar. 2000). Apart from the numbers, there seems to be a fast growing section of young people, mainly young women (without children), who are experiencing this.

tasks and decision making, and the complex view of the time dimensions involved. Compression is largely experienced as 'coming from outside the organization', as an effect of the societal flywheel of the industrial world, infusing organizations and not allowing people to ignore it. As a phenomenon it is not questioned; it is considered 'the way it is'—so people are engulfed by it, inclined to view its inevitable advantages largely without questioning its effects. Here management strategies come in: compression seems to be an individual strategy, an organizational necessity, and a societal norm.

Compression has a definite role in the areas of processing information, decision making, competing, and surviving. It is a highly complex phenomenon and it is difficult to assess whether it brings about transformation (of views, decision outcomes, strategies, individual or personal views, organizational goals, and so on.) or not. But assumptions can be made that this is the case, as so many instances point to an increase of short-term management and the surrender of managers to it.

Positive effects of acceleration are listed by top managers mainly in the area of 'processing information': compression is a way of leaving things out and getting to the 'essence' of things, probably parallel to the view of the computerization of society expressed by Daniel Lievegoed. It is hard to get a clear picture of what this 'essence' is supposed to be, apart from 'off-the-cuff' estimations, which imply ever shorter time frames: is it minimal information for decision making and a comfortable overview so that one can delegate the more time-consuming work to others and still be in control? It would appear that, to succeed in management, an ability to draw out 'the essence' from an overload of information is essential.

Looking at managerial work through the focus of compression reveals paradoxical effects in and over time. Managers tend to use the term solely in a positive sense. My research shows how ambiguous the meanings and effects of compression are, especially regarding long-term effects of organizational processes. Compression is seen by the managers simultaneously as a solution for acceleration and as another coping strategy in an accelerating world. The possible 'losses' are not understood or acknowledged because of pressures, the need for quick action, and an accepted level of (rational) efficiency. This underpins the taken-for-granted character of compression. If you do not comply with it, you are 'out'—you should find another job or you should not have been in this position in the first place. How does this fit in with the proclaimed need for creativity, invention, empathy, and open-mindedness (not to mention sustainability) in modern management? Compression ('gaining time') promotes acceleration by implying that rational reduction of information, emotions, and alternatives is necessary to reach organizational and individual goals. The image of compression is heavily influenced by the rationality of computerization and automatization. No one seems to be really in charge of deciding what is essential in flows of information. The criteria in deciding what is 'essence' and what is 'fuss' are vague. Yet, computers are not creative by themselves and in a way are rather time consuming, as most of us have experienced one way or another. Further questioning the taken for granted, as with compression, might reveal the disadvantages of using only rational time understanding and leaving out the genuine time needed for responsible, human-sized, and perhaps selectively decelerated management.

7

Cooperation Engineered: Efficiency in the 'Just-in-Time' System

Nishimoto Ikuko

INTRODUCTION

Kanban, kaizen, 'total quality control' (TQC) and 'quality circles' (QC), 'flexibility', and 'multiple processing'—since the 1980s Western companies have introduced concepts and practices such as these into their plants in the United States and Europe. They have done so to emulate Japanese cost-saving methods of production, or 'lean production', as it is known in the United States. Some figures may illustrate how the introduction of such 'Japanese' manufacturing techniques improved Western companies' performance. According to figures in 1989, the average number of hours required to manufacture a car in Europe was 35.5, and in the United States 24.9. In a 1993 survey the figures decreased. In southern Europe the hours were reduced to 22.9 and in American plants to 22.4. The same research, however, shows that Japanese transplants in North America took an average of 17.4 hours to produce a car, while Japanese plants located in Japan needed 16.5 (Womack *et al.* 1990: 85; Kochan *et al.* 1997: 93). The gaps are clearly diminishing; Western companies are fast catching up. Yet at the end of the twentieth century Japanese companies still seemed to be in a more competitive position.

The 'Japanese' production system seeks low-cost, high-quality products; it also attempts to manufacture a variety of products in relatively small quantities to meet the diverse and fluctuating demands of the market. Its basic idea is to produce what is needed, at the time needed, and in the quantity needed.

This chapter is based on research conducted for my article ' "Harmony" as Efficiency: Is "Just-In-Time" a Product of Japanese Uniqueness?', *Time and Society*, 8/1 (1999), 119–40. Japanese names in this article, including mine, are written in the order used in Japan—namely, the surname first followed by the given name.

The 'Japanese' method is thus seen as an alternative to Fordism, which is based on the principle of mass production. Ford, an automobile company, set the norm for manufacturing systems in the first half of the twentieth century; its 'alternative' in the second half of the century also came from a car manufacturer, Toyota. As against Fordism, the Japanese system is often called Toyotism, or more formally the Toyota production system. In industrial production, time and profit have an inseparable relationship. Maximization of profit is achieved by minimization of production time. Cost is saved by saving time. Toyota's fundamental aim is to maximize the profit by saving costs; in order to save costs, it attempts to eliminate all waste, including 'unproductive time'. It is very symbolic that Toyota's method of acquiring profit is also popularly known as JIT, or the 'just-in-time' system, bearing the word of time in its appellation. Benjamin Franklin's maxim of 'time is money' is clearly alive and well in this new approach to profit making. Toyota in this regard may agree completely with Alfred P. Sloan, once president of General Motors, who said that the business of the automobile industry was not to make cars but to make money.

My concern in this chapter lies in reviewing the just-in-time system in the light of time. One may immediately think of *kanban*, or information control used for the delivery of parts and supplies. Under a strict timetable, it embodies the quintessential feature of Toyota's mechanism: the precise timing of delivery, with a complex and multilayered system of subcontractors, and 'clockwork-like meshings' that 'tick' (Monden 1981, 1991: 98–136; Fruin 1992: 256). Speed-up is another important issue. Every worker at the assembly line experiences the computerized control of work. Finally, there is the principle of getting more work out of each unit of production. Forced overwork, in the most tragic cases, leads not only blue-collar workers but also white-collar workers to death (Sakuma and Ohmori 1991: 16–25).[1] My purpose, however, is not the exploration of such practices. The temporal element I would like to examine may fall into a more general category of time, efficiency. My concern, more specifically, is the efficiency achieved not by individual skilfulness but by teamwork. I am concerned about this because, while working as a team is a very common experience in the modern division of labour all over the world, it is often treated with a culturist emphasis on Japanese uniqueness. Some recognize that the just-in-time system is a rational manufacturing technique built upon and developed from the Western manufacturing system (Schonburger 1982; Cusumano 1985). Others, while allowing this point, nevertheless maintain that Japan's rise to an industrial power is largely due to the uniqueness of its culture or traditional organizational structure (Dore 1973; Ouchi 1981). When the culturists stress assets from the past, their arguments concentrate around concepts that attempt to characterize the Japanese by their preference for collective activity and their respect for 'harmony' and 'cooperation', thus

[1] During my studies at Manchester University another Japanese student told me that two of her uncles, who had both been working for Toyota, had died from overwork.

helping to reinforce the familiar dichotomy of 'Western individualism' versus 'Japanese teamwork'. Japanese companies, on their part, too, stress the need for harmony and cooperation. For these reasons, this article will reconsider the just-in-time system from two perspectives; one is to examine management's repeated stress on cooperation focusing on metaphors that appeared in managerial discourse; the second is to review the development of industrial techniques in Japan in the light of its post-war political history.

THE QUESTION OF COORDINATION

Modern industry takes the form of a division of labour. Car manufacturing, handling as many as 20,000–30,000 parts, involves a particularly complex division and subdivision of labour. While it is much more efficient to make a car this way than for one worker to do everything alone, it is also true that some elements of waste arise precisely because the work is divided. Toyotism removed the 'play' element from work (that is any non-productive time), as did Taylorism and Fordism. But Toyota's engineers were no mimics. They achieved something that the American industrial architects failed to see. Toyota technicians did not think that the sum total of maximum efficiency in each process was automatically identical with the shortening of the total production time. Taylorism distinguished value-adding from wasteful motion, in the sequence of the individual's work; Toyota distinguished profitable processes from wasteful ones within the whole productive sequence. The company saw a number of unprofitable points involving 'in-between labour' in existing manufacturing practices. Its primary concern was, while pursuing efficiency, how to reorganize the sequence of work, and therefore eliminate wasteful time.

Toyota, a Japanese automotive company, began to see the necessity for a new method when it faced a practical question. Toyota's historiography tells us an anecdote. In his struggle to manufacture passenger cars in emulation of Ford and General Motors, who were operating in Japan with considerable gain in the 1930s, Toyoda Kiichiro (1894–1952), the founder of Toyota Motor Corporation, decided to purchase the latest and the most sophisticated machine tools. Contrary to his expectations, mechanization was unsatisfactory; it did not produce a dramatic effect on overall efficiency. Each machine had a different efficiency level and machines were completing the jobs at different speeds. Kiichiro, seeing the synchronization of time as the critical aspect of manufacturing efficiency, envisaged a manufacturing process where each phase synchronized with each other in a smooth and coordinated flow. He then 'wrote the words "just in time" [jasuto in taimu] on a banner and hung it on the wall' (Toyota 1988: 69).

In production it is not only machines that need synchronization. Successfully efficient production involves an effective coordination of three elements: materials and human motion as well as machinery. In a factory where a number of workers with different levels of skill and experience work together, some may complete a task more quickly than others. It is management's task to teach a 'slow' worker how to abandon wasteful motion and work efficiently. This is where Toyota's engineers begin to speak in metaphors.

TEAMWORK AND SPORT METAPHORS

Ohno Taiichi (1912–1990), JIT's chief architect, drew the analogy between production and sports. 'Work and sports have many things in common', because both work and sports are 'done through teamwork.' But not all sports serve as a good example. Japanese traditional sports such as *sumo* wrestling, *kendo*, and judo are inappropriate analogies, for the contenders compete through individual skill and strength. It is organized team sports that can explain the nature of factory work: 'in modern industry, harmony among people in a group, as in teamwork, is in greater demand than the art of the individual craftsman' (Ohno 1988: 23). Ohno found the metaphor of baseball most suitable; he likens production to the defence aspect of the game.

...a player in the outfield has nothing to do as long as the pitcher has no problems. But a problem—the opposing batter getting a hit, for example—activates the outfielder who catches the ball and throws it to the baseman 'just in time' to put the runner out. Managers and supervisors in a manufacturing plant are like the team manager and the batting, base, and field coaches. A strong baseball team has mastered the plays; the players can meet any situation with coordinated action. In manufacturing, the production team that has mastered the just-in-time system is exactly like a baseball team that plays well together. (Ohno 1988: 8)

Teamwork is a very important element in JIT. Ohno repeatedly explained successful operation by cooperation through a variety of other sports, such as eight rowers in a boat race, eleven players on a football team, and the six players in a volleyball team. The idea is repeated in Japanese company 'transplants' in the United States. Laurie Graham (1995), herself working in a Subaru–Isuzu factory in Indiana, also notes the company's use of the team/sport metaphor. For the automotive company a person working in the factory is not a worker; he or she, in the firm's euphemism, is an 'associate', a member of a team. As the company explains, 'Team leaders are highly skilled Associates, like basketball team captains...A group leader is like a coach, responsible for several teams.' At the end of daily morning meetings, Graham records, 'Team members would huddle in a manner similar to that of a sports team before a game' (L. Graham 1995: 69, 108; see also Fucini and Fucini 1990: 43–4).

The track relay race has served as another powerful metaphor for production processes. It involves four individuals, whose skill at passing the baton affects the overall speed. Likewise, in the collective work of manufacturing, 'the parts should be handed over as if they were batons' (Ohno 1988: 25). This analogy marvellously corresponds to that used by Kamata Satoshi, a journalist who worked for Toyota as a seasonal worker, when he described the precise moment of the change in the shift: 'The first shift ends at 2:15 pm. Already, the man on the next shift is standing beside me, waiting for me to finish. As soon as I put my hammer down on the belt, he picks it up and begins precisely where I left off. A baton pass, and neatly done, too' (Kamata 1983: 23–4). In a track relay, unlike in a swimming relay where every swimmer swims an equal distance only after the foregoing swimmer has touched the wall, 'a strong runner can make up for a weak runner' in a relay zone. The same goes for manufacturing. 'If an operator in a later process is delayed, others should help set up his or her machine. When the work area returns to normal, that worker should get the baton and everyone should return to their positions' (Ohno 1988: 25).

We have seen some examples of metaphorical expressions used by the management of car manufacturing companies. Our question is why JIT needs to be promoted with such analogies. In Toyota, Ohno's answer (1988: 25) is, 'In work and sports, it is desirable for team members to work with equal strength. In actuality this is not always the case, particularly with new employees who are unfamiliar with the work.' Under Toyota's harsh working conditions, the rate of absenteeism and turnover is high. With both regular and seasonal workers, whether by dropout, transfer, or completion of the term, there is a constant flow of incoming and outgoing workers. In terms of cost saving, the use of new recruits and seasonal workers may be advantageous; however, frequent changes in deployment and the use of workers unfamiliar with the operations can be the source of delays in production. Kamata, the said journalist, for instance, took a full month to become 'independent'—namely, to be able to handle the assignment without any help (Kamata 1983: 42, 87). When one worker's delay can cause delays in the subsequent processes, such delays must be compensated for or even prevented through collective work. It is no exaggeration to say that without mutual assistance the whole scheme is impossible; nothing is produced 'just in time'. It is indeed the system of mutual assistance that fills the gap between the advantage of cost saving and the disadvantage of using inexperienced workers. There is a practical necessity to make a high level of synchronization possible. 'Teamwork' and 'cooperation' therefore are by no means 'cultural' or 'traditional', as some Japanologists would like us to believe. If there are indeed harmony and cooperation in the Japanese organization of labour, they are manufactured harmony and engineered cooperation. Cooperation, in short, is efficiency.

In order to emphasize this point, we may turn to some Western theory and experience. Max Weber argued that capitalism in the United States in its highest development assumed 'the character of sport' (Weber 1904–5/1958: 182). When the emphasis was placed upon gaining the highest score, he found the metaphor appropriate. In the same decade during which Weber was writing, Frederick Taylor explained before the US Special House Committee the importance of cooperation between workers and management. He spoke using the simile of baseball. A worker learning efficient motion, he said, was like a baseball player learning the best form; management giving instructions was like a coach giving signs and orders.

The players have not only been told the best way of making each important motion or play, but they have been taught, coached, and trained to it through months of drilling. And I think that every man who has watched first-class play, or who knows anything of the management of the modern baseball team, realizes fully the utter impossibility of winning with the best team of individual players that was ever gotten together unless every man on the team obeys the signals or orders of the coach and obeys them at once when the coach gives those orders; that is, without the intimate cooperation between all members of the team and the management, which is characteristic of scientific management. (Taylor 1912/1947: 46)

Both Taylor and Ohno use the baseball metaphor, but slight differences can be detected between them. While the former stresses cooperation between a worker and management, the latter places emphasis on cooperation among the workers. Baseball is a game of both offence and defence, but Ohno focuses exclusively on the defence aspect of the game. The stress is worth noting. Offence, after all, is the batter's individual fight against the pitcher. Only in defence is the analogy between sport and cooperation in teamwork all the more appropriate.

COOPERATION IS EFFICIENCY

The idea of cooperation as efficiency is familiar in European economic theory. Quoting G. R. Carling, Marx (1867/1976: 447), for instance, wrote in *Capital*: 'The strength of the individual man is very small, but the union of a number of very small forces produces a collective force which is greater than the sum of all the partial forces, so that merely by being joined together these forces can reduce the time required, and extend the field of their action.' He referred to this under the heading of 'Cooperation'. Once divided, labour should not be left divided but must be efficiently coordinated. If each process of work is not linked with the others, the division of labour eventually produces inefficiency. 'The isolation of the different stages of manufacture, consequent upon the employment of manual labour, adds immensely to the cost of production, the loss mainly arising from the mere removals from one process to another' (Marx 1867/1976: 463–4).

This is precisely the point upon which Marx disagreed with Adam Smith's account of the division of labour as efficient. Marx gave an example of the coordination of divided labour through glass-making (glass-blowing) in which five specialized workers (a bottle-maker, a blower, a gatherer, a putter-up, and a taker-in) work together. 'These five specialized workers are special organs of a single working organism that only acts as a whole, and therefore can operate only by the direct cooperation of all five. The whole body is paralysed if only one of its members is missing' (Marx 1867/1976: 466).

The whole interrelated labour process thus 'creates a continuity, a uniformity, a regularity, an order, and even an intensification of labour, quite different from that found in independent handicrafts or even in simple cooperation' (Marx 1867/1976: 465). If production is a continuous operation, it is not difficult to imagine that all sorts of pressures will be placed on each part not to be late, let alone absent. This is all for the purpose of achieving maximum efficiency. Marx detected the presence of 'peer pressure' in this arrangement. 'It is clear', Marx (1867/1976: 464–5) points out, 'that the direct mutual interdependence of the different pieces of work, and therefore of the workers, compels each one of them to spend on his work no more than the necessary time'. Efficiency is not achieved simply through the division of labour; it involves the question of the time spent on each labour process and the establishment of the connection between the processes. Toyota simply put this principle into practice in its own way given new technological circumstances. Cooperation, therefore, is nothing new, nothing peculiar to Japanese culture.

LEARNING FROM WESTERN TECHNOLOGY

Now, we may need to consider to what degree the so-called Japanese system owes its formation to cultural as well as institutional legacies. Delbridge (1998: 208) raises the issue when he urges us to ask the question about 'how "Japanese" the Japanese methods are'. In spite of culturist arguments, a different story is told about the making of the just-in-time system. It needs to be remembered that Ohno got the idea of implementing JIT from an American supermarket during his visit to the United States in 1956. He was staying in the country to learn about American techniques of car manufacturing. Ohno's visit was in no sense a special case. Its implication will become clearer if we consider Japan's technological development in the wider context of post-war political history. In the midst of the cold war, when nations all over the world were being grouped under either the American military alliance or the Soviet camp, the United States, spurred by the outbreak of the Korean War in 1950, saw the advantage of providing American technical expertise, including patents and licences, for the former enemy as well as other Asian countries. Supreme Command for Allied Powers (SCAP) officials invited a number of American experts to Japan to conduct seminars, which included W. Edwards Deming's lecture in 1950 on ideas of quality control. The United States, in turn, received many Japanese delegations. In 1953 and 1954 a total of fifty-three small groups visited, and in 1955 alone fifteen missions reaching as many as 174 members went to the United States to study industries such as steel and automobile (Saxonhouse 1983: 162; Hein 1993: 109; Morris-Suzuki 1994: 167).

Another aspect of post-war history should not be forgotten. In the aftermath of war and subsequent post-war social turmoil, Toyota management's efforts to recover their operations did not bring the satisfactory results they expected. With the conditions still worsening, the management followed financial guidance from General Headquarters of the Allied Occupation Forces (GHQ) and the subsequent Japanese government's deflation policy in 1948. Yet, reconstruction was all the more difficult. Management then resorted to cutting wages, and dismissed surplus labour in 1950. The massive lay-off lead to a ten-month labour strike, one of the biggest strikes in post-war Japanese history. (Another large strike took place in Nissan in 1953.) During the period, management succeeded in firing union leaders and crushing militant unions, whose organizing activities were gaining strength under a new Labour Union Law enacted with the GHQ initiative. In this way, from the early stages of post-war history, Japanese labour unions were emasculated and organized by the company to create a downward communication channel to serve the interests of management. The final step taken by management was to appoint Ohno Taiichi as the union president (Cusumano 1985: 137–85; Dohse *et al.* 1985: 133–41). Culturists present the course of Japanese labour organization as unilinear, a smooth trajectory with little trace of conflicts.[2] Their view then serves to make post-war radical unionism invisible. Emphasizing the company's fate as a whole, the ideology of class conflict was replaced with the discourse of cooperation (Gordon 1993: 375).

It is not only car manufacturing techniques that Japanese engineers learnt from the Americans. JIT's idea of time saving is without doubt based on Taylorist time-and-motion studies. William Tsutsui, in his analysis of the reception of scientific management in Japan, for instance, asserts that JIT is 'an heir to the Taylorist agenda' and a 'revised Taylorism' (Tsutsui 1998: 184, 187). Japan's concern for scientific management was almost coterminous with that in the United States. F. W. Taylor's *The Principle of Scientific Management* (1911) was translated into Japanese just two years after its publication in the United States. Japanese concern for and absorption of Western technology can be traced back even further. Putting forward slogans such as 'a rich country and a strong army' (*fukoku kyōhei*) and 'encouraging industry' (*shokusan kōgyō*) to catch up with Western nations, the Japanese government, since its establishment in 1868, systematically introduced Western institutions and technology in almost every sphere including law, politics, economy, medicine, education, railways, architecture, as well as art. When it comes to military technology, Japan's learning started much earlier, in the 1850s, still under the Tokugawa reign.[3] At these initial stages of 'modernization', 'hired foreigners' or foreign experts were invited to

---

[2] A somewhat similar view of unbroken continuity can be seen in T. C. Smith (1988), one of the few examples from literature on the Japanese sense of time available in English.

[3] The feudal government was opened up by Tokugawa Ieyasu in 1603 in Edo, now Tokyo, and ruled by the Tokugawa family for about 260 years until 1867.

Japan and appointed to help establish systems of Western methods throughout Japan. When Japan has been learning Western systems since the latter half of the nineteenth century, it seems rather strange to characterize the formation of the production system as the 'Japanese' model and attribute it exclusively to the country's past assets (Vogel 1979/2001).

THE SHOCK OF JAPANESE ASCENDANCY

For all his insistence on the Tokugawa legacies, Dore (1983), an expert on Japan, precisely because of his exquisite sociological insight, seems to contradict himself when he sees organizational affinity between two modern institutions: a Japanese factory and the military. 'The firm [Nippon Electric Company (NEC)] has very close connection with the Self-Defense Forces and makes a strenuous effort to recruit former soldiers and NCOs; 2,500 of its workers and a tenth of its foremen are ex-soldiers' (Dore 1983: p. xii). Significantly, the similarity is not limited to the Japanese SDF. Dore claims that Toyota even resembles the American army. 'Joining Toyota as a regular worker', Dore (1983: p. xii) suggests, 'is indeed rather more like joining the army in America than like going to work for General Motors'. Such contradictions and persistent arguments over Japanese uniqueness, in turn, seem to lead to a question that needs to be considered: 'why did Western corporations respond to Japan's industrial ascendancy in the way they did?' Admitting the increasing competitiveness of Japanese companies, Western counterparts began to consider the possibility of introducing the 'Japanese' manufacturing system. They pondered the question of the cultural difference, wondering to what extent it would be feasible to introduce the 'Japanese' system that had its roots in Japan's unique tradition. On the other hand, when the Japanese government and companies tried to import Western systems and methods, it did not occur to them to raise such a question. There was no room for questioning the conflict between Japanese collectivity and Western individualism. The issue of culture was totally irrelevant to them. Is there not then a psychological barrier, as it were, in the Western mind?

When Vogel's *Japan as Number One* appeared in 1979, it shocked the world as well as the Americans, to whom the book's message was primarily addressed. It was disturbing partly because the title suggested the demise of Western supremacy of industrial production. There seems, however, another, more fundamental reason behind it: that the American position as the economic superpower was now being conceded to an Asian country, which 'only recently had lain in ruins and been dismissed as a "fourth-rate nation"' (Dower 1999: 557). In almost every industry Japanese companies surpassed their American counterparts, achieving 'the Japanese miracle'. The United States, in guiding Japan into the industrial world, 'had single-handedly created its own nemesis' (Morris-Suzuki 1994: 167). Having tried to catch up with the West and when industries finally reached Western levels of competitiveness in the capitalist market, Japanese companies were not seen to be engaged in the same lucrative venture. The Western counterparts saw them as being driven and motivated by something entirely different. Not on the same plain, the Japanese seemed to belong to a distinct non-human category of 'economic animal'. (Is the same true of Taiwan, Korea, Singapore, and Hong Kong, which are likened to the imaginary creatures of Vogel's *The Four Little Dragons* (1991)?) The Japanese are heterogeneous, thus they need to be analysed from a different perspective: 'many...presumably expert accounts end up speaking of "secrets" and "miracles" which ultimately trace back to some non-discursive realm and quasi-mystical bonding unique to Japan' (Dower 1986: 312–13). The Japanese, it should be admitted, too, have attributed their growing economic power to their uniqueness.

CONCLUSION

The just-in-time system, as I have tried to demonstrate, has nothing to do with Japanese uniqueness; it is not the product of Japanese culture or the Tokugawa legacy, but the outcome of the careful study, application, and development of the Western—primarily American—system. Car manufacturing techniques, quality control and total quality control, industrial engineering, scientific management as well as the inspiration for the *kanban* system—all are imitations of the American system. The so-called Japanese model, more precisely, is all but 'a hybrid Japanese–American model' (Dower 1999: 558). Manufacturing techniques and devices were introduced in Japan at a particular historical moment. Politically, they were introduced in the years of American occupation and developed in the period of east–west polarization. In the light of labour history, the experiments began in times of low wage costs, just at the beginning of unionism. The companies' repeated emphasis on harmony, cooperation, and teamwork is the conceptual fortification to ensure the smooth running of the system built on complex and minute divisions and subdivisions of labour. Whatever their analyses may be, however, Western proponents of the Japanese system enthusiastically recommend its adoption as a means to catch up with Japan's efficiency. A sociologist urges people outside Japan to 'embrace the quality circles, embrace the assumption that workers can willingly contribute initiatives...to improve efficiency in the firm of which they are members' (Dore 1983: p. xxxvi). Womack and his co-authors uncritically extol the system, believing that it will 'spread to all corners of the globe for everyone's mutual benefit'. They too argue that responsibility involved in labour 'means freedom to control one's work—a big plus—' (Womack *et al.* 1990: 12, 13). But where is workers' freedom when workers cannot determine how many hours they will work, and are forced to do overtime against their will? It is as well to remember that Dore used the analogy of the army to characterize Toyota—the army, where not freedom but absolute obedience is required.

We might recall a report on a fire in February 1997, which broke out in a factory making parts for Toyota (Aisin Seiki Co.). The sudden halt of the supply of parts by the incident, it was thought, would bring total paralysis. The parent company was afraid that it would be a fatal blow to its proud efficient manu-facturing system, given the firm's high level of time coordination as well as complex multilayered webs of subcontractors. The damaged factory was in fact forced to suspend its operation for three days. But it returned to almost normal operation in only six days. Reports on the disaster and the subsequent recovery tended to shed light on the rapidity of the company's response to the crisis; the speed, indeed, is striking. Yet we must not forget what was behind the swiftness: the heavy burden on workers. In order to make up the leeway, a decision was made to bring in a temporary change of the shift in some of the production lines, from the two-shift, sixteen-hour labour to the three-shift, twenty-four-hour operation, with more frequent overtime work. Further, some Saturdays, which had been days off work, were made into working days, while other Saturdays, which had ordinary one-shift patterns were changed to the two-shift operation. The labour union eventually had to live with such company policies (J. Lee 1999*a,b*: 141–2). Behind the phenomenal recovery from the disaster lay workers' 'cooperation'—that is, compliance.

8

Hanging on the Telephone: Temporal Flexibility and the Accessible Worker

Emma Bell and Alan Tuckman

INTRODUCTION

In this chapter we consider the impact of flexible working time arrangements on the UK chemical industry. We focus on annualized hours agreements, which provide managers with a strategy for extending workers' temporal availability. First, however, and in order to begin to explore some of the consequences of this temporal redefinition of the employment relationship, let us consider the following examples, in which managers describe some of the difficulties encountered in implementing annualized hours.

There was a rumour around Eastham that, as soon as we put...in [annualized hours], Dixons sold more answerphones than they've ever sold any day of their lives. And with the BT systems now, and fancy phones, you can, you know...

Where we have tried to call people in, you'll phone their house and they'll be getting the wife [to answer the phone] now—or you won't get an answer [at all]. I've got to the stage where if I can't get anybody, I'll just call the contractors in.

Other stories from our research tell of employees' home telephone numbers having been changed and pagers being sabotaged. These accounts seem to reflect specific acts of resistance to annualized hours agreements, and to represent strategies for surviving the system of 'call out', which this form of temporal flexibility relies on. The examples are drawn from two separate and independent pieces of case study research on which this analysis is based. The first is an ethnographic investigation into two chemical companies conducted during 1996–7, and the second a longitudinal interview study of two different chemical companies undertaken between 1990 and 1997. On four of the five sites on which research was conducted, annualized hours agreements had been introduced.

Although these two pieces of research were conducted entirely independently and focused on different aspects of employment relations within the chemical industry—one on payment systems (E. Bell 1999) and the other on flexible working practices and employee representation (Tuckman 1998; Tuckman and Whittall 2002)—both highlight the importance of temporal changes within the employment relationship. The introduction and operation of annualized hours became the focus of separate papers presented within the 'Organization, Management and Time' stream at the EGOS 16th Colloquium (E. Bell 2000; Tuckman 2000). As well as making us aware of each other's research, through the conference we were able to recognize strikingly similar patterns of resistance to annualized hours within our data, even though the empirical work had been conducted at different times and in different locations. However, while there were clear symptoms within our data of what Noon and Blyton (1997) would describe as 'avoidance strategies', we interpreted these behaviours—the changing of telephone numbers, use of answer machines, or other strategies adopted by workers under annualized hours contracts—as means of accommodating new temporal arrangements.

This chapter therefore begins by exploring the implications of temporal irregularity associated with the flexible use of working time. It focuses on changing employment practices within the chemical industry and in particular on the introduction of annualized hours agreements. Whereas overtime and shift work have in the past represented the principal means through which management has sought to extend the period of daily productive activity (Blyton 1989), annualized hours agreements provide management with an alternative strategy for expanding workers' temporal availability. This is partly because, unlike overtime, which requires that the employee is financially compensated for the intrusion into his non-work time, annualized hours treats work beyond what was formerly defined as the standard day as part of an expandable day, which can be compensated for by fewer work hours on a later day, rather than by additional payment (Blyton 1994).

The chapter also considers some of the more general implications of annualized hours for the temporalities of work organization. In particular, the flexible use of working time under annualized hours agreements can be associated with a shift towards a more open-ended definition of work time. This reflects a broader societal transition enabled by the increased desynchronization of time and space, so that the use of particular spaces at particular times becomes steadily less predictable (Harvey 1989; Glennie and Thrift 1996). The expectation that employees become more temporally flexible is realized in part through the process of time–space desynchronization. This enables employers to expect workers to become more adaptable, both in terms of the times and places they do their jobs, as well as the range of tasks they are willing to do within them (Blyton 1992). In addition, temporal flexibility represents an attempt to desegregate work from non-work, based on the removal of former rigid, rule-based time-measurement structures, which have been a characteristic of modern, bureaucratic work organizations. Temporal flexibility has reversed patterns of time-segregated schedules, which allowed an apparent separation of home from paid work. This enables the increased penetration of work accessibility even for lower-status non-professional employees like chemical-process workers. Out of this conflation of private and public roles and the reversing of the privatization within the household (Goldthorpe *et al.* 1968; Zerubavel 1981) we see the emergence of management's ideal of 'the accessible worker'. This change is facilitated not just by flexibility within contracts of employment but also by technologies which make employees 'ever-available'.

The replacement of overtime, as a means of covering for the exigencies of continuous process manufacturing, with annualized hours agreements can be seen as an attempt by management to standardize the value of work time. Time spent at work is in this way defined in terms of a more homogenous time code (Clark 1990), by taking all units of working time to be of equal financial and social value. This despite the existence of irregular events in the calendar year, such as bank holidays or weekends, that give some time periods greater significance than others. By requiring workers to be accessible during periods when they are away from the work site, annualized hours agreements make the boundaries between workers' public and private time less distinct. Specifically, within such contracts we find unscheduled time that is designed for 'call-out', where the site worker is available for duties outside routine shift patterns. Away from the site in short or long periods of 'non-work', they are accessible for work and expected to be readily available to cover for absences or other exigencies. At times of supposed 'privatization', they are, almost literally, expected to be 'hanging on the telephone' waiting for a possible call-out. The erosion of these rigid boundaries between public and private time is enabled by the use of the telephone, instead of the clock, as the key device through which the temporal availability of an individual shift worker is negotiated. In this way, the telephone provides the means by which the boundaries between public and private time, work and non-work, are blurred.

THE OWNERSHIP OF PUBLIC AND PRIVATE TIME

Time ownership is commonly defined in terms of the dichotomous relationship between owners' time, the time for work, and own time, the time for leisure (Blyton *et al.* 1989; Adam 1990). This distinction is seen as a reflection of the struggle for control over time within the capitalist system, as a means of exploiting labour (Starkey 1988). Hence 'management tries to master time in order to prolong it while labour tries to master time in order to shorten it' (Gurvitch 1964: 44). The clock is claimed to be the central technical time-measuring device that has enabled the regulation and exploitation of labour. Its dominance, according to Thompson (1967), is marked by the shift away from disputes about the imposition of clock time in factories, fights *against* time, to contest over the detail of work time arrangements, fights *over* it. Control also relies fundamentally on the association of time with money, which turns time into a malleable commodity. Time is thereby constituted as a scarce and exploitable resource, able to be measured, bought, sold, and spent 'thriftily' (Ingold 1995). As a result of this process, time has become a means of defining labour itself, in terms of 'man hours', rather than merely a means of structuring any given work activity (Adam 1990).

Within industrial sociology, attention has been drawn to the social construction of organizational time within specific production sectors (Clark 1985; Whipp 1987) and areas of management (Whipp 1994; E. Bell 2001), which means that it is no longer possible to conceptualize time as a single, unitary, and absolute system. Furthermore, the development of information and communications technologies, combined with new forms of flexible working, implies that, in a number of work contexts, the clock is no longer the dominant time instrument. Instead, the tempo of modern life is increasingly defined by computer technology that fundamentally changes the way people relate to time by bringing its measurement below the threshold of human consciousness (Rifkin 1987). This same technology also allows the immediate surveillance of workers through the 'electronic panopticon' (Sewell and Wilkinson 1992). However, while the continuous monitoring of processes within chemical plants allows a degree of employee surveillance, we are concerned here with a more diverse and emergent technology including telephones, cellular phones, answering machines, and pagers, which we see as enabling the construction of the accessible worker beyond the physical boundaries of the workplace.

Time spent at work can also be understood relative to time spent away from it. In organizational research, domain analysis has provided a basis for understanding the temporal and spatial nature of this relationship (Near *et al.* 1980; Staines 1980). Domain analysis takes various spheres of life to be identifiable in terms of their temporal boundaries, although analysis can be based on quite different hypotheses. First, there are compensatory analyses, which suggest that human sacrifice in one context, such as work, tends to be made up for elsewhere, for example in the home. In relation to work, this position is illustrated by the stark fact that most workers must actually turn up at work in order to receive their wages (R. Edwards 1979). Consequently, time is spent at work primarily because one's bought labour is directed there (Willis 1979), mainly as a means of enabling a certain life outside it (Goldthorpe *et al.* 1968). In contrast, the alternative, 'spillover' hypothesis suggests that attitudes and behaviours within a work context have a ripple-like effect on other spheres of life (Near *et al.* 1980).

The spillover hypothesis draws attention to the way in which use of work time has an impact on time spent outside work. However, it continues to characterize time in terms of a dichotomy between work and non-work. Our analysis of annualized hours stresses the interpenetration of work and non-work domains, private and public time, following the expectation of increased accessibility of employees. As such we have drawn heavily on ideas developed from Zerubavel's studies of work time and organization in the hospital setting. Zerubavel's work pays attention to the processes whereby temporal segregation is achieved. This forms the focus for discussion in the next section, before moving on to our consideration of annualized hours.

THE ACCESSIBLE WORKER

The main focus of the work/non-work dichotomy has been on the use to which time is put. This can be contrasted with the distinction between public and private time (Zerubavel 1981), which concentrates on the extent to which one remains accessible, regardless of how this time is actually spent. Hence, in some time periods we must be accessible to others, whilst in others we may legitimately be inaccessible. However, accessibility to one group of people associated with one role is likely to make an individual inaccessible to others; accessibility to an employer, for example, is likely to make the employee inaccessible to friends and family. In this way, time regulates the social accessibility of the individual within the segmented social circles that define various roles within modern life. Public time is 'sociopetal', deliberately designed to promote establishment of social contact and draw people together, whereas private time is 'sociofugal', deliberately meant to prevent or discourage the formation of social contact (Zerubavel 1981). However, neither public nor private time exists in absolute form; instead they are hypothetical constructs that help us to assess the actuality of temporal situations. 'Privacy and publicity ought to be viewed as the ideal-typical polarities of a continuum rather than a conceptual dichotomy' (Zerubavel 1979*b*: 39). Each moment of an individual's time can therefore be regarded as a combination of both private and public elements and located somewhere along this continuum. Most importantly for Zerubavel, an important social function of time is to keep these private and public spheres of life apart. This is because 'the competing claims on individuals by the various social circles with which they are affiliated and the often-conflicting demands entailed by the variety of social roles they play make the institutionalization of periodic withdrawal from publicity into privacy absolutely essential to modern life' (Zerubavel 1981: 140).

Broadly speaking, working time is a form of public time, since it is characterized by situations in which the individual plays a role demanding only his or her partial involvement (Goffman 1959). The partiality of work role involvement reflects the distinction between person and role, private and public self. Therefore, it is in the domain of work that the temporal segregation of private from public spheres of life is best appreciated and the maintenance and erosion of these boundaries can be observed.

It is also from the notion of private time that the possibility of social inaccessibility arises. Zerubavel suggests that private time introduces the possibility of 'territoriality', a niche of accessibility in which we expect to have a high degree of control over our own social inaccessibility. Although the privacy or inaccessibility borne of territoriality is never absolute, its importance as an analytical concept is the key to our understanding of social time use. In the context of occupational roles, he argues that it has become generally accepted that the individual has a basic right to be inaccessible at certain times and has a right to claim control of his social accessibility during his private time as a kind of possession. Hence, 'it is officially agreed today that the person's accessibility in his occupational role is restricted to the temporal boundaries of that part of his time which he has "sold" ' to the organization (Zerubavel, 1979b: 46). Time beyond these boundaries, in the form of 'overtime', may be requested, but the individual also has the right to refuse. This is particularly true in organizations that operate 'around the clock'. Zerubavel draws attention to the temporal rigidity of modern society, where the patterning of events is dictated by the schedule, the calendar, and the clock. This, he argues, provides a rule-based structure that actually *protects* many individuals from being 'swallowed' by 'greedy institutions' (Zerubavel 1981: 166). Following his logic, it is the deregulation of employment relations, allowing for increased flexibility, that reverses this bureaucratic trend and allows for the creation of 'the accessible worker'.

In higher-status occupational roles, Zerubavel (1981) argues, time scarcity carries a premium, and individual 'ever-availability' has become a symbolic expression of being professionally committed in a way that is indirectly indicative of professional status and social value. Hence the use of cellular phones has become a modern status symbol for the corporate executive in the same way that the 'deliberate refrainment from ever taking one's telephone off the hook' (Zerubavel 1981: 146) was a former symbolic display of a valued social quality. Ever-availability is most often associated with professionals, where the individual is conceived of as inseparable from his or her occupational role. As a general rule, flexible boundaries of temporal accessibility are usually associated with higher-status occupations, and more rigidly defined boundaries with lower status.

In his ethnographic study of hospital life, Zerubavel (1979a) accounts for the occupational differences between doctors and nurses in terms of their social accessibility. For doctors, ever-availability is suggested to be a fundamental professional obligation. Electronic 'bleepers' mean that they can be reached at any time, and no periods of time are completely private. In contrast, nurses are paid by the hour and are expected to be active in their role only within the temporal boundaries of their duty periods. The rigidity of these boundaries of accessibility is built into the nursing system through fixed arrival and leaving times. In contrast to doctors, who always appear to be 'on call', nurses may be at their workstation but still able to claim legitimately that they are not yet on duty. If nurses are asked by a supervisor to work overtime, they have the right to refuse, and, if they agree, they are paid at a significantly higher rate, for having relinquished their claim over some of their private time.

Having set out some of the concepts associated with a time-ownership perspective, the remainder of this chapter undertakes to examine some of the specific temporal issues that are raised as a result of the implementation of annualized hours agreements. Zerubavel's work, which we have considered at some length, both identifies accessibility as central to understanding time and points towards the technology that facilitates this. Our analysis will enable us to explore the possibility of resistance to accessibility by focusing on some of the survival strategies utilized by workers in order to protect possession of their private time. It will demonstrate that the boundaries between work and non-work time have been eroded through the introduction of arrangements that require increased social accessibility. From there, the chapter will consider the possibility that annualized hours agreements represent a strategy that will lead to the emergence of the accessible worker.

ANNUALIZED HOURS AND TEMPORAL FLEXIBILITY

Annualized hours agreements allow employers to relate the hours worked by employees more closely to production requirements, by calculating an overall number of working hours based on an average twelve-month period. The various systems incorporate vacation time and days in lieu of statutory holidays into an overall annualized total, so that hours can be directed to times in the year when production demands are greatest. They thereby act to blur the distinction between holidays and rest days, workdays, and weekends (Desmons and Vidal-Hall 1987), by placing the same value on the working day no matter where in the calendar year it falls. Estimates in the late 1990s were that at least 600,000 employees in the UK were working on some form of annualized hours system (IDS 1999), although there were claims that this number could reach two million (IDS 1996). Agreements have been common in the employment of shift-workers in continuous-process industries (Beaumont and Hunter 1996).

Schemes differ in detail and in relation to specific shift patterns, but they all allow employers to relate the hours worked by employees more closely to production requirements. Employee availability is expanded by calculating overall working hours based on an average twelve-month period, so that hours worked can be varied according to demand, up to an annualized norm. Each pattern includes some unattached or unscheduled time to accommodate anticipated or unanticipated fluctuations. Annualized hours shift patterns also include unrostered or reserved hours, when employees are expected to be available for work if required. Shift patterns include relatively lengthy periods of non-work in the roster, referred to as the '16 days' at one site or 'long break' at another. Despite differences in the detail of particular annualized hours agreements, some basic similarities emerge: they present to the employee an irregular pattern of working time, based not only on changing shift patterns, but also on the anticipation of periodic call-out, which encroaches on private time.

Current pressure towards more flexible time use tends to be based on dismantling the notion of 'standard hours' and the accompanying wage systems that provide premiums for 'unsocial' or 'non-standard' time usage (Fagan and Lallement 2000). The introduction of annualized hours thus forms part of a broader managerial search for an alternative to the 'overtime culture', which has been blamed for producing an upwardly spiralling desire to work more overtime as part of a trade-off of non-work time in exchange for increased income (Blyton 1989; IDS 1999). The tendency to work overtime in the UK has been further reinforced by the payment of low basic pay rates, particularly in the employment of male, manual workers within manufacturing industries (Blyton 1994). Some annualized hours contracts are introduced by managers in response to a real or perceived crisis, such as possible site closure or redundancies. This not only allows a cost cutting through the abolition of overtime payments, but also offers a means of overcoming irregular demands on labour. Workers are drawn to accept such changes in the belief that they may create increased security of employment.

Managers in the chemical industry have argued that one of the advantages for workers of an annualized hours contract is that it increases employees' time out of work, in comparison with an overtime system. This is suggested to lead to an improvement in the worker's overall quality of life. Many employees, however, perceive annualized hours to be a threat to their control of working time, which is claimed to be the one resource that is, at least partially, still within their control. Lack of choice about time use can be resented by workers, who may have to take time off when it is allocated, when the rest of the family is out at work or school, for example, and not necessarily when they want it. In addition, imposed periods of time away from work can be perceived by some as leading to 'enforced periods of unwanted idleness' (Heyes 1997: 74). Being available for call-out, to provide holiday, sickness, and absence cover for teammates, can become like having 'a grey cloud looming over you' and a potential disruption to planned non-work activities. While employees appear to see long breaks within the shift pattern as a respite from the increasingly intensified work regime, this is fragile, since the threat of call-out still prevails.

Despite continuous process production within the chemical industry—seemingly the epitome of the logic of linear time frames—there are also continuous although irregular demands on labour. As Adam (1998: 140) has put it: 'The ideal of industrial production is for everything to be standardized. This means daily rhythms designed to secure maximum efficiency of operation.' But, she continues, 'in agriculture, more than any other industry...there are limits to the extent to which seasonal and daily variation can be rationalized to conform to a de-contextualized and de-temporalized standard'. We must look beyond the immediate plant and technology to see what differing time regimes articulate. Even within such a regime as a chemical plant there are limits to the degree they can be standardized. One site in our studies, for example, was producing fertilizers and was therefore precisely articulating the interface between the linearity of chemical process with the cycles of agriculture. Working patterns on the site needed to reflect the seasonal demands on the product, despite the potential for continuous and regular production throughout the year. More generally, irregularity may be because of the need for cover for absenteeism, the cycles of shutdown and maintenance of the plant, or the demands of some emergency. Traditionally these fluctuations have been accommodated through overtime working. However, overtime recognizes 'social' time through extra payment and a differential wage for working outside socially accepted times. Under an overtime system, working nights represents something different from working days, and bank holidays and weekends are more valuable than weekdays, whereas, under annualized hours, all time segments become homogenized and standardized and are considered equal in value.

Annualized hours agreements also mean that employees do not perceive as clear a direct or temporally sequential relationship between call-out and subsequent payment, as under an overtime system. Managers implementing annualized hours agreements encourage workers to see the benefits of a salaried system, in providing them with a more predictable monthly income. Employees, however, may continue to dwell on the fact that there is no extra, additional payment for call-out, now that an estimation of these hours has been previously calculated into the system. This response may relate to their structural position, since deferred gratification may be more acceptable to white-collar workers, who are in a stronger structural position and therefore have a more trusting relationship with the future (Adam 1990). As job insecurity is a dominant feature within all our case studies, this may be reflected in workers' responses to the annualized hours system.

Employees fall into two categories in terms of their response to annualized hours, depending on the way that the agreement is calculated. First, there are 'time-winners who are money-losers'. For employees who formerly worked high levels of overtime,. the introduction of annualized hours means a significant reduction in their overall earnings. They do not perceive the increase in time spent away from work adequately to compensate them for this financial loss and they may be resistant to providing holiday, sickness, and absence cover for others without the incentive of overtime payment. In some cases, they may even decide to take a second job—for example, truck driving during the 'long break' between shift patterns. The second group consists of 'time-losers who are money-winners'. Employees who have not tended to work overtime can gain an increase in pay as a result of annualized hours agreements based on the aggregation of overtime requirements. In the past, however, these workers were not under any obligation to be on 'standby' or to respond to 'call-out', whereas under annualized hours they can find their non-work time eroded to ensure the maintenance of a system to which they are not committed.

Although some workers do not fall neatly into either category, most recognize there are winners and losers within the system. Some employees in our study worked well beyond the required call-out hours, but the intensity of work left little available time for compensation through time off in lieu. At one site, the trade union found some resurgence as shop stewards monitored the upward drift in call-out and working hours. Annualized hours can then give rise to discontent, leading to the adoption of strategies of resistance to the erosion of individual social inaccessibility. Most notable among these is the struggle over availability for 'call-out'. This form of resistance relies on telephone use. Tactics involve arranging for wives or partners to answer the telephone, filtering all telephone calls using an answering machine, or even changing the home telephone number. In this way, workers attempt, on an individual basis, to secure a more favourable balance between the hours that are worked and the hours that the company has paid for. Managerial counter-strategies, however, are also diverse. They include the 'banning' of telephone answering machines, invoking disciplinary proceedings against employees who do not make themselves available for call-out, and bringing in outside contractors to do the work.

Conspiring against these individualistic strategies of resistance, however, is the process whereby annualized hours systems become 'self-policing' (Lloyd Smith and Wilkinson 1996). This is the result of peer pressure, which can be brought to bear on any individual employees who are putting pressure on the system. This ensures that the control of work time is achieved via worker, rather than managerial, supervision as a result of arrangements for call-out. For example, if a team member fails to respond to call-out, his teammate will be contacted. If the second team member finds out that he was called out because of his colleague's lack of responsiveness, this can develop into a situation of reciprocal absenteeism, a practice known as 'sticking it' (E. Bell 1999) or 'the knock' (Heyes 1997). In this way, self-regulation can cause workers to 'turn on each other' in a way that undermines workforce collectivity. This can undermine the social cohesion of the shift teams, so that, in the case of forced substitution of cover, workers' anger will be directed towards their absent teammate, rather than at the company (Heyes 1997).

CONCLUSION

The introduction of annualized hours agreements in the chemical industry has enabled the requirement of social accessibility within lower-status work roles that have been traditionally protected, as well as regulated, by the 'dominance of the clock'. Annualized hours, and in particular the mechanism of call-out, represents an attempt to debureaucratize accessibility through the removal of rigid boundaries that have traditionally segregated private from public time, in lower-status occupational roles, especially in modern, bureaucratic organizations.

According to this analysis, the telephone and not the clock is constituted as the primary technological device that enables management to expect workers to be socially accessible even when they are not physically present. Moreover, the condition of being on call whilst at home provides an example of the 'delicate combination of actual privacy and potential publicity, and indicates that private and public time do not form a mutually exclusive dichotomy, but are, rather, polarities of a continuum' (Zerubavel 1979b: 50–1). The analysis therefore supports the notion that time discipline can, and indeed does, exist within organizations independent of clock discipline (Glennie and Thrift 1996). Rather than liberating employees from clock time, the telephone enables management to overcome certain spatial boundaries between work and non-work in order to extend more effectively and control the time of its employees. However, the telephone also enables strategies of resistance to time control. Devices such as the 'home answerphone' enable employees to protect their private time and resist erosion of it.

The analysis also suggests that increased social accessibility, and perhaps even 'ever-availability', are being constituted as an expectation within lower-status occupational roles. These findings run counter to Zerubavel's prediction (1981: 153) that ever-availability is 'a gradually dying phenomenon'. Instead they suggest that the rigid boundaries that characterize lower-status work roles are gradually being eroded and, as a result, workers' private time is less protected. This leads us to suggest that time is becoming less institutionally regulated and progressively recast as a matter for individualized negotiation and potential conflict between employee and employer.

Finally, the analysis calls into question the dichotomous distinction between work and non-work, defined either in terms of time ownership or in terms of the use to which time is put, that has tended to form the basis of much work-time analysis. We suggest that the notional divide between work and non-work is an increasingly problematic dualism. The distinction between public and private time therefore provides an alternative, more subtle framework for the analysis of time use in work organizations.

A New Time Discipline: Managing Virtual Work Environments

Heejin Lee and Jonathan Liebenau

INTRODUCTION

For the most part, we live under a regime of temporality that has its origins in the early to mid-eighteenth century (Thompson 1967), but there is evidence that this is changing. Even beyond the actual experiences of those who seal foreign contracts over their mobile telephones, the virtual work environment provides us with the opportunity to experiment with new forms of time discipline. In particular, much can be learned from the extension of concepts of the multiple and qualitative notions of *times* (Whipp 1987; Glennie and Thrift 1996), in contrast to rigid concepts of time discipline based on clock time.

In this chapter, we apply and extend Glennie and Thrift's arguments to understand the temporal potential in new work environments. New structures such as the virtual office, virtual teams, and virtual organizations require new working patterns and provide opportunities for the emergence of new time disciplines. These emerging forms are represented here by virtual work environments where sets of people from different places, temporal locations,[1] and sometimes different organizations work together, primarily by interacting electronically. The first section presents how time disciplines are reflected in management and why time disciplines and their changes are important in managing employees in contemporary organizations. Section two presents two contrasting notions of time and dimensions of time discipline as suggested

---

[1] 'Temporal location' in a broad sense can refer to any of a variety of temporal circumstances, including time zones, night working, or different schedules. See Box 9.1 for a narrow meaning of the term.

by Glennie and Thrift (1996) and we apply them to the discussion of time disciplines in virtual work environments. Then in the third section we introduce some concepts of time we have developed in the context of information systems research (H. Lee 1999; Lee and Liebenau 2000) to compare time disciplines in conventional and virtual work environments. Trust is also included for this purpose. Finally, we conclude with implications and a research agenda arising from what we have discussed.

TIME DISCIPLINE AND MANAGEMENT

In his classic paper 'Time, Work-Discipline, and Industrial Capitalism' (1967), E. P. Thompson showed that the shift in time sense that was shaped by the mechanical clock affected labour disciplines. The new capitalist manufacturing systems made use of the clock and clock time to discipline workers and internalize new work practices. In this process, the 'task orientation' of time organization in which work proceeded to 'natural' rhythms (think of labour from dawn to dusk in a farming community) gave way to 'labour timed by the clock'. Task orientation is characterized by least demarcation between work and life; the working day lengthens or contracts according to the task. New capitalist manufacturing systems did not allow for this pattern of working and imposed rigid time disciplines instead. Timed labour implied a clear division between work and life. Thompson's account of time disciplines has dominated discussions of the relationship between time and society in England in the early days of industrial capitalism.

Rigid time disciplines, of which Thompson gave an account, have extended to influence management thoughts and practices in succeeding periods. Scientific-management movements in the nineteenth and early twentieth centuries inherited this tradition of time disciplines. This was epitomized by the time study of Frederick Taylor (1947). Taylor developed time study as an effort to gain control over the job. Mass production systems applied by Henry Ford subjected workers to the rhythm of conveyor belts. Abiding by rigid time disciplines is often described in a typical scene where workers are clocking in and out by inserting a card into a clocking machine. Even in the human-relations approach (Mayo 1945), the belief in rigid time disciplines as a main tool for controlling labour was not questioned. While Taylor dealt with the organization and control of the labour process, the practitioners of human relations dealt primarily with the adjustment of the worker to the process (Braverman 1974: 87). Likewise they were finding ways to select, train, and adjust the worker to the rigid time disciplines established by their predecessors. The rigid time disciplines that were shaped on factory shop floors to control manual workers were also extended to offices. Braverman (1974) revealed how the scientific management in general and the rigid time disciplines in particular invaded and controlled the world of office workers, who were deceptively described as white collars or 'mental' workers.

Time disciplines are still important in managing organizations and controlling employees, and the internalization of time discipline continues to play a role in organizations in the twenty-first century. Anderson-Gough *et al.* (2001) show how the internalization of time discipline changes trainee accountants to professional ones. It provides a key to socializing the trainees. Anderson-Gough *et al.* examine the socialization of trainees into beliefs about their time and the firm's time, and the flexible boundaries between them. In this process, audit trainees were made readily to accept weekend work at clients for stock counts as a common feature of their early years of training. They also acknowledged the importance of the annual cycle of work activity and time pressures, and in the busy season (January to March) no one 'could afford to be ill' (2001: 109). In the accounting firms studied, overtime was accepted as a norm. 'Service to clients' was used to 'rationalize overtime for trainees', and they were taught to 'put client's demand and loyalty to the audit "team" ahead of those for study and "private" time' (2001: 113). In summary, the organizational socialization of trainee accountants into particular forms of time discipline and thereby time consciousness is a fundamental aspect of securing and developing professional identity.

However, there are often cases where the discrepancy between the expectations for the time discipline of employees and managers leads to conflict. Despite the widespread use of flexible work and its high publicity, some managers are still reluctant to allow their employees to work in flexible patterns, especially in temporal terms. They tend to believe that rigid time discipline typically represented by '9 to 5' is the best way to control employees. This obstinacy to maintain normal working hours becomes a problem, particularly when it comes to working mothers who are struggling to maintain a balance between work and children (*Panorama* 2000). They typically blame their managers' reluctance to allow for flexible work. When professional women ask for a different type of time discipline, their managers generally insist on keeping the rigid time discipline that they worked in throughout their career and that they regard as a symbol of their authority.

Information and communications technologies have recently enabled new working patterns and new organizational forms such as telework, virtual teams, virtual organizations, and so on. 'Virtual' implies a fundamental transformation in temporal aspects of work and organization. One possibility is the reunion of work and life that have been separated since the imposition of timed labour and rigid time discipline in early industrial capitalism. Commonly, the clear distinction between work and life, and the lines between work and home, are blurring among some teleworkers. One of the difficulties facing managers in virtual environments is the control of employees who work out of their sight. Information technologies themselves provide increasingly reliable tools for managers controlling remote workers, for example, by measuring network connection time. When they are implemented, however, the merits of virtual working such as flexibility begin to evaporate.

Therefore, the time discipline that was shaped by the advent of industrial capitalism and has since dominated management thought may be challenged in the information age as many temporal (and spatial) constraints are transformed and transcended by technological developments. Rigid time discipline may not be an effective tool in virtual work environments. A new type of time discipline is required and may already be working in the current practices of virtual work. Inspired by Glennie and Thrift's analysis (1996) of time discipline, we aim to characterize this new type of time discipline and compare this with the conventional one by examining elements of time discipline and other temporal notions.

COMPOSITION OF THE TIME DISCIPLINE

In order to understand what effect technology might have if, for example, a virtual working environment is to supplant a set of office-based procedures, we must be able to analyse the temporal characteristics of work procedures.

E. P. Thompson stressed the shift from 'task orientation' to 'time orientation'. This shift includes 'one from natural, irregular, and humanely comprehensible time, blurring work and leisure ... to an "unnatural" life tyrannized by the clock and timed labour' (Glennie and Thrift 1996: 277). Initially new time disciplines were imposed externally by systems of communicating time to the workforce and enforcing continuous work during the working day. Then they became internalized as everyday time senses among the labour force, and came to dominate society as a whole at the same period when reliable mechanical clocks became widespread among the population.

Admitting that Thompson's account has had immense impacts, Glennie and Thrift (1996) argue that there has been much change in understanding time and time disciplines in the social sciences and humanities since 1967, the year when Thompson's paper was published. In contrast to emphasizing time disciplines based on clock time, they emphasize the multiple and qualitative nature of *times*. They also question the concept of time discipline and suggest that it must be elaborated. Focusing on the multiple and qualitative nature of time, they attempted to reformulate Thompson's account. The multifaceted nature of the concept of time discipline is also centred on their reformulation. In this chapter, we aim to contribute to such elaboration, too.

In the next section we present the two pillars of Thrift and Glennie's reformulation as a starting point of our characterization of new time disciplines in virtual environments.

Clock Time and Social Time

Thompson's rigid time discipline is based on clock time. Clock time is characterized as homogeneous and divisible in structure, linear and uniform in its flow, objective and absolute, that is, existing independently of objects and events, measurable (or quantifiable), and as singular, with one and only one 'correct' time (McGrath and Kelly 1986: 29; Hassard 1989: 17). This concept is the dominant one in our contemporary society, and is closely associated with the development of industrial society (Clark 1985: 45–51; Bluedorn and Denhardt 1988: 302–3). It is also the basic assumption upon which our society relies for its operation and management. Clock time is a fundamental part of many organizational control processes. In management, time has been closely related to productivity. An organization is considered more productive or efficient when it shortens the period of time it takes to accomplish a given amount of work. Time is viewed as a resource that should be 'measured and manipulated in the interest of organizational efficiency and effectiveness' (Bluedorn and Denhardt 1988: 303). This concept of time has dominated practice and research in management. As seen at the beginning, the time discipline based on clock time has also remained influential in different schools of management thought and practice.

Since Thompson's paper, the study of time has grown (Glennie and Thrift 1996: 278) and time is no longer conceptualized as a single unitary and absolute system. Instead, time is seen as intrinsically manifold, multiple, and heterogeneous, which is represented by the term 'social time'. Proponents of social time in management and organization studies (McGrath and Rotchford 1983; Clark 1985; Bluedorn and Denhardt 1988) argue that the clock-time concept is a very limited notion, and too simple to understand organizational phenomena. The clock-time concept should be complemented by concepts that have rich implications for a deeper understanding of organizations in the context of culture (Schein 1992). Bluedorn and Denhardt (1988) emphasize the plurality of time. Although our life is so embedded in time that people simply regard it as unchangeable and taken for granted, 'time is fundamentally a social construction that varies tremendously between and within societies' (Bluedorn and Denhardt 1988: 300). For example, the clock-time concept is just one historical concept that evolved with the development of capitalist society, and on which the contemporary industrialized Western societies are based. Whatever aspects of time may be emphasized, and whatever they may be called—social time (Lauer 1981), organizational time (Gherardi and Strati 1988), subjective time (Das 1993), and so on—they share an underlying assumption that time is socially constructed. It is also assumed that the clock-time concept should be complemented by these concepts of time (Lee and Liebenau 1999).

While conventional time disciplines are firmly based on clock time, the concept of social time will be increasingly necessary to understand time disciplines in virtual environments. For example, virtual teams tend to involve people of different affiliations or traits—that is, from different professions, different organizations, and different national cultures, to name a few. Their response to temporal markers—for example, deadlines—or their attitudes to temporal norms—for example, punctuality—may differ, in some cases primarily because of psychological factors, in other cases because of engineered features such as reporting systems or incentive schemes, all of which are under the influence of culture in its broadest sense. In virtual environments, therefore, time disciplines get complicated and need to take into account different notions of time each individual or group in virtual teams may have.

The Dimensions of Time Discipline

While the term 'time discipline' has been used in the singular, Glennie and Thrift (1996) argue that it should be seen as a multifaceted concept. It has three dimensions: standardization, regularity, and coordination. Standardization means the degree to which people's time–space paths are disciplined to be the same as one another's. Regularity refers to the degree to which people's time–space paths involve repetitive routine. Coordination is concerned with the degree to which people's time–space paths are disciplined to connect smoothly with one another's. Thompson's conception of time discipline represents a particular combination of high degrees of standardization, regularity, and coordination.

Glennie and Thrift suggest that various permutations of these elements are possible. For example, Fordist factory discipline involves high degrees of standardization, regularity, and coordination. Other sorts of industrial arrangements that function efficiently are also easily found. Flexible production systems are less standardized or regularized than those of Fordist production, but involve more intense coordination.

In virtual environments, these dimensions and their combinations become more complicated. Work in distributed environments may require other aspects of time discipline. Diversification is normally placed before standardization. Time discipline in virtual environments should be able to accommodate irregularity. Coordination also requires much more sophisticated skills than that of other work arrangements.

CHANGING WORK PRACTICES AND CHARACTERISTICS OF NEW TIME DISCIPLINES

To describe the characteristics of time disciplines appropriate for virtual work arrangements, we further employ some notions of time and temporality that we have developed in the study of time and information systems (H. Lee 1999;

Lee and Liebenau 2000). Trust is also considered, as it has become one of the essential aspects of understanding and managing virtual work arrangements (Handy 1995).

Monochronicity, Polychronicity, and Time Discipline

There are two different ways or cultures in which people organize time and process tasks, particularly at work: monochronic and polychronic. In the former, people do one thing at a time, while in the latter several things are done at once. This distinction is extended to imply that individuals following the polychronic way of working place less value on temporal order, accept events as they arise, and engage in multiple activities simultaneously, whereas people following the monochronic way seek to structure activities and plan for events by allocating specific slots of time to each event's occurrence (Barley 1988: 158).

Hall argues that 'without schedules or something similar to the M-time [monochronic] system, it is doubtful that our industrial civilization could have developed as it has' (Hall 1983: 48). This corresponds to Thompson's account on clocks and the shaping of the rigid time disciplines in early industrial capitalism. The monochronic system is one of the foundations of the time disciplines argued by Thompson. One of the implications of Thompson's work is that capitalist work disciplines or ways of working were made possible by the widespread use of reliable mechanical clocks. As clocks were the defining technology of Western Europe in the seventeenth to nineteenth centuries, computers define this age (Bolter 1984). Here we make a similar point that information and communication technologies are changing the way of working, especially in terms of temporality. For example, mobile computing technologies enable people to involve themselves simultaneously in several tasks that are located at different places. Even before we reap the supposed benefits of third-generation mobile communications devices, we already mix work and personal life while being engaged in neither. This happens as we use our mobile telephones on the train or check e-mails at airport public Internet terminals. Therefore, the time discipline developed to regulate monochronic work patterns requires modifications to regulate polychronic work patterns.

In common management practice, monochronic procedures are considered to be superior to polychronic ones. Schein (1992), for example, considers monochronic time to be easier to control and coordinate. Monochronicity is seen to be well suited to the management of large systems. As such, most organizations take it for granted as the only way to get things done efficiently. On the other hand, polychronic time is considered to be more effective for building relationships and for solving complex problems. It is therefore regarded as more suitable for the early stages of an organization, for smaller systems, and for organizations where one gifted person is the central point of coordination.

When information technologies are substantially involved in work processes, however, the opposite may happen. Information technologies are frequently introduced for the purpose of disrupting temporal order by shifting the ways in which people structure their work patterns. When this is done consciously, it can be integrated into standard management practices such as systems of reward and sanctions, or office architecture. Increasingly we see that information technologies are enhancing the polychronic dimension, and this should not be left out of organizational analysis. Conventional time disciplines may not be suitable for those working in the polychronic way in virtual environments.

Furthermore, we need to distinguish between two separate, though closely connected, domains to which discussions about monochronic and polychronic times can be meaningfully applied (H. Lee 1999). The first domain relates to the way in which tasks and events occur in a temporal sense. We call it the 'temporal behaviour of events and tasks'. While some events take place in an unexpected temporal way—that is, irregularly, sporadically, unevenly and not following a fixed schedule—others come in an organized temporal way—that is, regularly, following the predetermined, or at least predictable, sequence. The former is polychronic, the latter monochronic. The second domain relates to how workers organize their time to deal with tasks and events. This is concerned with ways of working, or the 'temporal behaviour of workers'. Some may deal with tasks and events spontaneously as they arise and may perform several things in any order during a given period of time, whether they occur regularly or not. This is a polychronic way. Others may deal with events regularly at specified times and conduct one thing at a time, designating some slots of time for specific tasks. This is monochronic. Fig. 9.1 shows modes of temporal behaviour.

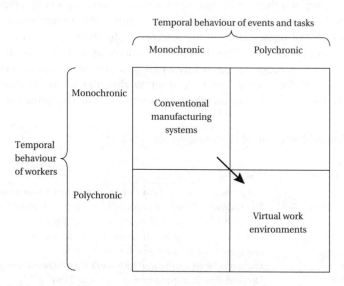

Fig. 9.1. Modes of temporal behaviour

In the upper-left area, events take place in a monochronic way—that is, regularly, in sequence, and at specific times. Workers in charge also operate in a monochronic way; they normally perform one task at a time. If a proper arrangement is made in order to coordinate temporality, things are more likely to move smoothly. This mode well describes the temporal profile of conventional manufacturing systems. Rigid time discipline can cope with managing and controlling workers working in this arrangement.

In the lower-right area, events take place in a polychronic way and workers operate in the same way. They can deal with tasks spontaneously as they arise and perform several tasks at a time. In this case, tasks are expected to be completed properly and in a timely manner without a separate coordinating arrangement unless there is too much work loaded on each worker. This mode describes the temporal profile of virtual work environments where tasks tend increasingly to take place in polychronic ways and workers are increasingly expected to work polychronically to deal with the tasks occurring in this way. Therefore, conventional time discipline to deal with monochronic ways of working cannot work properly in this polychronic pattern.

Temporal Dimensions of Business Processes

Temporal dimensions (Lee and Liebenau 2000) were developed as heuristics to investigate how information technology affects temporality in organizational work by describing and analysing changes in temporality. They are a set of concepts (Box. 9.1) that are devised to represent various aspects of temporality. They are based on some previous research on time, which examined temporal aspects of social organization in the workplace (Zerubavel 1981; Schriber 1986; Schriber and Gutek 1987). The six dimensions were used to describe temporal shifts in business processes caused by a new information system (H. Lee 1999). The temporal dimensions are here used to describe temporal differences between the nature of work for which conventional time discipline was made,

Box 9.1. Six dimensions of temporality of business processes

Dimensions	Definition
Duration	The amount of time spent to complete a task or an activity
Temporal location	The location of activities and tasks at particular points over the continuum of time; when they take place
Sequence	The order in which activities and tasks take place
Deadline	The fixed time by when work is to be done
Cycle	The periodic regularity in which work is completed repeatedly
Rhythm	The alternation in the intensity of being busy

on the one hand, and that of the work that is being conducted in virtual environments on the other. Thereby we demonstrate that conventional time discipline cannot afford to control the new patterns of working in virtual environments.

Generally, the duration that is required to complete a task in virtual environments is significantly reduced as compared with that in conventional work arrangements. As related materials are almost instantaneously downloaded and uploaded from the Internet and corporate intranets, and transmitted among team members, expectations for shorter duration are getting increasingly higher. Conventional work disciplines, which normally require direct inspection of the processes of work, cannot meet these expectations.

One of the assumptions of virtual work is that virtual workers are 'always on'— that is, available any time—though this assumption can cause a problem on the side of employees. As we can access the Internet at any time and transactions can be made independently of any working period, managers tend to assume that virtual workers should be accessible any time. To put it another way, work can be done in any temporal location—that is, any time. Therefore, time discipline devised to control work that is supposed to be done at a particular physical location at a particular time period may not be appropriate for the virtual work that is conducted by geographically and temporally dispersed workers.

Sequence also makes a difference. Normally, there are rigid procedures that should be followed in conducting tasks. People tend to feel uncomfortable when they find this sequence changed. The Internet is equipped with the facility of 'hypertext', which provides an alternative to linear reading. It allows people to read by instant needs of being inquisitive, if the objects of the needs are available (that is, linked), not dictated by the order. Now that the Internet is so widely used and embedded in work, new attitudes towards sequencing are emerging and changing sequences are more easily accepted. This also affects the way work is organized in terms of sequence.

Deadlines are a constant, static presence in our working lives and solidify our schedules. We can observe, however, that virtual work practices shift the concept and allow us to renegotiate the structure of deadlines. Increasingly, people can assume personally appropriate deadlines, after the last of which collective actions can be taken. Largely the differences in duration, temporal location, and sequence provide the opportunity to place deadlines at different positions in the course of a task.

Interaction among collaborators is conventionally marked by a combination of day/week/month/year demarcations and task cycles. As duration, sequence, and deadlines shift, new cycles are allowed to appear in virtual environments. Conventional time discipline is based on these demarcations. One representative demarcation is the weekdays' 9-to-5 working hours. Much work is organized on this basis. In virtual environments, the demarcation of this cycle is increasingly blurring. Even a basic tool like electronic mail has impacts on work time. 'Nine-to-five, five days a week, and two weeks off a year starts to evaporate as the dominant beat to business life. Professional and personal messages start to commingle: Sunday is not so different from Monday' (Negroponte 1995: 193). There are also possibilities of charting and managing numerous simultaneously operating cycles.

Rhythms of 'busy-ness' also shift when we use electronic media to take advantage of the opportunity to condense or disperse our working effort. Virtual environments equipped with electronic media put virtual workers under pressure with the expectation that they should be available any time and impose the discomfort that comes with the anticipation that they could become busier and busier. Simultaneously, they also give some discretion by which workers can choose when they are busy. For example, e-mail allows people to change their working rhythms by accumulating messages, or even messages of one particular type, and getting 'busy' with them at a chosen time.

Trust

Conventional management practices such as Taylorism and Fordism assume that employees gather to work at a common place like factory shop floors and offices during a designated period of time. This assumption can be represented by a panopticon metaphor, where the management can observe employees to control them. In this panopticon model, time is tightly regulated throughout the working hours, and all the control mechanisms are grounded on the assumption that workers cannot be trusted to work hard and efficiently without supervision and surveillance.

Thus one of the key difficulties facing managers in virtual environments is the control of workers who work out of their sight. Here the panopticon model is not applicable at least in the physical sense of the term. It is comparatively easier to manage people who are physically present in a particular place between certain fixed hours than those who are distributed in different times and spaces. Information technologies themselves provide managers with tools to control remote workers, for example, by measuring network connection time by the minute and even by the second. When this type of control is implemented, however, it tends to be considered by employees as surveillance rather than as an acceptable level of management control. Many mobile workers feel that companies use technologies to control them by monitoring their productivity and location (Davenport and Pearlson 1998: 54). Then the merits of virtual working such as flexibility begin to evaporate. This partly explains why trust has become a key word in managing virtual arrangements. People in virtual organizations are supposed to be more reliant on each other and require more trust than those in traditional organizations. According to Handy (1995), the increasing 'virtualization' of today's organizations prompts management to address the issue of trust. In virtual organizations where people need not be in one place to deliver their service and communicate electronically rather than face to face, trust is one of the important measures for managers to rely on to manage a group of people whom they do not see.

In this changed environment, employees want more control over their time, not necessarily fewer hours. Organizations also reconsider the appropriateness of the rigid time discipline to control the time of their workers. Some organizations are judging their employees by performance, not by time. They assess people by what they produce, not when they produce it and how long it takes. Thus significant changes in management styles and skills are required. Virtual offices demand radical new approaches in the management side to evaluating, educating, organizing, and informing workers (Davenport and Pearlson 1998: 54), and on the employees' part a certain level of self-discipline that has not been necessarily required in previous systems. Self-direction and self-control are likely to be a basis of social control in virtual work environments (Ishaya and Macaulay 1999). Paradoxically, in this new environment, trying to stick to conventional time management is an indication of poor management (R. Reeves 2001). However, managers accustomed to live and work in the rigid time discipline of the industrial age may find uncomfortable this new management practice based on trust.

As seen above, virtual environments are supposed to require more trust to manage people who cannot be monitored conventionally and controlled directly than traditional arrangements with face-to-face contacts. However, the type of trust in the virtual context cannot be the same one that is typically built on shared experiences over time while team members go through a lengthy team maturation process. Here we suggest 'swift trust' (Meyerson *et al.* 1996) as a type of trust that may be able to explain the trust in virtual environments. The concept was developed to explain behaviour in temporary teams such as film

Box 9.2. Characteristics of conventional and virtual time disciplines

Conventional time disciplines	Virtual time disciplines
Clock time • sharing one time standard in a shared physical place	Social time • possibly multiple and qualitative times operating
Dimensions of time discipline • standardization • regularity • coordination	Dimensions of time discipline • diversification • irregularity • coordination
Monochronicity	Polychronicity
Temporal dimensions	Shifts in temporal dimensions
No trust, control • assessment based on processes and time • trust built through experiences over time	Trust • assessment based on performance and results • swift trust

crews, theatre and architectural groups, and cockpit crews. 'Swift trust' has been used to show how individuals who are thrown together quickly become productive in spite of not developing solid interpersonal relationships. Swift trust occurs when team members assume that, like themselves, the other team members have been filtered for reliability and competence. Members set aside their suspicions and swiftly get into a trusting role. The team is keen to address the task at hand. Thus, they become productive quickly without going through the evolutionary and lengthy team maturity stages.

Box 9.2 compares characteristics of conventional and virtual time disciplines that have been discussed so far.

CONCLUSION

New technologies offer managers new forms of time discipline. This is what E. P. Thompson showed for the origins of factory forms of production system, though with some limitations (Whipp 1987; Glennie and Thrift 1996), and it can be applied to virtual work environments, too. When virtual environments substitute for traditional office procedures, for example, when previously monochronic practices become polychronic, new forms of time discipline appear or are imposed. That might happen as an unintended consequence of the new applications. This chapter has shown how analysts can discern the key temporal characteristics of existing work and can also judge how specific applications, by perhaps their architecture or functionality, might affect those temporal characteristics.

Although Barley (1988) shows that some interventions transform supposedly detrimental, 'chaotic' polychronic practices into efficient monochronic ones, this is not an inevitable consequence of the application of new technology. Other studies (e.g. H. Lee 1999) demonstrate how changes can bring effective polychronic characteristics into previously 'locked' monochronic work. The significance of these observations about the potential malleability of technology is that managers or other decision-makers have choices and consequent responsibilities over the temporal effects of their interventions. They have the opportunity to use new technology to increase surveillance and labour intensity, or to promote autonomy and the virtues of time discipline governed by trust. Therefore, proposed technological interventions should be assessed in relation to their temporal impact. This can be done through a consideration of the elements of time discipline and the assessment of the key temporal dimensions.

The temporal structure of sets of tasks is significantly disrupted by the introduction of new information technologies, and new forms of information technologies might reinforce or forcefully alter either sequential or parallel forms of working. It is also necessary to see whether workers have developed norms to accommodate certain kinds of temporal structures. Anderson-Gough *et al.* (2001) show how the internalization of time discipline is important in workplace socialization. This observation warrants a question of, for example, how this kind of temporal socialization can happen in virtual work environments. There is a clear need for empirical study.

The Use of Time by Management and Consumers: An Analysis of the Computer Industry

Paul Sergius Koku

INTRODUCTION

This study was conducted as part of my broader interest in innovations and information asymmetric conditions. Here, I focus rather narrowly on how managers in the computer industry strategically use the element of time in releasing new-product information. To guide the enquiry, I developed and tested two hypotheses on time whose implications are sufficiently broad to make them useful to managers in other competitive industries.

The element of time has been used by management in several different ways to gain a competitive advantage over rivals. For example, managers often strategize using the element of *time* together with other assets to gain the first mover's advantage by being the first to introduce a new product, enter a new market, or expand its distribution channel. Similarly, other managers use the element of time to shape their strategic decisions to be a market follower instead of a market leader. Indeed, using time as an important strategic variable that goes into the equation of production calculus is a well-established practice in management.

With new-product introduction, however, comes another crucial use of time. In this instance, management decides on the timing of releasing news regarding the innovation or new product. The heart of the timing issue involved in this context is that management makes a decision with regard to whether to use preannouncements or announcements as a means to communicate the innovation or new product to the external public. Preannouncing a product is defined as releasing information on a product to the public in excess of four weeks, typically several months, in advance of the product's arrival on the market (see Eliashberg and Robertson 1988). For example, Microsoft used a preannouncing strategy to release information to the market, indicating that it would come out with Windows 95, for over eighteen months before the product arrived on the market. Similarly, Intel preannounced the Pentium II micro-processor chip by making information available on the product in excess of twelve months before the product became available on the market.

Announcing a new product, on the other hand, is releasing new-product information to the public within four weeks of the product's arrival on the market. For example, IBM, in January 1986, released information on its powerful XT models less than four weeks before the products arrived on the market. Similarly, in October 1986 Data-Point without any prior news release unveiled its new workstations to broaden its office automation line.

In this study, I combine the traditional linearity concept of time—past, present, and future—in a production and consumption space using information as the common thread. I argue that management in producing firms (I use the term 'producing firms' to distinguish, in this case, firms that release new-product information from consuming firms, which, similar to households, are also in the market to purchase the new products) use the past and current information that they gather on products and consumers (households and other consuming firms) to shape the products that they bring to the marketplace at some future point (the term 'products' is used in the generic sense to refer to services as well).

Consumers also use the informational cues as well as information that is currently made available in the market by the producing firms to plan both their current and future consumptions (purchases). This information-gathering process is simultaneous and continuous. It is simultaneous because, while producers, on the one hand, tap into the consumers' purchase intentions and feelings about current and future products through the extensive use of marketing research, as they plan their new products, the consumers, on the other hand, are also gathering publicly available information (which has been released through announcements or preannouncements) to revise their intentions and plans.

Furthermore, the dynamic nature of conditions in the market and the economic environments in general also directly impinge on the consumer's purchase intentions. As a result, the consumer is often updating his information base and similarly revising his consumption intentions. Because this updated information is useful to producing firms in planning production, it too is sought, making the information exchange and gathering process continuous in addition to being simultaneous.

Within this broad outer perimeter of how management and consumers use time, the focus of this study is to examine how the element of time is used, by producing firms, in designing a communication strategy through which new-product information is released to the public. Specifically, I examine how firms and consumers simultaneously use time in their respective decisions to launch

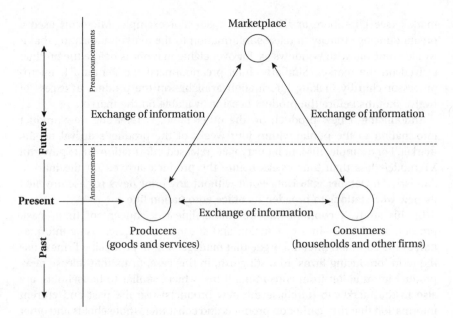

Fig. 10.1. Time, production, and consumption space

and purchase new products in the computer industry. I use preannouncements and announcements of new products as the critical linchpin of time between producers and consumers. The important question I wish to answer in this study is whether one means of communication—that is, preannouncement or announcement—accords a producing firm a different financial result. Even though the study focuses on the computer industry, its results could produce insights that could be invaluable to the practitioner in other industries, particularly in deciding whether to use preannouncements or announcements as a means to communicate new-product information to the public.

I will attempt to answer the question of whether there is a financial advantage in the mode of communication used by the producing firm by examining stock price returns associated with preannouncements and announcements of innovations in the computer industry. I chose the computer industry because it is one of the most competitive industries. As a result of the intensity of competition, the industry enjoys one of the highest rates of new-product innovation, which in turn allows preannouncements and announcements to be commonly used in the industry.

PREVIOUS STUDIES

Apart from being a subject of many philosophical enquiries, interest in time in the world of business has been more than cursory. Because of its role as an important strategic tool, time has been the focus of several studies in business and economics. These studies can be divided into two main groups—the macro-level studies and micro-level studies. The macro-level studies deal with time concept in the economy in general—for example, 'clock time' and cycles. The *economic cycle*, the time that it takes an economy to move from an economic downturn through an economic recovery, is one of the most well-known macro-level studies of time in business and economics.

The micro-level studies of time in business are focused on the application of time at the firm level. Most of these studies examine time in the innovation and production processes as well as in the management of inventory. For example, Kohli, Lehmann, and Pae (1999) examine the shortening of the new-product innovation process. Specifically, the authors examine the relationship between the shortening of the incubation time and the performance of the product in the market, and conclude that long incubation time means it would take the product a long time to reach peak sales. A study such as this is important because more efforts are being devoted to shortening the time spent between conceiving of a product idea to bringing the product to the market, thus a richer knowledge base, not only on the efficiency aspects of the production phase, but also on the effectiveness of those efforts, is important.

Another aspect of time in the new-product innovation process that has received a significant amount of research effort is the diffusion of new products. New-product diffusion is the length of *time* that it takes a new-product idea from conception to creation and adoption by the ultimate user (Roger 1983). Bass (1969), Dodds (1973), Akinola (1986), Bayus *et al.* (1989), and several other studies applied the basic and different variations of the Bass (1969) model to forecast diffusion of innovations in a wide area of products and services, including, but not limited to, retail service, industrial technology, agriculture, educational, pharmaceutical, and consumer durable goods.

In searching for new ways to reduce production costs, students of time in business turned their attention to inventory management and time-and-motion studies. These efforts yielded such new management techniques as the just-in-time approach and the more efficiently designed workplace that characterized McDonald's restaurants and the production platforms of Volvo, the automobile manufacturer. The far-reaching contributions of time-and-motion studies also led to the creation of an alphabet soup of acronyms derived from other time-based studies, some of which are less productive but were undertaken because of management's penchant for fads—issues discussed in other parts of this book.

Equally important, but less well studied, is how business organizations use the element of time as an integral part of their communications strategy—particularly how businesses use time in communicating innovations to their public. Also of interest is how the public reacts (if it reacts at all) to an advance notice of a product's arrival on the market. These issues are the concern of this chapter.

THEORETICAL UNDERPINNINGS

Because new-product information could be a useful intelligence to a firm's competition, the decision to preannounce or announce could have major financial consequences for a firm (Koku *et al.* 1997). Depending on conditions in the industry, there could be several advantages to the firm as well as to consumers when a new product is preannounced. By preannouncing, potential consumers of a product are provided with sufficient time to adjust their expectations, while current customers are given time to prepare for switching. In some cases, both the current and potential customers are given sufficient time to prepare mentally and psychologically to learn how to use the new product before the product arrives on the market. Innovating firms also benefit from preannouncing because they use preannouncements to shore up their reputation as being on the cutting edge of innovation and to keep competition away.

The product life cycle suggests that products that are currently the consumers' favourite and the manufacturers' cash cow will sooner or later become obsolete. As a result, firms that do not introduce new products will also sooner or later go out of business. To avoid this unwanted consequence, firms continually launch new products, and, to communicate information about these new products or their innovation to the marketplace, firms either preannounce or announce them. Because preannouncements are advance notices to the public, they indirectly reveal the preannouncing firm's competitive edge.

Thus, preannouncements also alert competition to what the preannouncing firm is currently working on. This way, preannouncements take away the element of surprise that an innovating firm would like to visit on its competition (giving competitors no time to react before the product reaches the market). By preannouncing, a firm becomes vulnerable to pre-emptive moves from competition. The decision to preannounce or announce must, therefore, be weighed carefully by taking the associated advantages and disadvantages into consideration. It should be noted that, in addition to informing current and potential consumers, a preannouncement can be used to send a signal to the preannouncing firm's competition about the extent of the preannouncing firm's arsenal. Such tactics are often used to ward off competition and leave a field open to the preannouncing firm.

If investors in the market perceive preannouncing as a wise strategic move that would increase the financial position of the firm, which could happen if preannouncements are successful in scaring competitors away, they would desire more of the preannouncing firm's stocks. This increased demand for the firm's stocks will lead to a rise in its stock price and a subsequent increase in the stocks' returns. However, if the market participants perceive a preannouncement as an unwise disclosure of a firm's strategic position that will subsequently have negative financial impacts on the firm, they will react

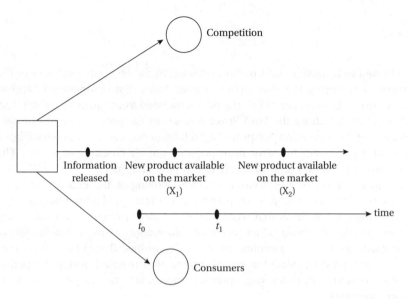

Fig. 10.2. Preannouncement and announcement dyad

negatively by selling off the firm's stocks. This will depress the firm's stock price and lower its stock returns. In this case, preannouncements and announcements have a direct connection to a firm's stock price performance. I develop two hypotheses on the basis of the discussions above.

First, it is important to realize that the industry structure has a significant impact on how the market and therefore stock prices react to preannouncements and announcements. Because of the fluidity of resources and the easy mobility of brain power, which fuels all the innovations in the industry, innovations in the computer industry, particularly innovations in the software area, can be very easily mimicked. Furthermore, unlike consumers of other durables such as cars, refrigerators, and washing machines, consumers of computers and computer-related products, particularly households, do not experience high switching costs or significant learning time. Moreover, preannouncements in the computer industry have not been particularly useful in scaring competitors away, thus they can be seen as an unwise exposure of a company's arsenal. As such, I hypothesize that:

H1: Stock prices will decrease with preannouncements in the computer industry.

Unlike preannouncements, announcements (information released close to the product's arrival in the market) still maintain the element of surprise and do not expose the announcing firms to pre-emptive strikes from their competition. Thus, I hypothesize that:

H2: Stock prices will increase with announcements in the computer industry.

DATA

I collected new-product information released in the computer industry in the United States using the *Wall Street Journal Index*. For completeness and to reduce error, I cross-checked all the data generated from the index in the *Wall Street Journal*. I chose the *Wall Street Journal* as the only source of our data because of its reputation for providing reliable coverage for business-related news and to prevent mistakes from possible double counting of events. The data covered a period of ten years between 1980 and 1989.

Because our method of analysis involves looking at the changes in stock prices that are associated with preannouncements and announcements, I limited the data to firms that were publicly traded. I obtained a total of 143, computer-related, new-product pieces of information. Using the definition of preannouncements and announcements, I determined that 71 (50 per cent) of the 143 new-product-related pieces of information released during the period in the computer industry were preannouncements; 72 (50 per cent) were announcements.

I obtained data on stock price returns using Center for Research in Security Prices (CRSP) tapes, and avoided confounding events by screening the data for other corporate events that might have had significant impact on the stock price. Specifically, I eliminated preannouncements and announcements that were made by the same firm within one week of each other, or within a week before or after a significant corporate event. Those events included such corporate news as the hiring of a new CEO, news of a pending lawsuit, and news of a product recall.

ANALYSIS

I used the standard event study methodology pioneered by Fama, Fisher, Jensen, and Roll (1969) in finance to detect the impact of unanticipated events on stock prices. This methodology is now widely used in marketing and management (see Kelm *et al.* 1995; Koku *et al.* 1997), and allows us to measure the market's reaction to new-product information. To examine the effect of *time* on the market's reaction to new-product information, I compared the market's reaction to preannouncements and announcements.

The technique uses the *efficient market hypothesis* (EMH), and the *rational expectations model* (REM). The former argues that publicly traded asset prices reflect all the information that is publicly available, while the latter maintains that current asset prices represent their discounted streams of future income. Using these two theoretical models together with the market model, I can investigate the effect of time as embodied in new-product information on the profitability of firms.

The market model succinctly combines the EMH and REM and argues that return on assets in the market model are linearly related. In algebraic terms, $R_{it} = \alpha_i + \beta_i R_{mt} + \varepsilon_{it}$, where R_{it} is the return to firm i at time t, R_{mt} is the return on the market portfolio at time t, and ε_{it} is the error term. I estimate the unknown parameters (α_i and β_i) in the model using returns data, and an equally weighted market portfolio from the CRSP tapes. The estimation period consisted of 224 days ($t - 245$ to $t - 21$). The market's reaction is measured as $ER_{it} = R_{it} - \alpha_i - \beta_i R_{mt}$. The excess abnormal return is the difference between the actual and the predicted return during the period $t - 20$ to t_0. I take the day that the preannouncement or announcement is printed in the *Wall Street Journal* as t_0, and therefore the day that information was released as day t_{-1}.

If the new-product information contains new and unanticipated news, then the excess returns are not equal to zero—that is, $E(\varepsilon_{i,t}) \neq 0$. Good news that is unanticipated will result in positive excess returns, while bad news that is unanticipated will result in negative abnormal returns. I argue that both pre-announcements and announcements are used to convey equally important news to the marketplace; however, the only essential difference between the two is the difference in the strategic deployment of the time variable. I use the two-sample means test to test for equality of means of the abnormal returns generated from preannouncements and announcements. The null hypothesis is that there is no difference in the means.

If there is no difference in the effect of preannouncements and announcements, then there will be no difference in the means.

RESULTS OF EMPIRICAL ANALYSIS

I analysed the results in two steps. First, I computed the abnormal returns and their t-values to determine their level of significance. Secondly, I used the two-sample means test of independent samples to test for the equality of mean abnormal returns of preannouncements and announcements.

The mean abnormal returns for preannouncements on day t_{-1}, the day on which information on the new product was made public, is -0.0657. This is not significant and therefore does not support H1. However, it is interesting to note that the direction of the abnormal returns is as predicted—negative. The mean abnormal returns of announcements on day t_{-1} is 0.0902. This is also not significant, and therefore does not support H2; yet again the direction of the abnormal returns is as predicted—positive. The coefficient of variation of the preannouncement is 989 per cent, while the coefficient of variation of the announcements is 794 per cent. The coefficients of variations suggest that the abnormal returns of announcements are less dispersed relative to the mean than the abnormal returns of preannouncements.

The results of the equality of means test are presented in Table 10.1. Because the null hypothesis states that there is no difference in the means, I use the

Table 10.1. Two-sample means test for equality of abnormal returns of announcements and preannouncements on day t_{-1}

Variable	Mean	Sample size	SD	SE
Announcements	0.0902	72	0.7171	0.0845
Preannouncements	− 0.0657	71	0.6498	0.0771

	T	DF	P	
Equal variance	1.36	141	0.1755	
Unequal variance	1.36	140	0.1716	

	F	NUM DF	DEN DF	P
Test for equality of variance	1.22	71	70	0.21

two-tailed test to evaluate the results. The results show that there is statistically no significant difference in the means. Even though the results of our empirical analysis did not come out as theorized, they nonetheless offer some interesting insights that have several implications. The findings of this study regarding pre-announcements contrast with the findings of Koku et al. (1997), who concluded, after analysing preannouncements and announcements in a cross-sectional study of twenty industries, that financial markets react positively only to pre-announcements and not to announcements. The lesson from comparing the results of this study with Koku et al. (1997) is that the market's reaction to preannouncements is industry specific and not a generalizable effect. This con-clusion is also consistent with Klein and Leffler (1981), who found that pre-announcements are a strategic tool in the manufacturing industry.

While the mean abnormal returns associated with preannouncements are not statistically significant, their negative direction indicates that there are no direct monetary gains from releasing information on new products in advance of the product's arrival in the market in the computer industry. Why then is pre-announcing so common in the computer industry? This study does not directly answer this question; however, it is clear from the intensity of competition in the industry that products in the computer industry have, on average, a shorter life cycle than products and services in other industries—for example, the phar-maceutical and automobile industries. Thus, unless the R & D department of a firm engaged in manufacturing in the computer and computer-related industry is prolific in coming out with new products, the firm will, in general, have a very short life. Furthermore, because of the intensity of competition, which has led into a short product life cycle in the (computer and computer-related) industry, it is possible that patents in the industry no longer offer the kinds of protection that patents offer in such other industries as the automobile and the pharma-ceutical industries. Thus, the monopoly of future streams of income that could be derived from innovations as a result of a patent protection is no longer effective in the computer industry. After all, the product will be obsolete in about three years. Preannouncing new products in the absence of such protections is, therefore, tantamount to revealing freely one's competitive strategy in a very competitive industry—hence the negative mean abnormal returns.

The question once again arises, why then is preannouncing so common in the computer industry? Although the study does not directly answer this question, it does proffer some plausible reason. Because of the short product life cycle and imminent death of non-innovating firms, there must be advantages associated with being perceived as being on the cutting edge of innovations in the industry. The opposite perception could have severe financial consequences.

For example, it would be difficult for a firm that is perceived to have a short life to secure lines of credit, as not many firms will be willing to sell on credit to a firm that may not be around to pay its bills. Furthermore, because of lack of viable products in the 'pipeline', such a firm will probably have a poor credit rating, which in turn will translate into higher costs for borrowing money and doing business. Because of these reasons, no firm would like to be perceived as lagging behind in innovation. Rather, they would like to be perceived as being on the forefront or at least having new products in the pipeline—hence the propensity to preannounce in the industry.

A poignant lesson embedded in these results is the fact that preannouncements can indeed be the double-edged sword that must be wielded rather carefully. On the one hand, they can be an effective instrument to take to war. They can be used to win fame and its associated fortunes. On the other hand, they can be fatal, even to one's own self-interest.

What about announcements? The results of this study on the market's reaction to announcements are also not statistically significant; they are, however, consistent with Wittink *et al.* (1982), who examined stock price reaction to announcements of new products in the computer industry and concluded that there was no significant reaction. However, the fact that the mean abnormal returns are positive is indicative of gains that could be had when one's competitors are taken by surprise. Ironically, one's consumers are surprised as well; this does not appear to be a problem in the computer industry, where switching costs are relatively insignificant, at least with households.

CONCLUSION

I have in this study attempted to examine quantitatively the simultaneous use of time in production and consumption space. Specifically, I have examined the reaction of the financial markets to new-product preannouncements and announcements in the computer industry. I argue that preannouncements (information released in advance of a new product's arrival in the market) and announcements (information released close to a new product's arrival in the market) serve as a critical linchpin of *time* between consumers and the producers of goods and services. Thus, an enthusiastic consumer response to the type of information released by producers would have profit implications for the firm. This in turn would translate into a higher demand for the producer's stocks, and result in positive abnormal returns. The opposite is also true.

While giving an advance notice (preannouncement) reveals a firm's strategic position, it has been argued in the strategic-management literature that it also enhances the firm's reputation and gives consumers adequate time to prepare for costs associated with switching. Our analyses of the type of information released (preannouncements and announcements) in the computer industry, however, show that there is no significant negative stock returns associated with preannouncing. However, the negative direction of the stock returns I found suggest that there could be disadvantages associated with preannouncing in the computer industry. This is generally consistent with the assertion that preannouncements in the computer industry unnecessarily alert the preannouncing firm's competition and therefore erode the firm's competitive position. This explanation may be particularly true in the computer industry, because the short product life cycle may make the monopoly of future streams of income conferred through patent protection less effective.

The extent of these disadvantages is mitigated by some major advantages. Possibly the penalty that the market exacts on firms that do not preannouce—which, in the market's perception, translates to absence of products in the pipeline—far outweighs the dangers associated with preannouncing. The results also seem to suggest that consumers in the computer industry, unlike consumers in other industries such as the automobile and other durable consumer appliances (washing machines and the like), do not need much time to prepare psychologically or financially for switching. As such, preannouncing a new product does not offer consumers much benefit as far as advance preparation is concerned.

It is important to realize that, while I have focused only on the time variable in new-product information, there are new-product information variables, such as the informational content of the new-product information—for example, detailed versus non-detailed information (see Koku *et al.* 1997)—that I have not addressed. Because all pieces of new-product information are different in terms of the degree of useful information provided to the public, a measure of the level of detail of new-product information is essential in explicating differences in the intensity with which the market reacts to new-product information. Detailed new-product information will convey much more to the market and the consumer about the new product than non-detailed new-product information. However, time being our focus in this study, I have acted as though all other variables were held constant and allowed only the time variable to vary as in announcements and preannouncements.

Time is one of the most widely studied concepts in philosophy, sociology, and lately in management, but the capacity of the dimension of time to be both ally and enemy in management needs to be studied further, particularly in more quantitative terms. After all, its effects could translate into real numbers, both in money—pounds, dollars, marks—and again in time—weeks, months, and years. Tangible contributions are yet to be made if quantitative models are to be developed to capture different aspects of strategic time-based models. Diffusion models have started us in the right direction, but the story needs to be updated.

Future studies that quantitatively model time dimensions in new-product information could provide a deeper insight. For example, instead of truncating time into a simple dichotomous variable of preannouncements and announcements as I have done in this study, treating time as a continuous variable and examining its impact on product delivery vis-à-vis the stock market reaction could provide a useful insight. Furthermore, the insights that could be gained from marrying the concept of time to the information content of new-product announcements could have far-reaching implications.

III

THE TEMPORAL IMPLICATIONS OF ALTERNATIVE APPROACHES TO MANAGEMENT

11

Contested Presents: Critical Perspectives on 'Real-Time' Management

Ronald E. Purser

INTRODUCTION

The real-time perspective has served as the foundation for the formation of new economy companies, as well as the adoption of e-commerce business models. Regis McKenna's book, *Real Time* (1997), seized the day, as it opens with the invitation: 'Imagine a world in which time seems to vanish and space seems completely malleable. Where the gap between need or desire and fulfillment collapses to zero. Where distance equals a microsecond in lapsed connection time' (1997: 3). The ideal for McKenna is to eliminate time entirely, to shrink to zero the gap or temporal distance between desire and the object of desire. With the emergence of digital technology, time negation is becoming a reality, for digital technology compresses the distance between 'here and there', 'now and then'.

Time compression of this sort, which for McKenna is the cause of celebration, is for Paul Virilio a matter of deep concern. 'With acceleration,' writes Virilio (1995*b*: 35), 'there is no more here and there, only the mental confusion of near and far, present and future, real and unreal—a mix of history, stories, and the hallucinatory utopia of communication technologies'. Geometry is negated with real-time technology, as one can be near anything in cyberspace, no matter what the distance. Hence, the need for cumbersome networks of distribution is abolished, and much physical movement can be eliminated. For example, commuting is replaced by telecommuting; attending meetings is no longer necessary with the availability of e-mail, groupware, and video conferencing; going to school is seen as a laborious inconvenience in the light of the choices that distance learning now offers.

Real-time technology compresses temporal distances, creating a sense of 'instantaneity' by processing information at increasingly faster speeds. Its concern, however, is with the future, which it aims to control through digital technology. Instantaneity supersedes the future, replacing it with a despatialized, dehistoricized, and detemporalized present (Adam 1988; Jameson 1997). The result is a managerial temporal orientation that is fixated on instantaneity, and an increasingly limited attention span. Knowledge is reduced to knowledge of the present, a bundle of information that can be instantaneously consumed. In so-called real time, there is no history or future—no time available for serious reflection or creative imagination. Nowotny (1988: 14–15) notes this trend: 'We are about to abolish the category of the future and replace it with that of the extended present . . . The category of the future is shrinking towards becoming a mere extension of the present because science and technology have successfully reduced the distance that is needed to accommodate their own products' (emphasis in original).

Interestingly enough, the accelerating forward trajectory of real time has its source in the past, and its acceleration is only the continued acceleration of past routines. Information processing necessarily depends on programs that are stored in computer memory, which are coded in the past. Managers operating in real time are forced to 'think and act immediately' (McKenna 1997), yet instant responses necessarily fall back on learned routines and unconscious cognitive biases (Purser *et al.* 1992). Operating in real time thus makes the future more unknowable than ever. Rather than developing the ability to engage the changing realities of their situation, managers find themselves trying to map learned routines and algorithms onto what time presents. Their instant responses always come a moment too late, and fast is never fast enough. The real-time manager is caught in a continuous instant replay, with each performance demanding greater speed and efficiency. The 'speed-slippage-more speed' model is a vicious causal loop, intensifying the inadequacy of a limited attention span.

Real time is a model of reality, an approach that is based on what Arendt (1958/1998) called the 'means-end paradigm', according to which the aim of any action or strategy is to do whatever it takes to bring about a desired result. In this model, time is conceptualized as an obstacle to the attainment of future desires. McKenna (1997) goes on further to define what he means by to operate and to do business in 'real time': 'Almost all technology today is focused on compressing to zero the amount of time it takes to acquire and use information, to learn, to make decisions, to initiate action, to deploy resources, to innovate. When action and response are simultaneous, we are in real time' (McKenna 1997: 4). Typical innovations and applications of real-time technologies are heralded in the popular business press and digital zines as a positive advance by both consumers and producers alike. Rarely are such real-time technologies assessed for the disorienting effects they may have on our personal, social, and collective perceptions. Even McKenna (1997) recognizes that real-time technologies will alter our cultural sensibilities, but his rhetoric bespeaks of an uncritical, inexorable, economic and technological determinism.

These instances of instant satisfaction change our frame of reference. They provide different patterns and signals for setting expectations and for judging what is reality, what is truth or fiction, what is good or bad service, what is satisfaction. The cultural and value-laden patterns of our society change as we are taught by our environment to adapt to new ways of doing things (McKenna 1997: 5).

McKenna does not discriminate between our sense of time passing—what I refer to as lived time or 'psychological time'—and compressed clock time. Indeed, McKenna (1997) not only conflates clock time with lived time, but he privileges clock time and its associative links to technology as deterministic of our consciousness. He defines his position, stating:

Real time is what I am calling our sense of ultracompressed time and foreshortened horizons in these years of the millennial countdown. The change in our consciousness of time is the creation of ubiquitous programmable technology producing results at the click of the mouse or the touch of the button or key. Real time occurs when time and distance vanish, when action and response are simultaneous.   (McKenna 1997: 4–5)

McKenna's *Real Time* is among a genre of management books that dictate the need for greater speed and acceleration in organizations, and highlight the importance of challenging time limits. These books share a common and flawed assumption: objective, physical time is superimposed onto lived/psychological time, and conceptualized as time *per se*. In other words, the ideas put forth in these books do not distinguish the acceleration of technological time from our psychological time consciousness. For example, McKenna's conception of real time has a psychological-time component as evidenced in his observation of 'our sense of ultracompressed time', but he devotes the entire book to a discussion of economic and technological imperatives for shortening clock-time units. Further, the implicit conceptualization of time as money is treated as incidental and unproblematic. Adam (1998) argues that associating time with money actually has the effect of 'detemporalizing time', making it into a quantifiable commodity that is decontextualized and disembodied from events. Mechanized and commodified time is dissociated from the contingent flux of everyday life.

Real time promises autonomy and independence from the flux of life, but its method for doing so is to deliver us up to the constructs of the past. As Adam (1998) puts it, real time does not depart from the mechanistic principle of repetition without change—a standardized order that is intolerant of all variation. In addition, once time is equated with money, human consciousness is entrained to the rhythms of the dominant economic order, conditioned to follow the demands for the maximization of speed. In this respect, the real-time perspective can be viewed as a temporal regime, characterized by such assumptions that time is exclusively objective, decontextualized, and external to human consciousness. In essence, McKenna and other authors of 'fast' books in this genre have privileged clock time, albeit an accelerated version, and commodified it, ignoring the fact that human and social time cannot fully be explained by the former.

DROMOSPHERIC POLLUTION AND CHRONOSCOPIC TIME

Real-time technologies are radically altering our everyday experience of space, time, and knowledge. Spatial distance and temporal relief are collapsing, while our creative intelligence is diminishing. Space feels more claustrophobic, as if it was closing in on us. In a context of increased capacity for instantaneous communication, time is accelerating and knowledge is becoming more voluminous, but simultaneously more superficial, as our attention is distracted and overloaded. The benefits appear to be a double-edged sword. We are attracted to the convenience of being technologically connected in 'real time', yet we are often overwhelmed by the increased demands that come with being wired, plugged in (Gleick 1999). In this respect, our 'real space' is increasingly being crowded out by the network of digital devices at our fingertips—e-mail, cell phones, voicemails, palm pilots, and the Internet. Enticed by the increases in efficiency that these real-time technologies offer, we also tend to feel more stressed out by the increasing demands made on our time and attention. New advances and changes in the world happen with such rapidity that we find it difficult to keep up. With little time available to digest experience, or reflect on intentions and actions, knowledge that could improve the quality of our lives seems out of reach.

As pointed out in the introduction to this chapter, the ultracompressed time speed of a real-time environment demands instant reactions to events. The time required for sound human judgement, communal reflection, and deliberation— the sort of relief necessary for making sense of the world—is simply not available in real time. Perhaps the greatest danger and threat to our temporal ecology are the erosion of human judgement (Postman 1993). Consider this futuristic scenario, which illustrates the loss of temporal relief on the human mind:

You can call for a dual-language text of Marcus Aurelius, or the latest paper in Malay on particle acceleration. Your reading can be interrupted by the appearance of a friend in your portfolio, a look at the actual weather in Djakarta, a film clip of Lyndon Johnson's inaugural, or, for that matter, anything, summoned by voice, available instantaneously, and billed to your central account...The man of 2016...is no longer separated from anyone. Any of his acquaintances may step into his study at will—possibly twenty, thirty, forty, or fifty a day. If not constantly interrupted, he is at least continually subject to interruption, and thus the threshold of what is urgent drops commensurately....No matter how petty a matter, a coworker can appear to the man of 2016 in a trice. Screening devices or not, the modern paradigm is one of time filled to the brim. Potential has always been the overlord of will, and the man of the first paradigm finds himself distracted and drawn in different directions a hundred times a day... (Helprin 1999: 263–5)

We have given little serious consideration in organization and management studies to the fact that the new information economy is producing an invisible form of pollution with very real consequences—what Paul Virilio (1997) calls 'dromospheric' contamination. The term dromospheric comes from the Greek *dromos*, meaning a race, running. Virilio's 'dromology' (1997) is an apt term for the study of speed in society, and how the dynamics of power are tied to the acceleration of socio-technical systems. Dromospheric pollution has to do with the unperceived contamination of 'time distances' and compression of our 'depth of field' (Virilio 1997: 40). Just as physical pollutants released by the old economy exceed the carrying capacity of the Earth's ecosystems, so the temporal pollutants that are being released by the new economy are exceeding the carrying capacity of the human nervous system and consciousness. The will-to-speed unleashes the absolute speed of real-time technologies, annihilating real space. The result: a loss of appreciation for the vastness and qualities of space, a dimension that provided protected intervals of time, periods of delay and relief between events and action. Management now occurs in a technologically mediated landscape, in the virtuality of *nonspace*, and in the temporalities of *distraction* (Morse 1998: 102).

Real-time technologies are, in effect, distorting and diminishing our perceptual 'depth of field'. According to Virilio's theory, a fundamental perceptual distortion is occurring because of a mutation of our cultural aesthetic. We are moving from the passive, small-scale optics of geometric linear perspective, to the active large-scale optics of digital media. Small-scale optics—which is derived from the linear perspective, a development in art during the Renaissance period—is an extension of human vision as expressed in painting, photographs, and film. An apparent and visible horizon serves as a key point of perceptual orientation for making sense of scale and perspective, and a deeper horizon grounded in our collective imagination is instrumental in deriving meaning from our situated experience. For some thing or object to exist, it literally must stand out against the background of a horizon. The depth of field in small-scale optics is based on the preservation of spatial distance, giving rise to such distinctions as 'near versus far', 'here versus there', and so on. In contrast, with real-time/large-scale optics, time moves at the speed of light, erasing distinctions based on spatial distance. Having instantaneous access from any point in space to virtually any other point in a 'real-time instant' renders such spatial notions as 'near versus far', 'here versus there', meaningless. The result: a distortion of our depth of field and fundamental disorientation.

The 'transapparent horizon' of digital media supersedes physical and cultural horizons, where 'the far prevails over the near and figures without density prevail over things within reach' (Virilio 1997: 26). Moreover, real-time technologies introduce a 'bug' or mental virus into the perceptual field as a new transapparent horizon, generated purely by digital media and electronic transmission of images that takes hold over the normal boundary line of the physical horizon, and also plays havoc on the deep horizon of our collective imagination and memory (Virilio 1997).

In what amounts to a fundamental confusion of natural, collective, and technological horizons, Virilio posits that dromospheric pollution, if left unabated and unregulated, will lead to a sharp loss of cultural memory and a degradation of collective imagination. Virilio (1997: 25) laments this loss as

a practical consequence of the emergence of a third and final horizon of indirect visibility after the apparent and deep horizon: a transapparent horizon spawned by telecommunications, that opens up the incredible possibility of a 'civilization of forgetting', a live live-coverage society that has no future and no past, since it has no extension and no duration, a society intensely present here and there at once—in other words, telepresent to the whole world.

In contrast, McKenna (1997: 6) rejoices in this state of affairs, as he exclaims: 'We will increasingly find that the technologies of speed will not give us the time to see or plan beyond the horizon. We will have to think and act in real time. We cannot choose to do otherwise.'

'We cannot choose to do otherwise?' This technological imperative sounds dangerously totalitarian. For McKenna, the demand for speed overrides human intelligence and judgement. Fast decision making in real time requires instant answers. In order for us to 'adapt', we will have to develop a hyperintelligence (we have no choice), that is situated not in the horizon of human-scale optics, but in the transapparent horizon. Hyperintelligence is pure algorithmic knowing, indifferent to, and decontextualized from, local spatio-temporal horizons. The totalitarian overtones are indicative of the fact that the techno-fundamentalism inherent in the real-time perspective will redefine and alter the very meaning of human intelligence. To think and act in real-time terms requires a certain kind of wilful blindness to the past and future.

From Chronological to Chronoscopic Time

Virilio (1977/1986, 1980/1991, 1995b,c, 1997, 2000) has gone to great lengths to show that the essence of post-war telematics involves the virtual elimination of both spatial and temporal distances. Speed is no longer limited by moving across geographic distances by means of physical transport—that is, movement through chronological time. Rather, speed is equated with real-time data transmission moving at the speed of light—giving rise to what is now understood as instantaneity. Virilio characterizes this digitalized speed-up as a shift from chronological to chronoscopic time.

A key driver of chronoscopic time is the shift to digital interactive media—the conduit for an instantaneous mode of production and consumption. This shift entails a dramatic transformation in forms of cultural communication, in our sensibilities and conception of knowledge, which are imperceptibly changing our lived experience in space and time. As communication is increasingly being transmitted through the media of digital, real-time technologies—where vast increases in speed and expanded volume are key drivers—the form of everyday culture shifts to keep up with the rapid transmission and exchange of information. Not only does cultural life become increasingly commodified as it is forced to adapt to the frenzied pace of chronoscopic time, but basic capacities for sharing meaning—the stuff culture is made of—begin to atrophy (Rifkin 2000). Instead of sharing meaning, or engaging in what Borgmann (1984) refers to as 'focal practices', cultural activity is reduced to the transmission of information, for the expressed utility of procuring ephemeral desires and increasing consumption (Simpson 1995).

Chronoscopic time, however, is still bound to and dominated by a clock-time world, but it represents a movement away from a cultural rhythm based on analogue and spatial sequences, to a world punctuated by distinct, identical, still, digital time units (Rothenberg 1993: 205). Symbolically, such a shift from chronological to chronoscopic time is analogous to the difference in how time is read out on an analogue versus a digital watch. Chronological time is apparent in the mechanical and sequential movement of the analogue clock, as we 'tell time' by noting the spatial location of hour and minute hands. Unlike their analogue counterparts, digital clocks continually flash an instantaneous read-out of the temporal present instant. Digital clocks flash a 'real-time' display, erasing the sense of transitional sequential movement. In some respects, it is not so much that we 'tell time' when looking at a digital clock, as that the clock 'tells us'.

The shift from chronological to chronoscopic time involves a radical change in temporal orientation and the very means by which we make sense of our lives. In a chronological world, time as duration was coupled with space as extension. Calendars and clocks served as the dominant means for regulating and synchronizing political, social, and economic activities. The emergence of a chronoscopic world parallels the advance of electronic data transmission technologies, which send and receive signals at the speed of light. This amounts to a new time standard based on real-time capability for instantaneity, and an accelerated perspective focused on intensive duration of the 'the real' moment replacing extensive duration of history.

The extensive time of history, chronology, and narrative sequence implodes into a concern and fixation with the real-time instant. What used to comprise a narrative history—sense making based on knowledge of the past, present, and future—contracts into the buzz of a flickering present. For Virilio (1997), the metaphor of 'photographic exposure' replaces the sensibility of time as a succession of moments of present duration and that of extension in space. Digital media produce a temporality akin to photographic time, where time does not so much pass or move sequentially, but erupts, is exposed, and breaks the surface (Virilio 1997: 27). Rather than making sense of time through the unfolding of a narrative (before, during, after), time is perceived more in terms of abrupt and discontinuous irruptions of varying intensities (underexposed, exposed, under-exposed). Virilio claims that real-time technologies have an effect of narrowing our time sense, refocusing our attention exclusively on the present, or what Benjamin (1993: 32) simply calls 'now-time'. Thus, a key feature of real-time technologies is that they function as a sort of monochronic filter that screens or cuts out concern for the past and future. Noting this trend, Virilio (1997: 137) states: 'the time of the present world flashes us a glimpse on our screens of another regime of temporality that reproduces neither the chronographic succession of the hands of our watches nor the chronological succession of history. Outrageously puffed up by all the commotion of our communication technologies, the perpetual present suddenly serves to illuminate duration.'

High-impact media messages are designed to captivate attention, narrowing our temporal orientation to a flashing series of now moments. A constant stream and barrage of media images results in a distracted form of hyper-attention. The real-time instant of economic transaction eclipses the consumer's sense of situated presence in time (Wood 1998). Indeed, in chronoscopic time the postmodern subject is constituted as a dutiful consumer, what Deleuze and Guattari (1977) would call a 'desiring machine', or Baudrillard (1983: 57) an 'operator without subjectivity or interiority', a human terminal who clicks a mouse to satisfy every passing whim and desire.

Because time in chronoscopic environments is experienced as flashes, a 'series of pure and unrelated presents' (Jameson 1997: 26), it becomes increasingly difficult to construct and weave together one's life as a coherent narrative (Sennett 1998). Postmodern temporality

can be characterized as an attitude toward time or an experience of time that...places emphasis upon maximum intensity in time, not the living in time that would be a form of praxis, but a more passive fascination or playing...The result is a flashing pointillism, a lived experience as a series of disconnected intensities. Not being able to commit to a future or to take the past seriously, the postmodernist makes do with the present. (Simpson 1995: 144)

As Paul Klee (quoted in Virilio 1997: 10) put it, 'To define the present in isolation is to kill it.' Virilio likens the psychological experience of chronoscopic time to a sort of 'time freeze'.

Temporal Alienation in Real Time

In the chronological epoch, modern collective malaise was expressed in terms of alienation: alienation manifested in forms of withdrawal or feelings of estrangement from one's spatial surroundings—for example, alienation towards poor working conditions, urban sprawl, and large impersonal bureaucracies. Other psychological maladies such as depression were symptomatic of such spatial alienation. Metaphors for depression are primarily spatially oriented, 'feeling down', 'downtrodden', 'under the weather', and so on. In chronoscopic environments, temporal alienation becomes more salient. Wood (1998) des- cribes temporal alienation as a mismatch or discordance between rational/ clock time and lived time. Similarly, McGrath (1988) notes the importance of such mismatches between rhythms of clock time and subjective time as sources of stress in organizational settings. Temporal alienation is contingent on two key factors that are inversely related: (1) the degree to which one obeys clock time; and (2) the sense of one's own presence (Wood 1998: 97). In other words, the more one tends to embody and obey the mechanical/digital rhythms of clock time, the greater the feeling of loss of situated presence in time.

Common symptoms of temporal alienation are chronic stress, various forms of rage (which are expressive of an intensified impatience), and work addiction. Such behaviours are rooted in the temporalities of distraction—consolidated and perpetuated by habitual routines enacted in the daily operation of digital real-time technologies. Just as the mechanical clock commanded and regulated social behaviour in the industrial era, the real-time perspective transmitted by digital media is also taking command of social and organizational life. Consider, for example, how telecommunications and computing technologies have blurred the boundaries between work and home. People now talk about having '24/7' access, meaning, of course, that with the electronic prostheses of cell phones, e-mail, voicemail, faxes, pagers, and palm pilots they are continuously 'plugged in' to the global information network. Even Steve Jobs, the man who made it his mission to get an Apple computer on everyone's desk, confesses how intrusive these devices have become in his own life, and just how obsessive- compulsive his behaviour has become as a result of having '24/7' access:

Technology cuts both ways. It's a double-edged sword.... with high bandwidth to my home in place, people can send me e-mail over the Internet and I receive it instantly. What this means is that they learn very quickly that, if I want to, I can respond imme- diately, even if I am sitting at my computer at home at midnight. But this also means that if I don't respond instantly, there's no cover for me to hide behind. So, at nine o'clock at night, when I'm with my family, it's very hard to resist the urge to take fifteen minutes and go check my e-mail. It really has invaded my personal life, I have to say. It follows me everywhere, there is no escape anymore.   (cited in McKenna 1997)

What Jobs fails to recognize is that the increase in technological bandwidth has led to a subsequent narrowing of his temporal world. He, like millions of others, is ensnared by the demands of 'real time', is experiencing a diminishing sense of 'real presence' in lived time. One wonders even when Jobs is with his family in the evening if he is really 'there', 'fully present'?

The automatisms associated with the habitual use of real-time technologies are not only insidious, but also pervasively demanding of conformity

(Morse 1998: 118). As Jobs admits above, the compulsive checking of e-mail throughout the day is now a common occurrence and expectation in managerial work. Distracted attention and compulsive behaviour are highly correlated with immersion in real-time work environments. Performing tasks half-aware, talking on the cell phone while driving in traffic, and other so-called multitasking activities are not only signs of temporal alienation, but also illustrate productive forms of discipline that are not imposed, but self-initiated, requiring very little surveillance. Morse (1998: 118), drawing from Foucault's *Discipline and Punish* (1979: 103), argues that the disciplinary power of real-time technologies (and its associated mental states of temporal distraction) are built upon an 'empire of the habitual' and 'layer upon layer of built environment and representation', or what she refers to as 'zones of ontological uncertainty'.

Chronoscopic temporal environments tend to foster what appears to be a postmodern form of malaise—what Rappaport (1990) calls 'telepresssion'. The symptoms of telepression combine a cognitive hyperactivity that is immobilized and fixated on the present. As outer events are accelerating at a rapid pace, telepression manifests as a defensive reaction to an unknown futurity. Describing the typical profile of the telepressed individual, Rappaport (1990: 191–2) states:

The future of this type of individual does create an illusion of successful future extension.... they have 'marks' on their time lines that give the appearance of plans. The typical problem, however, is that the future is narrowly defined in terms of present business plans, so that the future is usually not very distant. In addition, this 'near-future extension' is often crowded and unrealistic. The overconcentration of goals makes the temporal experience of this person disjointed because time moving too quickly means time not personally controlled. It is precisely this sense of no control that causes the feeling of 'inauthenticity' that Heiddegger expounded in his philosophical work. The experience of desynchronization with objective time creates the general feeling that there is no clear purpose to life.

...It is possible to sail a boat, for example, without charts or a compass. However, the absence of a chart prevents the possibility of a journey. One is limited to 'day' sailing, so that new destinations and new challenges are out of reach. Eventually the same seascape and circumstances will produce a tedium not unlike the absence of meaning associated with a present-centered existence.

Rappaport's clinical observations are suggestive of an often overlooked relationship between time and meaning. Indeed, knowledge of time is intimately tied to the meaning and the quality of our lived experience, as the research of Ida Sabelis (this volume) on top managers shows. Nihilistic attitudes towards life in the new economy are becoming more widespread. Relationships and activities are viewed in instrumental terms, subject to a calculative means–end analysis, 'What's in it for me/the corporation?'

Sennett's latest critique (1998) on the personal consequences of the new capitalism goes to the heart of temporal alienation and complements Rappaport's analysis of telepression. For Sennett, temporal alienation in the new economy, where there is 'no long term', is manifest in the demise of character. Character, according to Sennett (1998: 10), is shaped by the 'ethical values we place on our own desires and on our relation to others'. The loss of long-term commitments, the destruction of loyalty, and the inability to delay gratification make character development difficult and set our inner life adrift. Yet, the lack of temporal attachments is propagandized (by those who stand to benefit) as the sort of 'competencies' needed to flourish in the new flexible economy. For Sennett (1998: 62), such an appetite for flexibility that demands weak temporal attachments is pathological, as it encourages a greater tolerance for fragmentation.

REIMAGINING TIME

Clock time can be thought of as an 'extension' that, according to Hall (1983: 29), is an 'externalized manifestation of human drives, needs, and knowledge'. Extensions function like language in culture, and when they take on a life of their own, we are engaged in what he calls 'extension transference'. Extension transference is apparent when the substitute takes the place of the process that was extended. Commenting on how this occurred with clock time, Hall (1983: 131) states, 'This principle is illustrated by the way in which we have taken our biological clocks, moved them outside ourselves, and treated the extension as though they represented the only reality.'

Industrialization of culture was imbued with the clock metaphor, which permeated images of social organizations. With the real-time perspective, extension transference shifts to the computer, the new cultural idol. Extension transference involves a kind of collective amnesia. Clock time is a collective representation for organizing social and economic activities, which has become abstracted and detached from its roots in consciousness. This process resembles what Barfield (1988) refers to as *modern idolatry*. We commit idolatry in the way we relate to clock time and its real-time compatriot, for we have forgotten that temporal phenomena are a collective representation, a human creation, an extension of a deeper topography of time. We are idolaters not because we create idols, but because of our blind worship of externalized clock time. We are left with a modern picture of time that ignores the central role of human consciousness and imagination, and, in so doing, treats time as an independent, external phenomenon (which we have slavishly to adapt to).

Given the insights of twentieth-century physics, it is commonplace to know that the activity of the observer is implicated in what is observed. While perception relies on sense organs, it is human consciousness that perceives. It is also an epistemological truism to recognize that the phenomenal world, the world of appearances, is not to be equated with the ultimate reality. When we see a 'chair', ultimately what is 'really there' is but a pattern of moving particles.

Barfield's famous analogy (1988) of the rainbow can help shed light on the epistemological issue having to do with temporal phenomena. When a rainbow appears in the sky, we can all point to it. But if we were to actually walk over to the end of the rainbow, and look directly at it, there would not be anything actually there. What we call a rainbow is the conjunction of particles of water, the sun, and human vision. Like a chair, the rainbow is a collective representation. It is not a hallucination, for we all claim and agree that we see such an entity called a rainbow.

We can extend this analogy to time, since time is also a collective representation. While we all can point to the clock and agree that time is passing, if we go to look directly for time, we cannot find it. Even our sense of the present is a conventional notion, a relative term. If we attempt to look for the present, it slips away. Time appears to be always moving, never fixed. The 'present' (and for that matter the past and the future) is very much like the presence of a rainbow, the outcome of a very powerful collective representation. Moreover, the present is not independent of some object that changes as we normally assume. So-called real time appears to be a counterfeit. As Morse (1998: 23) states, 'real time depends for its very existence on the creation of unreal time that can mimic the clock'.

One reason time is such a slippery concept to understand is because it is not based in matter. Our conventional approach is to treat time as some independently existent objective referent. This seems misguided, as we do not have any sense organs for perceiving time. Noting this fact, Adam (1998) argues that, in order to appreciate the complexity of time, we need to embrace our sensual embodiment and tap the evocative power of our imagination. As she states: 'Since we have no sense organ for time, we need—even more than for the landscape perspective—the entire complement of our senses working in unison with our imagination before we can experience its working in our bodies and the environment. Such an effort at the level of imagination is needed if we are able to take account in our dealings with the environment' (Adam 1998: 55). It is interesting to note that 'pre-perspectival' cultures (Gebser 1985: 11) were not detached from their own collective representations as we are with our perspectival world view. Barfield notes that, for us moderns, 'the only connection of which we are conscious is the external one through our senses. Not so for them.' Given our bias toward the senses, it is understandable then why we have so little connection and such a superficial relationship to time, which is not material in nature. This leads us to consider that the epistemological link between time and mind, between human beings and the phenomenal world, may be of a different, perhaps 'super-sensory' order. That order, as suggested by Barfield, is one of *participation*, or, to use Coleridge's term, the 'primary imagination'. To function as moderns, we have suppressed our awareness of participation with the representational nature of the phenomenal world as a whole, including that of time. Our dominant mode of thinking relies on models (constructed from analytical thought about thought) and we perceive such models as if they were actually and literally true (rather than as representational and relatively true). In this sense, we have gained the ability of scientific rational analysis, attained the powers of perspective by positioning ourselves as separate from phenomena, but all at the expense of maintaining a non-participatory consciousness. As noted above, this has been the function of modern idolatry. Thus, it should come as no surprise that time has been regarded as totally independent of our own consciousness and such empty notions as 'real time' accepted uncritically.

Recognizing the role of participation and imagination in the figuration of temporality leads us to consider other topographies and textures of time. Our dominant cultural concept of time has been limited to the topographical surface—a spatialized view of time—which has led to our propensity to idolize outward-directed extensions. As an alternative, a focus on the participatory nature of temporal perception can help us to 'own' and take more responsibility for our own extensions. Critical to this process is an examination of how primary imagination (or figuration) constructs our collective representations of temporal experience. Rather than limiting our participation to the surface of time, participatory consciousness offers us a way of exploring the complex topography of 'whole time'. Reimagining time to be a complex, multidimensional whole can serve as a counterbalance to the real-time perspective with its insatiable appetite for speed, power, and negation of lived human experience.

12

The Rhythm of the Organization: Simultaneity, Identity, and Discipline in an Australian Coastal Hotel

Dirk Bunzel

INTRODUCTION

While the issue of time has recently received increased attention in the field of organization studies, *rhythms* and their role in the creation of (organizational) identity are issues still to be discovered for the field.[1] This chapter, then, attempts both raising awareness of the issue of rhythmicity and illustrating its relevance to organization studies. Accordingly, I will describe aspects of organizational life at an Australian coastal hotel that seem to convey a sense of the rhythm of the organization.[2] Based on this account, I will briefly address the constitution of rhythms and reflect on their role within society, highlighting their socially integrative function. Linking these thoughts back to the example

A number of people have offered helpful advice and comments on different drafts of this chapter. Most notably, I would like to thank Chris Baldry, Stewart Clegg, Jeff Hyman, Rolland Munro, and Richard Whipp, as well as the participants of the 'Organization, Management and Time' stream of the 16th EGOS Colloquium, where an earlier version of this paper was presented.

[1] A notable exception is Zerubavel's study (1979*a*) of the temporal structure of hospital life.
[2] The account provided in this chapter is based on findings of my Ph.D. research, an organizational ethnography that focused on issues of power and identity within a five-star hotel on the Australian east coast. During the fourteen-month research period, I conducted formal and informal interviews with management and staff in the hotel, worked together with, or followed, managers in the conduct of their everyday routines, and attended regular meetings by management as well as training courses and other social events. Additionally, I recorded my personal experience of life at the hotel (for example, routines, rituals, ceremonies, extraordinary events) including the (varying) aesthetic composition of the hotel. As will become clear, a

of the hotel, I will argue that, today, the socially integrative function of rhythms unfolds around the creation of a sense of simultaneity among individuals or collectives separated across time and space. However, I will also argue that the subjection to rhythms corresponds to a certain form of domination. The chapter concludes by pointing out how a concern with rhythms can inform organization studies.

THE NUMBERS, THE RACE, AND THE FAMILY: SYMBOLIZING THE RHYTHM OF THE GRAND SEASIDE HOTEL

The Grand Seaside Hotel is a five-star luxury hotel in a small town on the Australian east coast. At the time it was studied, the hotel had just changed ownership. The new Hotel Management Company appointed Tim Chang General Manager to implement an extensive restructuring programme. Top of his agenda in order to render the Grand Seaside Hotel into an efficient and profitable business was the provision of service excellence. Tim not only introduced a *customer service programme* to generate a culture of service excellence within the hotel; he also sought to create a collective form of identity, *the Grand Seaside Family*, to balance the alienating experiences of the restructuring process and to foster a common sense of belonging among members of the organization. This community, as was made clear, however, was a contingent one; it evolved around the dedication of staff to the principles of service excellence and, hence, their contribution to the overall profitability of the business. As this may not have been an innate concern to most employees, management did not cease stressing that the organization was in intense competition with other hotels in the area, fighting fiercely about every inch of the market. As a result, efficiency and excellence in the provision of customer service were presented as imperatives to (economic) survival and thus constituted fundamental obligations to every 'family member'. In effect, the Grand Seaside Family *offered membership (identity) in exchange for commitment.*

The image of the Grand Seaside Family as a contingent bond was projected by various means. Training programmes communicated a proactive attitude to customer service that sought to anticipate even imaginary customer wants and needs, while awards were granted to staff who delivered 'service beyond customer expectations'. However, staff were also frequently reminded of their duties and, occasionally, were reprimanded for negligence or failure in the provision of service excellence. Twice a week, during the Morning Briefings, the Controller of the hotel informed attending managers and supervisors how

pivotal aspect of my research was the attendance at regular management meetings, the 'Morning Briefings', and the account here provided draws substantially on observation notes of thirty-seven of these meetings, which I coded and entered into a NUD-IST database.

the hotel's latest economic performance figures related to the targets specified in the budget.

CONTROLLER. We were fully booked again on Friday. We have an average rate of 220. 45 per cent on Sunday. Monday on 33. So, we are pretty good so far. The October-Fest seems to be really working well.

BAR MANAGER. Yeah, they were quite busy the whole weekend in the bar. It's going extremely well.

CONTROLLER. So, we are going extremely well for this time of the year. Only the functions-revenue is still a bit behind budget, but they will certainly make that up with the incoming conferences now. [*Controller looks to one of the Conference Coordinators, who nods her head.*] All the other departments are ahead of budget.

Short pause.

CONTROLLER. As I said. We are going OK so far. We have started this month very well, so that I expect us, actually, to end even further ahead of budget. Currently, we are just 50 ahead of budget. But, with this result we are just over last year's result. Last year we had been behind by this time. Remember, last year we were behind almost until February by about 250. Somehow, we were still able to catch up and finish 250 ahead of budget.

MANAGER. That was quite amazing. I mean, this was actually after the boom period. And we still caught up and finished ahead. [*Many people nod their heads, which seems to suggest concurrence.*]

CONTROLLER. Yes, it's funny. We were picking up almost 2 per cent per day at that time. But again, I don't want us to have to achieve such a miracle again. So, there is still a lot to do to not fall behind again.

She sorts out some of her pages, and continues to read from those pages.

CONTROLLER. November looks above budget so far, but also not really great. December is a little bit softer. January and February sitting well so far. But as I said, we are not that well ahead, so we really have to be on top of the cost this time, from day one on. [*She looks up.*] So, that's it.

In response to the reading of 'the numbers', managers and supervisors were usually expected to report on the activities of their respective department or unit. Such exchange of information included reports on targets, the announcement of incidents or activities relevant to the hotel, or strategies developed for the acquisition of new business. Overall, the reading of 'the numbers' seemed to convey variable senses of urgency to all participants with respect to the diverse, spatially and temporally segregated business operations. The less favourable the figures reported, it seemed, the more attendees of the meetings stressed their efforts to increase efficiency and profitability of the hotel.

Within the image of the Grand Seaside Family, we are encountering a metaphor common in management theory. The organization envisaged as a *sociological organism* (Morgan 1997) finds itself engaged in *a struggle for survival in a hostile economic environment*. The frequent references made by managers that reminded staff of market pressure from competitors, budget demands, and the importance of performance indicators represented this struggle. This struggle seemed to know no difference between the various members of the organization and it seemed to unite them through a common fate—a fate that was perhaps best visualized by a slide that the Human Resource Manger presented to staff on the occasion of the annual All-Staff Meeting. This slide showed a cartoon with two groups of three people each engaging in a tug of war. The whole scene was located on a tiny island, which provided just enough space for the six people to stand. This small island appeared like a platform on the water—a platform surrounded by huge crocodiles with widely opened mouths. The rope on which both groups were pulling was already tearing apart, so that each group was about to fall into the sea and to get caught by the crocodiles. The Human Resource Manager commented on this slide stating: 'Yes, this makes it clear. We are a great team here, and only by working together will we succeed.'

In the light of the metaphor of the hotel as a sociological organism, some sequences of the Morning Briefings also appear in a different light. During the early stages of my research, I was wondering why 'the numbers' were announced with a degree of regularity unmatched by any other aspect of the meetings. I was also puzzled as to why the Controller would announce those figures with an incredible speed, almost bombarding people with targets, performance indicators, and occupancy rates, giving them hardly any chance to keep track with the pace of her reading. After all, I do not recall that I ever saw anyone seriously attempting to jot down those figures. Most of the time, people's behaviour seemed to indicate attitudes ranging from indifference to polite interest towards this ritual component of the Morning Briefings. My suspicion that hardly anyone was seriously interested in the concrete value that those figures represented was confirmed in conversations with several attendees of the Morning Briefings. 'No, I don't really know what these numbers are about,' said the Conference Manager. 'And I think most other people don't know either. Those numbers just give you a feeling of how we are going.'

Yet, if no one really understood these figures, how could they provide such a feeling? And if they were more or less non-intelligible to the recipients, why were 'the numbers' read out at all? It was the remark of another manager that unravelled the symbolism of 'the numbers'. On that occasion, the respective manager characterized the Grand Seaside as being 'simply a very *number-driven* organization', a statement that I could confirm only from my observations. Yet, what if it was not the manifest, obvious meaning of the numbers as representing parameters of the hotel's performance that mattered? Perhaps, it was less the concrete value of the numbers announced that mattered; instead, it was the illustrative phrases and idioms accompanying the reading of those numbers that gave them their particular meaning: 'a feeling of how we are going'.

Suddenly, some sequences in the meeting appeared to me in a different light. Was it possible that the reading of those numbers symbolized the struggle of the organization with the market? Emanating from that assumption, standard phrases such as 'we are ahead of budget', 'we are behind budget', 'we have to make up ground', 'we are gearing up', and the like, which were routinely uttered during the Morning Briefings and which constituted established parts of the hotel jargon at the Grand Seaside, received a different meaning. All of them seemed to symbolize the hotel as struggling, as *moving* relatively to some external entity. In the light of this symbolism, one could envisage the Grand Seaside as engaged in a *race against the budget*, the latter representing the external forces of the market. In the logic of this metaphor, phrases like 'being ahead of (or behind) budget' clearly convey a sense of the organization's performance, independently of the concrete and often unintelligible meaning of the figures presented. In short, 'the numbers' seemed to symbolize a particular collective state of being: *the rhythm of the organization.*

The idea that, by focusing on symbolic aspects of organizational life, we can sense the rhythm of an organization provokes a number of questions. Most importantly, questions arise regarding the constituents of rhythms and their relevance to organization studies. Consequently, we shall now consider how rhythms emerge and address the role of rhythms within society. Linking these considerations to the example of the Grand Seaside Hotel, we shall then address the significance of shared concepts of time to the creation of collective identities.

RHYTHMS AS LIVED EXPERIENCE

Let us, briefly, consider the constitution of rhythms. Contrary to the objectivist 'error of seeking the origin of the rhythm within the object', rhythmicity results, ultimately, from the creative activity of the *rhythmizing consciousness* and unfolds around the (dis)satisfaction of certain expectations (Abraham 1995: 67). While sitting in a train compartment and (initially rather unconsciously) tapping his foot to the sound of the wheels, Abraham analyses the constitution and efficacy of rhythmizing consciousness:

I am no longer at the mercy of external forces; on the contrary, it is now they who obey me. At just the right time, I tap my foot and instantly I trigger the event. My expectations have no other meaning: in reality, they are desires, demands, incantations. When the event occurs, I experience the satisfaction of my efficacy. Thus, rhythmizing consciousness is apprehended as activity, as spontaneity.   (Abraham 1995: 70–1).

Rhythms are spontaneous, creative, and intentional; yet, they also constitute a *particular form of existence*. It is, therefore, 'erroneous to speak of a perception of rhythm or of a perceived rhythm. What occurs, in fact, is the *rhythmization of perception*, a creation within a consciousness of unreality' (Abraham 1995: 73; emphasis added). Movements—for example, the tapping of the fingers or the sequential steps of dancing—represent *mediators* that not only *realize this unreality* but allow for recognizing the true object of rhythmic contemplation: *coessentiality*. Yet, the fundamental role of coessentiality does not confine to the triggering of rhythmic experience; it also represents the very *criterion* for the rhythm thus created. Importantly, such coessentiality includes other individuals. Hence, time (rhythm) is significantly involved in the creation/experience of intersubjectivity (see Noss, this volume).

With Abraham, then, we can reject rhythmic objectivism[3] and qualify rhythms as the creative accomplishment of rhythmizing consciousness, as a form of (collective) sense-making. Rhythms are not so much 'products' of this mode of consciousness, as they represent a particular form of being. While this form of being ultimately unfolds from an act of will, it cannot be evoked entirely voluntaristically. Rhythmizing consciousness is not autarchic: it responds to the phenomenal world as much as it imposes rhythmic qualities upon the latter.

THE ROLE OF RHYTHMS IN SOCIETY

Having identified rhythms as a particular form of being, as unfolding from the creative activity of rhythmizing consciousness, we shall now consider their role within society. Authors from the fields of anthropology, sociology, or social psychology have described rhythmicity as the *temporality of nature* (Adam 1990), as the most *fundamental form of human time experience* (Kaempfer 1996), or as *underlying the normalcy of everyday social life* (Zerubavel 1981). The anthropologist Leroi-Gourhan, for example, conceives of rhythms as underlying any form of time and space appropriation/construction. 'Rhythms are the creators of time and space, at least for the individual. Space and time do not enter lived experience until they are materialized within a rhythmic frame' (Leroi-Gourhan 1988: 309). Highly significant for the context of our argument is Leroi-Gourhan's assertion that human conceptualizations of time–space—and, hence, rhythms as a most fundamental form of time and space appropriation—are *crucial to social integration*. During thousands of years of evolution, the biological reality of human existence has become increasingly superimposed and replaced by an ethnic order that is wholly symbolic in nature. This process of symbolically 'domesticating' time–space implies the substitution of 'natural' rhythms through rhythms based on social convention; a process that renders human

---

[3] In this respect, the title of this chapter seems somewhat misleading, as it suggests the rhythm of the organization to be an objective property of the latter. Instead, this rhythm represents the creative accomplishment of a (collective) rhythmizing consciousness that imposes rhythmic qualities upon its object of contemplation.

time–space into a *scene*, replacing the 'chaotic rhythmicity of the natural world' with 'regularized cadences and intervals' (Leroi-Gourhan 1988: 313). The rhythms that rule (post)modern life have changed over time, as have the contexts of their symbolic creation. What has endured, though, is the fundamental role of rhythms for the appropriation of time (and space) and, hence, their socially integrative function: that is, their relevance to the coordination of social interaction and to the creation of social identity.

In premodern societies, social interaction tended to be temporally and spatially confined to the level of local communities. With a simple division of labour and rare cross-communal interaction, the regulation and integration of the group activities into a commonly shared temporal frame appeared less complex and tended to be solved at intra-communal level (Sorokin and Merton 1990). In other words, the predominantly contextualized course of behaviour in premodern societies made the integration of different temporal perspectives superfluous. This limitation of social interaction to the local and intra-communal level meant that different concepts of time—which tended to be naive, egocentric, group specific, and socio-centric (Elias 1988)—could coexist peacefully, integrated into a framework of *non-simultaneous synchronicity* (Esposito 1998).

It was not until the spread of the capitalist mode of production that such interactions were *lifted out* of their contextual constraints on a broader scale (Giddens 1990). With the increasing division of labour under the capitalist regime of production, the issue of coordinating social activities across communal boundaries and of integrating people into a commonly shared inter-communal temporal frame became imminent. It was the bourgeois society that brought about a dissociation of social time from individual time, of public time from private time, and of internal time (*Eigenzeit*) from external time (Nowotny 1993). The *individualization of social time* that emerged with modernity led to a multitude of local times and rendered the (temporal) coordination of social activities more complex (Elias 1988). What modernity demands, then, is an *abstract chronology* capable of integrating the various unregulated yet interrelated social activities into a *non-synchronized simultaneity* (Esposito 1998). The attempts to standardize time by making it quantifiable, which marked the whole period of industrialization, can be seen as tributes to the individualizing and potentially 'centrifugal' forces released within modernity. Within the latter, simultaneity is produced, most prominently, through the abstract chronology of *clock time*, which seeks to govern, meticulously, even the most mundane social activities (Zerubavel 1981).

The diversification of social time in modernity is perhaps most clearly exemplified by the segregation of home (time) and work (time) (see Bell and Tuckman, this volume). Significantly, this segregation of social time coincides with the development of *new forms of personal and social identity* manifest in the dissociation of the individual's self into different roles. In this respect, the standardization of time as achieved in abstract chronologies not only facilitates the coordination of social activities but also has implications for the constitu-tion of social identity. Chronologies provoke the creation of an *intersubjective* *(temporal) frame of reference*—one that makes local experiences of social time communicable across local and communal boundaries and that is fundamental to the creation and maintenance of *imagined communities* (B. Anderson 1983). In modernity, where interactions are increasingly anonymous, *distanciated* over time–space (Giddens 1990), a commonly shared concept of time helps sustain faith in the existence of a communal bond among individuals separated in time–space. It contributes a form of (systems) *trust* indispensable to the maintenance of such communities (Giddens 1990).

Today, social life is not only increasingly fragmented, giving way to a mul-tiplication of temporal experiences (Gergen 1991); society itself seems progress-ively in motion (Virilio 1999) with the result that 'time itself becomes more dynamic: it develops into *accelerated innovation*' (Nowotny 1993: 11; trans. DB). Increasingly, people discover that they have to run faster only to remain on the spot, to keep up with the fulminate developments within society—developments that expose the relativity of any notion of progress (Nowotny 1993: 86): 'place becomes more important than the destination: those who persist will stagnate: everything, most notably the time, becomes rapid movement' (trans. DB). Similarly, identity has become increasingly saturated, fragmented, and tentative. Consequently, both social time and identity have become increasingly complex and fragile accomplishments (Gergen 1991).

TEMPORAL SEGREGATION AND ACCELERATION OF LIFE AT THE GRAND SEASIDE HOTEL

With respect to both the acceleration of social life and the diversification of activities across spatio-temporal boundaries, the Grand Seaside Hotel seemed to represent a microcosmic image of contemporary society. Besides its spatial segmentation into 'front of house' (where service encounters take place) and 'back of house', the hotel was segregated along temporal lines. While activities in some departments (for example, administration) evolved around regular weekday work and were performed, typically, in '9–5 jobs', other departments worked much more flexible and extensive hours. Many jobs 'front of house' were built around customer needs or preferences. Staff working in the hotel restaurants or at concierge used to work in shifts, covering large parts of the day from early mornings to late at night. The same applied to jobs in the 'back area' that catered or supported those departments, such as kitchen staff. A number of other departments had staff constantly on duty (twenty-four hours a day, seven days a week) such as the Duty Managers, responsible for the safety at the hotel. Similarly, the reception desk had to be attended around the clock, despite the fact that the intensity of work increased during certain peak periods of the day and slowed down considerably at night. Work at the conference department, perhaps the most illustrative example, evolved around a form of project management with lead periods of up to several months from the first contact with the client through to the hosting of the event and to the follow-up letter or interview in the aftermath. With every stage of this form of project management, the contact with the client and with the supporting departments of the hotel became more intense and complex. The days immediately before and during an event were the most hectic and stressful ones. Conference Coordinators not only had to fine-tune the preparations for the event but also had to respond quickly to assist its smooth running, liasing and cooperating with clients and other departments.

In the context of such spacio-temporal segregation and diversity, it may be useful to think of service provision as a *symphony* that requires the contribution of several soloists, all with their specific peak times, deadlines and schedules (Reeves and Bednar 1995). Rhythms can assist the orchestration of such diverse activities. The rhythm of the Grand Seaside, for example, did not replace or discard all other temporal experiences at the hotel: the rhythmic mode of being is not substitutive but *co*essential (Abraham 1995). It integrates the various temporal experiences within the hotel into a common rhythmic frame—a frame that

allows us to get free from the complete synchronization of each event with all others and to give place to completely independent rhythms, temporal projections, accelerations, and slowdowns. This holds particularly for the various functional precincts of society: economy, politics, religion, families each have their own temporal organization, with their own rhythms, deadlines, priorities, that cannot and must not necessarily be synchronized with those of other precincts. In order to secure connection...it is enough to be able to stage in each moment what is simultaneous with what (or has been, or will be). (Esposito 1998: 22–3.)

The *rhythmic simultaneity* created around the reading of 'the numbers', allowed different departments to run on different clocks, while it also provided a common 'sense of how we are going'. This way, it signalled the need to alter the intensity of the work and thus assisted the coordination of various activities without necessarily levelling or eliminating the diversity desired in the context of customized service.

Life at the Grand Seaside also seemed to have *accelerated* in the wake of the restructuring programme. The abolition or integration of positions at all hierarchical levels led to a noticeable intensification of work, particularly for managers and supervisors. Many of those who survived the restructuring found themselves in often unfamiliar positions and had to cope with significantly increased levels of work intensity and overall responsibility. Often, they had to work extra time or long hours to get their work done. Frequently, such time pressures generated frictions between work and private life.

The metaphorical *race against the budget* not only symbolizes the acceleration of life at the hotel; it significantly contributed to the latter. The element of fatality that underpins this metaphor seemed to unite management and staff and bound their (common) future to their capability of withstanding the challenges of the race. Simultaneously, the recurrent reading of 'the numbers' also defined obligations attached to membership. Only those who were fast and efficient enough to contribute to the hotel's performance in the race were considered worthy of being part of this community.

This constellation seems significant for contemporary social life well beyond the context of the hotel. In today's society, the obligation to perform translates into the demand to be fast, quick, efficient. Those who are slow, who cannot keep up with the pace of (public) time and life, are not only disadvantaged; they are also marginalized or socially excluded (Nowotny 1993). Perhaps it is the underlying obligation to contribute, to perform in 'the race against the budget', that explains another habitualized performance during the Morning Briefings. Whenever someone was supposed to report on his or her department or function and had actually no information he or she considered relevant or important enough mentioning, the usual reply was: 'Nothing from me—just busy'. This phrase reassured the other members of the 'family' that the person concerned was still performing his or her obligations, despite the fact that the details of this performance were considered as constituting more or less insignificant information. It also conveyed a sense of movement, of urgency, of keeping up the pace—no matter what.

In short, we could claim that most departments or units at the Grand Seaside seemed to run on different schedules and had developed different internal times (*Eigenzeiten*). They were, in effect, *running on different clocks*. Within the Grand Seaside's 'race against the budget', *speed* (as metaphorical for economic performance) became *imperative to survival* of the group. Consequently, both *rhythm and community* were experienced as *interlinked social constraints*: individuals were obliged to conform to the temporal demands imposed upon them at the risk of social exclusion.

THE GRAND SEASIDE AS RHYTHMIC COMMUNITY

To some authors, the diversification and acceleration of (post)modern life ask for new integrative measures (Nowotny 1993). As indicated above, the ritual events, ceremonies, and daily routines of communal life that reproduce rhythmic simultaneity also help in creating and sustaining a *sense of community*. Although the subject of his considerations is the nation, we can extrapolate some of Benedict Anderson's insights (1983) to the case of the Grand Seaside Family: 'The idea of a sociological organism moving calendrically through homogeneous, empty time is a precise analogue of the idea of a nation, which is also conceived of as a solid community moving steadily down (or up) history' (B. Anderson 1983: 31).

In the light of Anderson's metaphor, we may suggest that one ought not to conceive of the hotel as an entity rigidly fixed in time–space. The hotel as a sociological organism appears to live a quite vivid life—drifting along the line of sociocultural standardized temporal frames: season, week, day, special occasions. It changes its face with the seasons, offering different visual, oral, or culinary experiences to its guests, adequate to the occasion. It contracts and expands with the unfolding of the week, swallowing up masses of guests on Friday night only to ejaculate them again on late Sunday. It speeds up during peak times in the morning and late afternoon, with guests arriving or departing, whilst somewhat slowing down outside these periods. In short, the hotel seems to possess its very own life and rhythm. While its 'pulse' increases during peak times (high season, weekend, or peak times of the day) when the race is on most intensely, it also enjoys periods of relative rest (off season, working week, off peak times of the day) when the pressure eases somewhat. Maintaining a basic level of continuity, the rhythm of the organization thus gives way to different tempos.

The experience of the hotel as a social organism, the sensing of its 'pulse', which is probably all too familiar to employees and which can be discerned by guests and external observers as well, can be said to represent one of its most distinctive features. If identity is the 'capacity to keep a certain narrative *going*' (Giddens 1991: 54; emphasis added), then rhythmic experience, which allows for sensing '*how* we are going', is a fundamental aspect of that identity. It provides a sense of continuity in the face of unsteadiness and volatility. The rhythm of the organization integrates the different temporal experiences within the Grand Seaside Family into a *communal rhythm of work* (Hatch 1999), thus contributing to the trust required for maintaining this community. As Benedict Anderson (1983: 31) explains: 'An American will never meet, or even know the names of more than a handful of his 240,000,000-odd fellow-Americans. He has no idea of what they are up to at any one time. But he has the complete confidence in their steady, anonymous, simultaneous activity.'

'Nothing from me—just busy', used as a standard response during the Morning Briefings, represents one way of preserving such confidence.

THE POWER OF RHYTHMS

From another perspective, the social integration provoked by the rhythm of the organization constitutes a form of domination. By this we mean not merely the subjection of individuals to a common temporal structure. Rhythmic subjection is not passive; on the contrary, it is fundamentally *active*. It not only demands the creative contribution of rhythmizing consciousness; it also implies a certain obligation. To achieve the rhythmic coessentiality desired, individuals/ groups have to *act*. Dancing, perhaps the best example, asks for coordinated movements to evoke and sustain the rhythmic experience (coessentiality) desired—in fact, this is what qualifies dancing as such. In other words, rhythms are *calls for action*. In the context of organizations, such subjection takes on different forms. Most directly this is the worker's subjection to the rhythm of machine technology, as exemplified in Charlie Chaplin's movie *Modern Times*. On a more symbolic level, we could claim that the rhythm of the Grand Seaside Hotel carries a similar obligation: the obligation to perform within the race against the budget. In this sense, rhythms are experienced as obligation, as subjection towards some normative demand.

Consequently, we can argue that the rhythmic capacity for social integration corresponds to a certain form of domination. More precisely, in the context of organizations such as the Grand Seaside, we can assert that rhythms subject individuals to a certain form of discipline. As Foucault (1979) has elaborated, discipline is neither purely coercive nor descending. Rather, it implies both *technologies of power* (which are descending, directed at others, and coercive) and *technologies of the self* (which are self-directed, more voluntary, and productive).[4] Whereas the former constitute control and surveillance in medieval monasteries as much as in modern institutions such as prisons, schools, or factories, the latter are vital to the construction of individual and collective identity. Most relevant to the context of contemporary organizations are those instances where both technologies overlap or merge, thus provoking a form of *subjugation* 'which produces self-disciplining subjectivity' (Knights and Willmott 1989: 550).

In other words, rhythms correspond to a certain form of domination. They not only discipline individuals by subjecting them to a specific temporal frame—be it the rhythmic sequences of a dance, the flow of the assembly line, or the dictate of 'the numbers'. Their power also subjugates individuals into a self-disciplining identity. The member of the Grand Seaside Family is asked to *act* upon him or herself so as to perform well in the race against the budget. This way, he or she contributes to the survival and prosperity of the organization. 'The numbers' communicate this obligation; their call for action not only conveys a 'sense of how we are going'; it also *normalizes* life at the hotel and thus imposes a certain *rhythmic discipline* upon the Grand Seaside Family.

IMPLICATIONS FOR ORGANIZATION STUDIES

Summing up the main arguments of this chapter, we can say that the reading of 'the numbers' conveyed to members of the Grand Seaside Family 'a sense of

---

[4] For the sake of brevity, this qualification of both Foucauldian technologies has to remain rather crude and superficial. For a more extensive discussion, see Foucault (1979, 1988) and, for the context of the Grand Seaside Hotel, see Bunzel (2000).

how they were going' in their metaphorical 'race against the budget'. It provided the occasion for members of the 'family' to share their (temporal) experiences and it helped them coordinate their activities by establishing a *sense of simultaneity*. The 'product' of this process, *the rhythm of the organization*, can be said to have represented a distinctive (collective) form of being—the identity of the Grand Seaside Family significantly evolved around this rhythm.

The account provided in this chapter has some implications for organization studies. First, our rejection of rhythmic objectivism in favour of a perspective that stresses the creative activity of rhythmizing consciousness as a particular form of being makes erroneous any attempts at measurement. Rhythmicity is *not* periodicity! Rhythmic consciousness as creative, intentional activity is perfectly capable of integrating non-periodic events. Instead, our concern was with rhythms as collectively created meaningful phenomena and, as such, was descriptive. It proceeded from a description of (collective) rhythmic experience to the identification of contextual factors that triggered that experience only to demonstrate that both were mutually constitutive. Strictly speaking, the reading of 'the numbers' neither 'represented' nor 'caused' the rhythm of the organization; it provided occasions for the (collective) invocation of rhythmic experience and it was from that that 'the numbers' derived their ('rhythmic') meaning. In this sense, our approach sought to eschew the representational epistemology of both objectivism and subjectivism (see Odih and Knights, this volume) in favour of a perspective on *rhythms as lived experience*, as (collective) accomplishment of individuals jointly sensing and making sense of their world. However, our concern with rhythms has been far from exhaustive and has left room for further explorations. Meetings, for instance, are a common but certainly not exclusive occasion for (collective) sensemaking. Further, rhythmizing consciousness may be evoked in very different ways: planned or spontaneous, coordinated or chaotic, habitual or sporadic. Similarly, the reading of 'numbers' may be one method of evoking/communicating rhythmic experience; yet other more or less effective means may exist to create/convey such experience. In other words, for a better understanding of the role that rhythms play in contemporary organizational life, the various ways in which rhythmizing consciousness is evoked and communicated require further investigation.

Secondly, a focus on rhythms seems instructive in an era where organizations have become increasingly flexible, virtual, and semi-structured. Paying tribute to this development, a number of authors have recently focused on organizational *improvisation* drawing for that purpose on the metaphor of *Jazz* (e.g. Weick 1998; Hatch 1999). Today, the argument goes, organizing resembles increasingly the performance of a Jazz band, with various actors improvising around a fixed canon of routines ('tunes'). As this chapter sought to demonstrate, *rhythms* provide an equally useful concept to approach performance within contemporary organizations. Rhythmic performance is not entirely rigid but may be performed within different tempos. This way it allows for *flexibility*, as when the intensity (tempo) varied with which certain routines at the Grand

Seaside were performed. As rhythmic performance is only partially ordered (semi-structured), it allows for *spontaneity* and *creativity*. This is important for the provision of service excellence. While performance at the Grand Seaside (for example within service encounters) was generally planned and based on routines, staff were also asked to 'expect the unexpected' and to 'exceed customer expectations'. In other words, we may argue that many of the activities performed within contemporary organizations are rhythmic. Again, it remains to future research to approach organizing as rhythmically arranged process. Such an approach may be particularly useful in the context of intra- and inter-organizational project management where coordination and temporal integration are complex yet imperative processes.

Finally, a concern with rhythms can not only conceptually link the issues of coordination, identity, and time; the socially integrative function attributed to rhythms closely relates to discussions of power and domination. Beyond the well-established role that time plays within the subordination of labour to the factory regime, a focus on rhythms allows for conceptualizing power as being both enabling and constraining, directed at the self and others, submissive and creative. Further, *rhythmic discipline* is continuous yet sporadic and is experienced to varying degrees and intensities. In other words, governance within contemporary organizations may well be conceived of as *rhythmic domination*. However, it still remains to be explored exactly how individuals are socialized into a particular communal rhythm and how pervasive is the subjection thus achieved.

In sum, the task of this chapter was to raise awareness for the issue of rhythms and to demonstrate its relevance to organization studies. While it has left a number of issues unexplored, I hope that the story of the Grand Seaside Hotel and its 'rhythmic community' has not merely been entertaining but that it may have inspired other researchers to pay more attention to the rhythmic aspects of organizational life. However, in order to sense it, '*you* have to *feel* the rhythm' of the organization.

13

Interpretative Times: The Timescape of Managerial Decision Making

Tom Keenoy, Cliff Oswick, Peter Anthony,
David Grant, and Iain Mangham

PROLOGUE

Remember, what we are trying to do is to say: 'can we take an incident in a real organization's life and create something out of it which reflects something of the wider level from which we can learn about issues like our politics, emotions, dynamics, change, whatever?

This discursive fragment is taken from a conversation between a small group of senior academics conducted intermittently over a period of about fourteen weeks. Their task was to reconstruct or—perhaps more accurately—attempt to 'relive' a critical incident they had been involved in before reconstituting it as a thirty-minute script. Our task in this chapter—which, from a different perspective, replicates what the academics were doing—is to reconstruct what they said during that process in order to illustrate the significance of 'time' in the decision-making process. In particular, we attempt to identify the timescape (Adam 1996) of decision making with a view to reinforming our understanding of how organizational decisions are shaped and formulated.

THE ANALYTIC ASPECT

Generally, the linear touchstone assumption that continues to underpin most management texts is that organizations are disembodied rational–economic phenomena guided and informed by the tenets of legal–rational authority. We are presented with an image of managers whose decisions in the presumed clinical pursuit of strategic goals are invariably shaped by a variety of contingent and contextual market factors. Their behaviour is fuelled by instrumental rationality and the values of efficiency and effectiveness. However, despite Fineman's characterization of organizations (2000) as 'emotional arenas', emotion and emotional engagement remain marginalized in the lexicon of managerial practice. In our view, emotion has been singularly neglected and undervalued in most approaches to organizational analyses. Moreover, we think it plays an unacknowledged and perhaps critical role in shaping the processes of social construction and, in consequence, infuses organizational behaviours and the interpretative frameworks participants deploy to understand such behaviour. A fuller appreciation of the impact of emotions on managerial practices and procedures will, in our view, greatly enhance our understanding of organizations (see also Edwards 1987; Damasio 1999; Fineman 1999; Ashkenasy et al. 2000).

We set out to develop a methodology through which we could research the apparent absence of emotion in management processes. Our approach is informed by the dramaturgical perspective on organizational analysis (Goffman 1959/1990; Mangham 1986; Mangham and Overington 1987), which problematizes the more conventional notions of role playing and forces the analyst to confront a wide range of issues about actor authenticity, feelings, and identity; about how organizational actors script their performances; and, more fundamentally, about how actors socially construct and reconstruct their organizational performances. Reflecting the social constructivist epistemological stance that informs this chapter (Gergen 1999; Searle 1999; Hacking 2000), our preferred approach to the data is through discourse analysis. For present purposes, this involves contextualizing the 'drama' we witnessed and examining the actors' discursive practices—that is, identifying how the actors' utilize and deploy discursive resources to (re)construct the 'realities' of the organization they inhabit (van Dijk 1985; Fairclough 1995; Keenoy et al. 1997, 2000; Grant et al. 1998).

The substantive research focus is on the process of organizational decision making. We needed what appeared to be a universal but reasonably identifiable managerial process and 'decision making' emerged as, perhaps, the archetypal organizational activity that is deemed to be an essentially rational 'objective' activity. One assumption that informs our analysis is the conviction that, while managerial decisions are often fuelled and conditioned by emotional responses, publicly they are framed in terms of legal–rational legitimations. Such assumptions inform what might be termed 'foundational' decision theory (March and Simon 1958; Cyert and March 1992). Subsequent analyses have consistently acknowledged the situational context of decision making (Lindblom 1959; Cohen et al. 1972); and Mintzberg (1973, 1979; Mintzberg and McHugh 1985) has long emphasized the constitutive and generative significance of the informal realm over formal processes and structures. However, fundamentally, the presumed linear and utilitarian (Etzioni 1961) character of decision processes has remained largely unchallenged (March 1994; see also Mintzberg et al. 1990).

For these reasons, decision making appeared to offer us a potentially fruitful empirical focus.

THE METHODOLOGICAL ASPECT

To put the matter sharply, our central methodological problem concerned how to 'observe' the impact of emotions (however defined) on a decision process. Conventional managerial sensemaking (Weick 1995) privileges legal–rational norms and marginalizes emotion as a legitimate basis of organizational action. It is a rare manager who would confess that anger, jealousy, love, or guilt was the prime motivational rationale behind a particular decision. Further, we would anticipate that the emotive triggers for any decision and the emotive responses to any decision are invariably disguised—perhaps even suppressed—in any account of a decision (Marshak *et al.* 2000). Thus—short of being present in 'real time'—it is simply not possible to observe such phenomena directly. And, unsurprisingly, it is part of our argument that any conventional *post hoc* account of a decision process will, almost inevitably, be 'explained' in terms of some emotionally homogenized rationale.

We needed to devise some means of providing a non-threatening and—in so far as is possible—an emotionally secure environment within which managers could discuss decision processes in a reflexive manner. Thus we asked a set of managers—in this case a group of senior academics at a Graduate Business School—to write a short drama, which was to be based around a critical incident (that is, a particularly emotive decision process) with which they were familiar. Initially, they were required to reconstruct the decision from start to finish including as much detail as they thought necessary to expose the underlying issues, rationales, and motivations. Thereafter, they engaged in a process of 'fictionalizing' the events in a thirty-minute 'script'. In this respect, actors were permitted to change, distort, and invent material in order to 'tell a better story'. Such a process is not unproblematic, but, in manufacturing this artificial 'research space', our intention was to create a permissive atmosphere for managers to 'reflexively reconstitute' a managerial process. (More detail on the methodology is provided in Oswick *et al.* 2000; and we have commented on some of the potential research advantages of employing 'fiction' to examine 'reality' in Oswick and Keenoy 2001.) Their focus was on the outcome—the script; ours was on the discursive processes they employed to arrive at that outcome. In our view, as a research method, it liberated the managers openly to acknowledge their own partiality and provided them with the discursive space to explore the underlying values that informed their decision values and decision criteria (see also Gergen and Thatchenkery 1996*a,b*). That said, we would certainly accept that the proof of such experimental puddings is in the eating.

THE DRAMATIC ASPECT

On the surface, the critical incident they decided to reconstruct was a routine and intrinsically uninteresting issue: the absence of any formal specification concerning the work roles and function of part-time lecturers. The 'organizational progress' of the issue is represented in Box 13.1, which reconstructs 'what happened' in terms of the stages in a conventional decision model. The left-hand side indicates the putative stages; the right-hand side indicates where and how those stages were accomplished. As ever with such depictions there is a decontextualized linear progress from problem identification to problem solution.

Hence, formally, if the organizational 'record' were examined, a researcher would find that the Director of the School identified a 'problem' relating to the apparently casual controls exercised over part-time lecturers. After predictably grinding bureaucratic consideration, *it was decided* to draft and formalize a general job description for such posts. Thus the issue appeared resolved. As ever with such records, there is no hint of anything except a sensible, instrumental goal orientation leading to an organizationally 'progressive' decision. However, in the process of reconstitution, it emerged that the historical context in which the issue arose and the way in which it was handled caused considerable angst and frustration and was a source of continuing peripheral friction even after it had apparently been resolved. Significantly, and perhaps curiously, no one lost out over the decision; no one was directly affected; but, at least temporarily, it soured relationships, was a continuing source of irritation, and, apparently, marked a sea change in the atmosphere at the Graduate Business School.

With respect to our dramaturgical expectations, the actors fulfilled their roles. As anticipated, their account indicated that 'in public' they drew on conventional order and efficiency values in processing the decision. Indeed, they were

Box 13.1. The decision process

Decision model	Our case
Problem identified	Unspecified role of part-time lecturers
Action	Agenda item at committee(s)
Identify parameters	Discussion at meeting(s)
Collect evidence	Discussion at meetings(s)
Evaluate evidence	Discussion at meeting(s)
Identify options	Discussion at meeting(s)
Evaluate options	Discussion at meeting(s)
Decision	Job description written
Outcome	Problem solved

instrumental in devising the 'solution' to the 'problem', even though, privately, they would not have chosen to make the decision at all. In contriving a preferred solution, they acted out the roles of good organizational citizens. However, our actors also detailed the significance of backstage (Goffman 1959/1990) private conversations in which defensive stratagems were devised, and hinted at how these were deployed to engineer both the character of the discussions and the final outcome. All of which is unsurprising, for, unlike minimalist textbook models, 'real' decisions are taken in 'real time' and are the artefacts of historically situated socio-political relations (not all of which can be located 'within' the organization; see below). Our model procedure (see Box 13.1) projects a bloodless rational process and gives no indication whatsoever of the *actual* decision process, nor any clues about the situated factors, forces, and values informing 'the decision'. Moreover, from their reconstruction, it seemed clear this particular decision was seen as reflecting a much more complex set of issues and concerns about what could be described as the 'strategic direction' of the Business School. These included: the fact that the Director was new to the job; that he was said to be trying to impose 'alien' values on the organization and refocus the way actors conducted their affairs; that his attempt to formalize the informal represented a direct challenge to the pre-existing social norms and values and, thus, an attempt to change accepted behaviour. In addition, those who opposed him could be seen as representing the 'old guard'. In effect, his action appeared to criticize the way they had run things. As such, he was portrayed as a 'modernizer', a 'controller', a creature of the 'establishment', and a facilitator of 'alien' and, by implication, negative values. His 'academic' values and priorities were said to be different (and, again, 'by definition' not legitimate). In the early stages of resimulation (but, significantly, not later) his behaviour was also portrayed as an attack on academic freedom.

Hence, the decision was both embedded in and the outcome of a complex of personal, professional, and organizational issues and conflicts, which, in consequence, meant that the formalized 'non-decision' was like a peace treaty that (to the outside world) could be projected as an image of progressive change. In effect, everything changed but everything remained the same—and the symbolic significance of the decision far outweighed its operational impact.

With respect to decision theory, our findings merely confirm the well-rehearsed critiques of the conventional models (Whittington 1989; Mintzberg *et al.* 1990). First, as ever, the problem with such terms as 'rational', 'optimal', or 'satisficing' (that is, a 'satisfying' but not an optimal decision) is that they are all reflective of the detemporalized, linear machine model of organization that imposes an idealized invariant sequence on social action and banishes ambiguity and complexity (see Introduction and Burrell 1998). They bypass the intrinsically negotiated character of organizing and the ubiquitous influence of historically situated political, social, and—indeed—personal values. As is well known, the latter not only shape perception, interpretation, and evaluation (and thus the presumed nature of 'social reality'), but also the decision choices. Secondly, while the formal decision outcome was, *by definition*, of a satisficing character, as indicated above, operational decision values may draw on an indefinably wide variety of motivations and legitimations. Our volunteers mobilized a wide range of values to sustain their collective opposition to the decision that had been pursued by the new Director. (To complicate the matter further, it needs to be remembered that, while 'opposing' the decision, they had also been pro-active in designing it to ensure the Director's presumed control objectives would be subverted.)

As noted above, our interest was not in the issue as such but in the discursive resources utilized by the actors as they reconstructed what happened and in how they translated that into a fictionalized script. In this way—if only through the partial memories of those involved—we managed to chart how they *said* the decision was made. Initially, our empirical interest lay in the emotive basis of the decision values actors used to legitimize their positions. But, as events proceeded, it became clear that the social processes they utilized in actually reconstructing and reconstituting social reality are intrinsically time dependent.

THE TEMPORAL ASPECTS

We have used Barbara Adam's concept of timescape (Adam 1996, 1998) to draw attention to the complex of mutually implicated temporalities and sedimented 'time layers' embedded in the social process(es) we explored. The particular analytic advantage of the notion of 'a timescape' is that it permits us to identify and discuss each different temporal aspect without losing sight of the facticity of their simultaneous coexistence. At any one moment in the drama, each temporality unfolds, so to speak, 'at its own pace and in its own time'. For example, 'real-time' social action may skip unreflectively over the surface of the *longue dureé*, yet each is in continuous interaction with the other. Further, elements within the timescape coexist both independently and interactively—thus career cycles coexist with and interpenetrate annual work cycles. In this respect, our data illustrate Adam's insistence that social phenomena have multiple temporalities and that these temporalities are mutually implicated.

Initially, perhaps the most obvious point to make is that, with few exceptions, conventional accounts of decision processes tend to project them as taking place in a 'time vacuum'. At best, the temporal aspects remain marginalized. There is an unreflective assumption that decisions are self-conscious discrete proactive 'real-time' responses taken 'in the now', which can be assumed to have a clearly directional impact on organizational behaviour. But, as we will try to demonstrate, both the substantive decision process and decision outcomes may be better understood as the enfolded events (Keenoy 1999) of the numerous temporalities that can be shown to influence these phenomena.

Constitutive Temporalities

On the 'surface' of our discursive data, there are two interactive temporalities that have shaped—some might even say, constituted—the events we are attempting to analyse.

First, there is what might be called *managerial time*. This refers to the linear calendar and clock time that elapsed between the public emergence of the 'problem' and the point at which the 'actual decision' was made. We are accustomed to see such episodes as taking place within defined parameters—as symbolized by the formal (and appropriately termed) 'minutes' that record and fix organizational behaviour in space and time. In terms of the calendar, it took about 6–8 weeks from apparent start to apparent finish. This aspect of the social action unfolded in real time and embraced the 'hot cognitions' (see below) surrounding the critical incident; the various meetings, both formal and informal; the time–space between meetings; and the publicly declared 'resolution'.

MARK. The least accurate record is probably the minutes, isn't it, if you ask anyone that was there?

However, despite the comforting precision of allocating 'minutes' to 'spent' managerial time (whatever they describe), in terms of clock time, we can have no accurate estimate of 'how long' the decision process took. We do know that the key events took place at three formal meetings each of which lasted between two and three hours (and, at which, other issues were also discussed). But the issue itself had originated in an informal exchange between two managers and we also know that, in between the meetings, a variety of other informal discussions took place. However, it is important to recognize that even this account is abstracted from the complex of constitutive temporalities within which the decision was embedded—some of which went back several years. The latter were identified, revealed, and, indeed, *created* during the recon-struction process.

Secondly, there are what we might call the *research times*. These relate to the temporalities that encompass both the period of 'time' it took to reconstruct the decision and the temporal device that our actors employed to access their understanding of the decision process.

In calendar time, the research task—reconstructing the decision and starting to script the play—lasted for 12–14 weeks, with the actors meeting for a day or half a day as and when they could. In other words, this social action took place in *intermittent* real time. However, it would be mistaken to assume that 'nothing' happened in between these meetings—there is some evidence sug-gesting that the 'space' between meetings permitted actors to reflect privately and review and revise their previous understandings. Perhaps unsurprisingly, over time, they appeared to moderate their perceptions and produce more rounded accounts of what had 'really happened'. For example, John, initially fairly critical of the Director, reflected:

JOHN. You know, you actually need...somebody like him in a funny sort of way...Now, we were going along fine before...it's all about organizational change as well, isn't it? I think...maybe we got a bit slack?

Such changes of view not merely arose from individual reflection but were also an artefact of the method used to *research* the decision. In this context, 'researching' the social event involved attempting to arrive at a plausible narrative account of it by 're-experiencing' it. The actors had to simulate the decision process by attempting to relive their feelings, actions, thoughts, and interpretations to each other in real time while, at the same time, relating to each other as colleagues, friends, and research informants. In one sense, we might regard this as a fairly banal process, for it involves resort to the commonplace and ubiquitous social practice of attempting to describe 'what really happened' by going through the 'he-said-she-said' routine of doorstep discourse. What seems notable about such routines is the extent to which they are infused with temporal reference points employed to 'fix' reality.

MATTHEW. Right, so...let's put our minds back if we can to this critical school staff meeting which took place where? Here?
MARK. In this very room I believe.
MATTHEW. During the day was it, afternoon?
MARK. 2 o'clock in the afternoon.
LUKE. It was a sunny day...[*laughter*]. I could go and get the minutes if you like.
MARK. That might be difficult/
JOHN. So the next item is/
MARK. 'Next item is recruitment, part-time lectureship'. Er...I can word for word remember saying 'John, you're down on the agenda as wishing to bring this item up'...yeah, I can remember...
JOHN. I've no idea what I said...[*overlap*]
MARK. /or 'brought this item forward' and there was a palpable silence actually/ ...Everyone was waiting/
LUKE. A nice long pregnant pause/
JOHN. /don't remember, never do. I don't know what happened but I would have said that this came up at the research committee. [*The Director*] wanted to talk about it/
LUKE. No, no, no...no you didn't. I'll tell you what you said and I'm fairly certain that it was more or less word for word what you said as well...John said something along the lines of um 'this was an issue that came up at the last research strategy meeting'...'research committee' rather um...'given it had wider implications', or 'given that it was of interest to everyone' that 'perhaps this was a better forum in which it might be raised'...

In this exchange, two actors present at the key meeting appear convinced they 'really know' what was said; but each remembers something different and they provide different emphases. The third actor—whom they are quoting—claims not to remember what he said with any precision. Similarly, not long afterwards, Luke says:

LUKE. I can remember what other people say very vividly at meetings but I can't remember what I say...

This is curious; and it may indicate something about how we experience the 'immediate present'. While it seems obvious that speakers and listeners engage differentially in social action, why should speakers appear to remember less than listeners? It was this phenomena that led us to the conclusion that the 'he-said-she-said' taken-for-granted feature of social life is a much neglected and, perhaps, fundamental source of social sensemaking. As a process, it is intrinsically social in that it involves actors relating to each other as significant others while providing (perhaps) competing accounts in order to arrive at a more 'acceptable' story. During the process, each contribution 'of fact' appears to be considered and reconsidered, refined and reinterpreted, until the actors arrive at an albeit temporary agreement as to 'what really happened'. In Weick's terms (1995), this routine is a highly complex social process grounded in identity construction (and, we would add, identity confirmation). Actors utilize what, for them, are privileged social cues about 'how-the-world-is' to make an ongoing social *judgement* about a particular event (that is, by its very nature, sensemaking goes beyond mere description of an event—it involves an evaluation of competing discursive accountings). Since sensemaking is a reflexive process, it is necessarily retrospective and the objective is to arrive at a plausible rather than what might be deemed an 'empirical' account. In passing, it is worth remarking upon the extent to which 'daily discourse' is constituted by the telling and retelling of organizational events. This appears to be the discursive wallpaper of organizational meanings, if not, indeed—and here we are guessing—much of what passes for organizational 'life'.

More pertinently, the fundamental social resource required to enact the 'he-said-she-said' scenario appears to be *virtual time*. We use this term to refer to the social space routinely constructed by our actors in order to 'tell their stories' of the decision process. In contrast to the linear character of managerial time, virtual time is a free-floating cognitive resource that social actors employ to make sense of the present by locating the present simultaneously in the past, present, and future. As such, it offers almost limitless possibilities to—and we use this word advisedly—*speculate* about the range of potential motivations and explanations of organizational behaviour. However, such speculation is always constrained. In practice, in the process of 'rationalizing' the decision events in terms of their 'he-said-she-said' memories, our actors embedded their sensemaking accounts in their taken-for-granted organizational time–space. This involved calling on a multitude of episodes from the organizational history and mythology; on their presumed shared values; on related histories and myths; and on cognate stories from similar organizations. In other words, fragmentary details from other events taking place at different points in time and in different social locations were employed to make sense of the specific decision they were analysing. In this respect, 'virtual time' can be seen as a collective reservoir of judgemental experiences employed to 'fix' an ever-transient 'present' (see also Adam 1990: 38–42). Analytically, it is important to note that their engagement in this process, *of itself*, changed our actors' understanding of the decision process they were reconstructing. For example, towards the end of their reconstruction, the participants concluded:

MATTHEW. We've ended up in this position of total ambiguity and uncertainty...
    [*murmurs of agreement*].
JOHN. There's a lovely kind of balance at the end of uncertainty which is...
    maybe that's the way the world is sometimes—maybe that's the way the
    world is all the time?
MATTHEW. I think that's the way the world is in good pieces of literature or good
    pieces of dialogue and you're left with an ambiguity...if you look at.../
JOHN. /But you don't think that's how it is in real life?
MATTHEW. Yeah/
LUKE. /Yes I'm sure it is.
MATTHEW. It's just you don't usually get into these kind of discussions.

Reconstructive Temporalities

It is difficult to find a suitable generalization to characterize the reconstruction process. As one might expect from academics, it was a long-winded, tedious, and occasionally tortuous process, which—while it lacked order—did have some direction. In retrospect—that is, by using the transcripts as a guide—it appears to be somewhat chaotic in that it was rare for actors to focus exclusively on one issue or event at a time. Actors would start to relate an episode, doubt their own memory or be corrected by someone else, refer to another similar episode of behaviour, reinterpret events in the light of some 'new' information, call up some historical parallel and/or relocate the discussion in a debate about the local or wider politics of their situation, before returning to their point of departure. And, at each of these junctures, they could get side-tracked on the detail of an apparently marginal issue. While it *is* possible to abstract a linear narrative from the transcripts, in our view, this risks misrepresenting how actors reconstitute 'reality', because it obliterates the kaleidoscopic points of reference employed to fix recollected experience. Our preferred alternative is to say that reconstruction is not a linear but an iterative process triggered by emotive cues and shaped within situational factors

(Keenoy *et al.* 1999). In this respect, apparently marginal details seem to be central to 'securing' memory:

JOHN. Did he [*really*] say that?

LUKE. Yeah, he did; he said [*John laughing in background*] 'how many times might we require them to be in?' 'What we actually get for our money' was the phrase he used... [*murmured assent in the background*].

One particularly striking feature of their meandering progress is the fact that, even during the script-writing phase of their deliberations, the actors continued to reconstitute and revise their understanding of how and why the decision was made. Their 'accounting for' the decision appeared to be a never-ending process. Indeed, it seemed as if our actors were 'deciding' what 'had happened' during the *process* of reconstruction (cf. Boje 1995). In this respect, it appeared that they only came to 'know' what had transpired *after they had reconstructed it*—in making sense of it, they apparently transformed the experience. It was this particular finding that led us to focus on the temporal aspects of the process and, in particular, the properties of virtual time.

Virtual time, we suggest, is a sensemaking discursive resource through which we 'talk out' experience. However, when, as in this instance, the experience is more emotionally charged than usual, finding appropriate language may prove difficult. In our view, such events involve 'hot cognition'—an instantaneous mixture of adrenal reactions, strongly felt emotion, sharpened perception, and instantaneous judgement. We feel; we react: the social interaction is not merely a 'linguistic exchange' but also involves a more or less powerful physiological response. Of course, it is impossible to reconstitute such experience. The best we can do is to say 'what it *felt* like' by translating the emotive content into linguistic (linear) representations that are unlikely to be adequate to the task. This might help to explain why our actors found it extremely difficult to arrive at anything but a working consensus on what had 'really happened'. Virtual time, it would seem, *necessarily* involves an attempt to differentiate the elements of 'hot cognition' and—because it is a discursive medium—privileges the 'cognitive' element (see also Damasio 1999). Given the cultural marginalization of 'feelings' in organizations (and the generally cerebral inclinations of academics), it is perhaps unsurprising that our actors had difficulty in focusing on the emotive and favoured 'rationalized' accountings.

LUKE. /the whole event was pre-determined... [*the Director*] was going along there to get you basically. In a non-emotional way, nothing personal, but he was there... But you know what I mean, it's about power relationships/

JOHN. /Oh, it's about power, it's all about power/

But this is not the only time-dependent factor influencing the outcome of the reconstruction process. There are at least four other interdependent temporalities that the actors drew on as judgemental reference points during the course of their discursive interactions. Each of these also appear to be implicated in and, indeed, to further 'recondition' memory.

Government policy cycles. Contextually, it is important to remember that, indirectly, the emotion and intra-organizational conflict may have arisen because of the scheduling of the governmentally sponsored productivity measurement mechanism. The Research Assessment Exercise (RAE), which takes place in the UK about every five years, includes an evaluation of staff research activity. The next exercise was looming and the new Director was seeking to include everyone in the official return. In this respect, the 'problem' was timely. In explaining the Director's behaviour and motivations and his emphasis on 'performance', much of the actors' discussion was taken up with debating the impact of this governmental initiative on academic decision values. They made numerous references to the way in which this had impacted negatively on the notion of academic scholarship.

JOHN. Well, that reflected his concern that we get 'value for money' . . . Do we get value for money in terms of RAE publications; 'what are they writing?' . . . not what are they doing, what are they writing . . .

LUKE. /and research income . . . So, he extended his original remit . . . And he went on to say: 'And we have to be sure' and he used the word . . . it was an adamant phrase like 'sure'; 'We have to be sure' or 'We have to ensure' that we get four publications from anyone that we appoint to these posts.

Organizational action cycles. Contextually, it is also significant that the decision outcome was, to some degree, dependent on the calendar dates of the cycle of the school meetings. By chance, the timing of these permitted actors to engage in a range of 'preparatory activities', which had clearly shaped the decision. Indeed, without the extra time, it is possible the formal outcome might have been different. But it also reflected the longer-term developmental organizational cycle:

MARK [*sighing*]. /well, yes . . . Well, it's just part of . . . at the moment I feel resigned to it as if it's part of the natural evolution of the school. I mean almost taking [*the Director*] out of the equation, I think with increases in size and . . . if you look back at the history . . . when I first joined . . . in many respects it was a depressing place to work . . .

Mark went on to reconstitute the problem in terms of a change in management style.

Career cycles. The actors' point in their career cycle reflected not only their judgemental time frames but also their career aspirations and expectations. For example, some had never known a time when the RAE had not been in place. In this respect, the older actors tended to be more hostile to the implicit control objectives of the decision. This may have reflected both their grounding in the more traditional pre-RAE academic values and also the fact that they were under less pressure to perform.

LUKE. I mean his [*the Director's*] position is legitimated in terms of the RAE...that provides him with a very strong platform that this is what ought to be happening...I do quite like the whole twist about, you know, the way it starts to challenge what's important...I'm fortunate, I've got four articles out already so I'm OK for the next exercise...

JOHN. /[*But*] it's like Catch-22, you see, as soon as you get four, we up the number of submissions [*laughter*]...

LUKE. /oh yeah, I'm sure [*they*] will. In that sense...I can afford to say 'this is great'...[*But*] If I didn't have four, would I be in that position?...there's a tension, a trade-off.

Then, referring to the older managers present, he continued:

LUKE. You don't have to have to worry about building reputations, yeah?... Now, our jobs are still to build those sort of reputations, you know. [*Turning to one of the younger managers*] What are you, 33?

MARK. I'm 35 now so, you know, getting on a bit and it's a question of really driving for recognition and one route through to that in terms of the RAE is output. So there is a bit of a...you know...so I could quite easily end up siding with [*the Director*]. Numbers are important the more I think about it [*laughter from all*].

Personal life cycles. As this last quote indicates, the actors' personal biographies, professional relationships, and personal life cycles reflected not only their varying ages (which ranged from mid-30s to early 60s) and social commitments but also their differential knowledge with respect to the range and type of previous experiences, their political memories, their previous jobs, and their socio-political values.

THE IMPLICATE ASPECTS

It has long been said that a way of seeing is also a way of not seeing. In this chapter we have sought to begin to outline—if not a new—then an alternative way of investigating decisions and decision processes. However, once we acknowledge the representative limitations of linear accounting procedures and begin to explore the complex sensemaking activities of both those being researched and the researchers themselves, a range of mutually implicated possibilities present themselves for consideration.

We set out, in linear fashion, to examine the relationship between emotion and decision making. Intuitively, we felt that there was something to be learned from utilizing the dramaturgical perspective to explore the actors' normally unspoken assumptions and covert motivations. And, during our own sensemaking, we have become aware of potential significance of time and temporality for understanding these social processes. As we have tried to demonstrate, there is indicative evidence suggesting that decision processes and decision outcomes are not linear temporal processes but draw on a sometimes confusing complex of temporal reference points. It appears that decision processes implicate not only ongoing judgements about the perceived past, present, and future of the organization but, simultaneously, the perceived and projected pasts, presents, and futures of the individuals involved in the decision process. Such temporal factors appear to play an unremarked but, on occasion, critical role in shaping decision outcomes. This is not to imply that decisions are not rational; but that—at least in our instance—the rationality they display is a *post hoc* socially constructed overlay that homogenizes a complex of sometimes incommensurate individual rationales into the organizational 'lifeworld'. In this way, decisions become 'normalized' and simultaneously 'alienated' phenomena for—as our evidence also indicates—decisions *become* linear 'rational' phenomena only once they have been formally recorded.

Secondly, to return to the impact of emotion with which we started, it seems that *time passing* may play a critical role in mediating the 'experience' of social reality and, thus, permit us to rationalize our feelings in terms of more conventional organizational scripts and legitimizing texts. The initial emotional temper, personal antipathies, and personal motivations gradually became part of the background 'explanation' and were replaced by a series of ever more complex rationalizations that permitted actors to distance themselves from their emotional engagements and feelings. In other words, the phrase 'time heals' seems to have an empirical basis.

Perhaps less surprisingly, in reconstructing it, they also imposed an order and a logic on it, which the original 'experience' itself did not possess. It appeared that, having 'got beyond' all the emotions, which had fuelled their experience of the events, gradually they produced a more rational and objective narrative—that is, they distanced themselves from the emotion—the 'hot cognition' that had been engendered at the 'onset' of the experience. But, crucially, the incident was no longer 'explained' in terms of how it had been *experienced*—it was reconstituted in terms of 'what really happened'. This seems to suggest that 'experience'—or what we usually refer to as 'immediate experience'—is itself rather 'fuzzy'. More precisely, we might conclude that our accounts of emotive experiences are little more than linear rationalizations informed by subsequent events and rereadings, subsequent knowledge, situated interests, and (re)interpretations of behaviours. While this seems to have something to do with protecting our own sense of identity, we suspect it may also have something to do with our incapacity to *articulate* emotive states. In short, time has to pass *before* we can 'make sense' of such events, but, paradoxically, in making sense of such experience, it seems as if our accounts are necessarily distortions of the experience itself. It may be that there are no words to describe what happens during 'hot cognition'.

REFERENCES

Abraham, N. (1995). *Rhythms: On the Work, Translation, and Psychoanalysis*. Stanford, Calif.: Stanford University Press.

Adam, B. (1988). 'Social versus Natural Time: A Traditional Distinction Re-examined', in M. Young and T. Schuller (eds.), *The Rhythms of Society*. London: Routledge, 191–226.

—— (1990). *Time and Social Theory*. Cambridge: Polity; Philadelphia: Temple.

—— (1992). 'Modern Times: The Technology Connection and its Implications for Social Theory'. *Time and Society*, 1/2: 175–91.

—— (1993). 'Within and Beyond the Time Economy of Employment Relations: Conceptual Issues Pertinent to Research on Time and Work'. *Social Science Information*, 32: 163–84.

—— (1995). *Timewatch: The Social Analysis of Time*. Cambridge: Polity.

—— (1996). 'Timescapes for Posterity: Critical Issues for Managing the Environment'. Paper for 'Between Tradition and Innovation: Time in a Managerial Perspective' conference, ISIDA, Palermo, May.

—— (1998). *Timescapes of Modernity: The Environment and Invisible Hazards*. London: Routledge.

Ahola, H. (2000). 'Internet Marketing—Literature Review and Research Agenda'. http://www.tekniikka.oamk.fi/netties/2000/papers/InternetMarketing.

Akinola, A. A. (1986). 'An Application of the Bass Model in the Analysis of Diffusion of Coco-Spraying Chemicals among Nigerian Cocoa Farmers'. *Journal of Agricultural Economics*, 37/3: 395–404.

Anderson, B. (1983). *Imagined Communities: Reflections on the Origin and Spread of Nationalism*. London: Verso.

Anderson, J. C., and Narus, J. (1999). *Business Market Management. Understanding, Creating and Delivering Value*. Englewood Cliffs, NJ: Prentice Hall.

Anderson, P. F. (1989). 'On Relativism and Interpretivism with a Prolegomenon to the Why Question', in E. C. Hirschman (ed.), *Interpretative Consumer Research*. Provo, Ut.: Association for Consumer Research, 10–23.

Anderson-Gough, F., Grey, C., and Robson, K. (2001). 'Tests of Time: Organizational Time-Reckoning and the Making of Accountants in Two Multi-National Accounting Firms'. *Accounting, Organization and Society*, 26: 99–122.

Ansoff, H. I., and MacDonnell, E. J. (1990). *Implanting Strategic Management*. 2nd edn. New York: Prentice Hall.

Academy of Management, AoM. (2000). *A New Time*. Conference programme. Toronto.

Araujo, L., and Easton, G. (1996). 'Networks in Socioeconomic Systems', in Dawn Iacobucci (ed.), *Networks in Marketing*. Thousand Oaks, Calif.: Sage, 63–107.

Arcaya, A. (1992). 'Why is Time not Included in Modern Theories of Memory'. *Time and Society*, 1/2: 301–14.

Arendt, H. (1958/1998). *The Human Condition*. Chicago: University of Chicago Press.

Arndt, J. (1985). 'The Tyranny of Paradigms: The Case for Pragmatic Pluralism in Marketing', in N. Dholakia and J. Arndt (eds.), *Changing the Course of Marketing; Alternative Paradigms for Widening Marketing Theory*. Greenwich, Conn.: JAI Press, 3–26.

Arthur, W. B. (1990). ' "Silicon Valley" Locational Clusters: When Do Increasing Returns Imply Monopoly?' *Mathematical Social Sciences*, 19: 235–51.

Ashkenasy, N., Hartel, C., and Zerbe, W. (2000). *Emotions in the Workplace: Research, Theory and Practice*. Westport, Conn.: Quorum Books.

Bakhtin, M. M. (1981). *The Dialogic Imagination, Fours Essays*. Austin, Tex.: University of Texas Press.

Barfield, O. (1988). *Saving the Appearances: A Study in Idolatry* (Wesleyan Revised Edition). Hanover, NH: University Press of New England.

Barley, S. R. (1988). 'On Technology, Time, and Social Order: Technologically Induced Change in the Temporal Organization of Radiological Work', in F. A. Dubinskas (ed.), *Making Time: Ethnographies of High-Technology Organizations*. Philadelphia: Temple University Press, 123–69.

Barnett, L. (1957). *The Universe and Dr Einstein*. New York: William Sloane.

Bartels, R. (1986). *The History of Marketing Thought*. Columbus, Oh.: Grid.

Bartky, I. R. (2000). *Selling the True Time: Nineteenth Century Timekeeping in America*. Stanford, Calif.: Stanford University Press.

Bass, F. M. (1969). 'A New Product Growth Model for Consumer Durables'. *Management Science*, 15 (Jan.), 215–17.

Bastien, D. T., and Hostager, T. J. (1988). 'Jazz as a Process of Organizational Innovation'. *Communication Research*, 15: 582–602.

Baudrillard, J. (1968/1996). *The System of Objects*, trans. J. Benedict. London: Verso.

—— (1975). *The Mirror of Production*. St Louis, Mo.: Telos Press.

—— (1981). *For a Critique of the Political Economy of the Sign*. St Louis, Mo.: Telos Press.

—— (1983). *Simulations*. New York: Semiotext(e).

—— (1988). *Xerox and Infinity*, trans. Agitac. Paris: Touchepas.

Bauman, Z. (1988). *Freedom*. Milton Keynes: Open University Press.

—— (1998). *Globalization: The Human Consequences*. Cambridge: Polity.

Bayus, B. L., Saman, H., and Labe, R. P., Jr. (1989). 'Developing and Using Forecasting Models for Consumer Durables'. *Journal of Product Innovation Management*, 6 (Mar.), 5–19.

Beaumont, P. B., and Hunter, L. C. (1996). 'Continuous Process Technology, Annualised Hours and National Bargaining'. *New Technology, Work and Employment*, 11/2: 118–24.

Beck, U. (1992). *Risk Society: Towards a New Modernity*. London: Sage.

Becker, G. (1965). 'A Theory of the Allocation of Time'. *Economic Journal*, 75 (Sept.), 493–517.

—— and Michael, R. (1973). 'On the New Theory of Consumer Behaviour'. *Swedish Journal of Economics*, 75 (Sept.), 493–517.

Bell, E. (1999). 'A Cultural Analysis of Payment-Systems-in-Use in Three Chemical Companies'. Unpublished Ph.D. thesis. Manchester University.

Bell, E. (2000). 'Bought, Sold and Controlled: Conflicting Temporal Orientations in the UK Chemical Industry'. Paper presented at the EGOS 16th Colloquium, School of Economics and Business Administration, Finland, 2–4 July.

—— (2001). 'The Social Time of Organizational Payment Systems'. *Time and Society*, 10/1: 45–62.

Bell, V. (1999). *Belonging and Performativity*. London: Sage.

Benhabib, S. (1992). *Situating the Subject*. London: Sage.

Benjamin, Walter (1993). 'Writing, Time, and Task', in *Walter Benjamin's Philosophy*, ed. P. Osborne and A. Benjamin. London: Routledge, 33–49.

Bergadaa, M. (1992). 'The Role of Time in the Action of the Consumer'. *Journal of Consumer Research*, 17 (Dec.), 289–302.

Bergson, H. (1950). *Time and Free Will*, trans. A. Mitchell. London: Macmillan.

Bernstein, R. (1980). 'Philosophy in the Conversation of Mankind'. *Review of Metaphysics*, 32/4, 762.

Berry, L. (1979). 'The Time Buying Consumer'. *Journal of Retailing*, 55, (Winter), 58–69.

Bertalanffy, L. von (1950). 'The Theory of Open Systems in Physics and Biology'. *Science*, 111: 23–9.

Bettman, J. (1979). *An Information Processing Theory of Consumer Choice*. Reading, Mass.: Addison & Wesley.

Bluedorn, A., and Denhardt, R. (1988). 'Time and Organizations'. *Journal of Management*, 14: 299–320.

Blyton, P. (1989). 'Time and Labour Relations', in P. Blyton, J. Hassard, S. Hill, and K. Starkey (eds.), *Time, Work and Organizations*. London: Routledge, 105–31.

—— (1992). 'Flexible Times? Recent Developments in Temporal Flexibility'. *Industrial Relations Journal*, 23/1: 26–36.

—— (1994). 'Working Hours', in K. Sisson (ed.), *Personnel Management*. Oxford: Blackwell, 495–526.

—— Hassard, J., Hill, S., and Starkey, K. (1989). *Time, Work and Organizations*. London: Routledge.

Boden, D. (2000). 'Worlds in Action: Information, Instantaneity and Global Futures Trading', in B. Adam, U. Beck, and J. van Loon (eds.), *The Risk Society and Beyond: Critical Issues for Social Theory*. London: Routledge, 183–98.

Boje, D. (1995). 'Stories of the Storytelling Organization: A Postmodern Analysis of Disney as *Tamara*-Land'. *Academy of Management Journal*, 38/4: 997–1035.

Bolter, J. D. (1984). *Turing's Man: Western Culture in the Computer Age*. London: Duckworth.

Borgmann, A. (1984). *Technology and the Character of Contemporary Life*. Chicago: University of Chicago Press.

Bourdieu, P. (1979). *Algeria 1960*. Cambridge: Cambridge University Press.

—— (1990). *The Logic of Practice*. Cambridge: Polity. Originally published as *Le Sens pratique*. Paris: Éditions de Minuit, 1980.

Braverman, H. (1974). *Labour and Monopoly Capital*. New York: Monthly Review Press.

Brews, P. J., and Hunt, M. R. (1999). 'Learning to Plan and Planning to Learn: Resolving the Planning School/Learning School Debate'. *Strategic Management Journal*, 20: 889–913.

Brown, J. S., and Duguid, P. (1991). 'Organizational Learning and Communities-of-Practice: Toward a Unified Way of Working'. *Organizational Science*, 2/1 (Feb.), 40–57.

Brown, S. L., and Eisenhardt, K. M. (1997). 'The Art of Continuous Change: Linking Complexity Theory and Time-Paced Evolution in Relentlessly Shifting Organizations'. *Administrative Science Quarterly*, 42: 1–37.

——— (1998). *Competing on the Edge: Strategy as Structured Chaos*. Boston: Harvard Business School Press.

Brownlie, D., Saren, M., Wensley, R., and Whittington, R. (1994) (eds.). *European Journal of Marketing 'Rethinking Marketing'*. Special Edition, 28/3.

Bunzel, D. (2000). 'Real Numbers, Imaginary Guests, and Fantastic Experiences: The Grand Seaside Hotel and the Discursive Construction of Customer Service'. Unpublished doctoral dissertation. Sydney: University of Western Sydney.

Burke, K. (1950). *The Rhetoric of Motives*. New York: Prentice Hall.

Burrell, G. (1992). 'Back to the Future: Time and Organization', in M. Reed and M. Hughes (eds.), *Rethinking Organizations*. London: Sage, 165–83.

——— (1998). 'Linearity, Control and Death', in D. T. Grant, T. Keenoy, and C. Oswick (eds.), *Discourse and Organisation*. London: Sage, 134–51.

Butler, J. (1990). *Gender Trouble*. New York: Routledge.

Butler, R. (1995). 'Time in Organizations: Its Experience, Explanations and Effects'. *Organization Studies*, 16: 925–50.

Callon, M. (1998) (ed.). *The Laws of the Markets*. Oxford: Blackwell.

Carlstein, T., Parkes, D., and Thrift, N. (1978) (eds.) 3 vols. *i. Making Sense of Time, ii. Human Activity and Time Geography, iii. Time and Regional Dynamics*. London: Edward Arnold.

Castells, M. (1996). *The Rise of the Network Society*. Oxford: Blackwell.

Chia, R. (1997). 'Essai: Thirty Years On: From Organizational Structures to the Organization of Thought'. *Organization Studies*, 18: 685–707.

Child, J., and Kieser, A. (1981). 'The Development of Organizations over Time', in P. C. Nystrom and W. H. Starbuck (eds.), *Handbook of Organizational Design*. New York: Oxford University Press, i. 28–64.

Chung, C. H. (1999). 'Balancing the Two Dimensions of Time for Time-Based Competition'. *Journal of Managerial Issues* (Fall), 299–314.

Clark, P. A. (1982). 'A Review of the Theories of Time and Structure for Organisational Sociology'. Working paper. Birmingham: The University of Aston Management Centre.

——— (1985). 'A Review of the Theories for Time and Structure for Organizational Sociology'. *Research in the Sociology of Organizations*, 4: 35–79.

——— (1990). 'Chronological Codes and Organizational Analysis', in J. Hassard and D. Pym (eds.), *The Theory and Philosophy of Organizations: Critical Issues and New Perspectives*. London: Routledge, 137–63.

Clarke, D. (2000). 'Space Knowledge and Consumption', in P. Daniels, J. Bryson *et al.* (eds.), *Knowledge, Space and Economy*. London: Routledge, 209–26.

Cohen, M. D., March, J. G., and Olsen, J. (1972). 'A Garbage Can Model of Organizational Choice'. *Administrative Science Quarterly*, 17: 1–25.

Coleman, J. S. (1990). *Foundations of Social Theory*. Cambridge, Mass.: Harvard University Press.

Collins, D. (1998). *Organizational Change: Sociological Perspectives*. London: Routledge.

Cook, K. S., and Emerson, R. M. (1978). 'Power, Equity, and Commitment in Exchange Networks'. *American Sociological Review*, 43: 721–39.

Cooper, R., and Law, J. (1995). 'Organization: Distal and Proximal Views', in S. Bocharach, P. Gaghardi, and B. Mundell (eds.), *Research in the Sociology of Organizations*, 13, Greenwich, Conn.: JAI Press, 237–74.

Cummings, S. (forthcoming). *ReCreating Management: Strategy from the Inside-Out*. London: Sage.

Cummings, T. G., and Worley, C. G. (1993). *Organization Development and Change*. 5th edn. St. Paul, Minnesota: West.

Cusumano, M. A. (1985). *The Japanese Automobile Industry: Technology and Management at Nissan and Toyota*. Harvard East Asian Monographs, 122. Cambridge, Mass.: Harvard University Press.

Cyert, R., and March, J. (1992). *A Behavioural Theory of the Firm*. Oxford: Blackwell.

Damasio, A. R. (1999). *The Feeling of What Happens*. London: Heinemann.

Das, T. K. (1987). 'Strategic Planning and Individual Temporal Orientation'. *Strategic Management Journal*, 8: 203–9.

—— (1991). 'Time: The Hidden Dimension in Strategic Planning'. *Long Range Planning*, 24/3: 49–57.

—— (1993). 'Time in Management and Organizational Studies'. *Time and Society*, 2/2: 267–74.

Davenport, T., and Pearlson, K. (1998). 'Two Cheers for the Virtual Office'. *Sloan Management Review* (Summer), 51–65.

Davies, G. (1994). 'What Should Time Be'. *European Journal of Marketing*, 28/8–9: 100–13.

Davies, K. (1990). *Women and Time: Weaving the Strands of Everyday Life*. Aldershot: Averbury.

De Grazia, S. (1964). *Of Time, Work and Leisure*. New York: Doubleday.

Delbridge, R. (1998). *Life on the Line in Contemporary Manufacturing: The Work place Experience of Lean Production and the 'Japanese' Model*. New York: Oxford University Press.

Deleuze, G., and Guattari, F. (1977). *Anti-Oedipus: Capitalism and Schizophrenia*. New York: Viking Press.

Derrida, J. (1978). *Writing and Difference*, trans. A. Bass. Chicago: University of Chicago Press.

Desmons, G., and Vidal-Hall, T. (1987). *Annual Hours*. London: Industrial Society.

Dhar, R., and Nowlis, S. (1999). 'The Effect of Time Pressure on Consumer Choice Deferral'. *Journal of Consumer Research*, 25: 369–85.

Dicken, P. (1998). *The Global Shift—Internationalization of Economic Activity*. London: Paul Chapman.

Dodds, W. (1973). 'An Application of the Bass Model in Long-Term New Product Forecasting'. *Journal of Marketing Research*, 10 (Aug.), 308–11.

Dohse, K., Jurgens, U., and Malsch, T. (1985). 'From "Fordism" to "Toyotism"? The Social Organization of the Labor Process in the Japanese Automobile Industry'. *Politics and Society*, 13/22: 115–46.

Dore, R. (1973). *British Factory—Japanese Factory: The Origins of National Diversity in Industrial Relations*. London: Allen & Unwin.

—— (1983). 'Introduction', in Kamata Satoshi, *Japan in the Passing Lane*. London: Allen & Unwin, pp. ix–xi.

Douglas, J. D. (1970). *Understanding Everyday Life*. London: Routledge & Kegan Paul.

Douglas, M., and Isherwood, B. (1978). *The World of Goods: Towards an Anthropology of Consumption*. London: Allen Lane.

Dower, J. W. (1986). *War without Mercy: Race and Power in the Pacific War*. New York: Pantheon Books.

—— (1999). *Embracing Defeat: Japan in the Wake of World War II*. New York: Norton.

Dubinskas, F. (1988). 'Janus Organizations: Scientists and Managers in Genetic Engineering Firms', in F. Dubinskas (ed.), *Making Time: Ethnographies of High-Technology Organizations*. Philadelphia: Temple University Press, 170–232.

Dunne, J. S. (1973). *Time and Myth: A Meditation on Storytelling as an Exploration of Life and Death*. London: SCM Press.

Durkheim, E. (1912). *Les Formes elémentaires de la vie religieuse*. Paris: F. Alcan.

—— (1915). *The Elementary Forms of Religious Life: A Study in Religious Sociology*, trans. J. W. Swain. London: George Allen & Unwin.

Easton, G., and Araujo, L. (1994). 'Market Exchange, Social Structures and Time'. *European Journal of Marketing*, 28/3: 72–84.

Ebert, R. J., and Piehl, D. (1973). 'Time Horizon: A Concept for Management'. *California Management Review*, 15: 35–41.

Edwards, D. (1987). *Discourse and Cognition*. London: Sage.

Edwards, R. (1979). *Contested Terrain: The Transformation of the Workplace in the Twentieth Century*. London: Heinemann.

Eisenhardt, K. M. (1989). 'Making Fast Strategic Decisions in High-Velocity Environments'. *Academy of Management Journal*, 32: 543–76.

—— and Bourgeois, L. J., III (1988). 'Politics of Strategic Decision Making in High-Velocity Environments: Toward a Midrange Theory'. *Academy of Management Journal*, 31/4: 737–70.

Eliade, M. (1949). *Le Mythe de l'éternal retour. Archetypes et repetition*. Paris: Librairie Gallimard.

—— (1949/1954). *The Myth of Eternal Return: Cosmos and History*, trans. W. R. Trask. London: Arkana.

Elias, N. (1988). *Über die Zeit*. Frankfurt/Main: Suhrkamp.

—— (1992). *Time: An Essay*, trans. E. Jephcott. Oxford: Blackwell.

Eliashberg, J., and Robertson, T. S. (1988). 'New Product Preannouncing Behavior: A Market Signaling Study'. *Journal of Marketing Research*, 25 (Aug.), 282–92.

Elliot, R. (1999). 'Symbolic Meaning and Postmodern Consumer Culture', in D. Brownlie, M. Saren, R. Wensley, and R. Whittington (eds.), *Rethinking Marketing: Towards Critical Marketing Accountings*. London: Sage, 112–26.

Engel, J., Kollat, D., and Blackwell, R. (1968). *Consumer Behavior*. New York: Holt, Reinhart & Winston.

—— Blackwell, R., and Minard, P. (1986). *Consumer Behavior*. 5th edn. New York: Holt, Reinhart & Winston.

—— —— —— (1990). *Consumer Behavior*. 6th edn. Chicago: Dryden Press.

—— —— —— (1995). *Consumer Behavior*. 7th edn. Chicago: Dryden Press.

Ermarth, E. (1992). *Sequel to History. Postmodernism and the Crisis of Representational Time*. Princeton: Princeton University Press.

Esposito, E. (1998). 'The Hypertrophy of Simultaneity in Telematic Communication'. *Thesis Eleven*, 51: 17–36.

ESRC (2001). *Postgraduate Training Guidelines*. Swindon: ESRC.

Etzioni, A. (1961). *A Comparative Analysis of Complex Organisations*. New York: Free Press.

Fagan, C., and Lallement, M. (2000). 'Working Time, Social Integration and Transitional Labour Markets', in J. O'Reilly, I. Cebrian, and M. Lallement (eds.), *Working-Time Changes: Social Integration through Transitional Labour Markets.* Cheltenham: Edward Elgar, 25–60.

Fairclough, N. (1995). *Critical Discourse Analysis.* London: Longman.

Fama, E. F., Fisher, L., Jensen, M. C., and Roll, R. (1969). 'The Adjustment of Stock Prices to New Information'. *International Economic Review,* 10: 1–21.

Faulkner, D., and Campbell, A. (2002) (eds.). *The Oxford Handbook of Strategic Management.* Oxford: Oxford University Press.

Featherstone, M. (1991). *Consumer Culture and Postmodernism.* London: Sage.

Filipec, J. (1986). 'Society and Concepts of Social Time'. *International Social Science Journal,* 107: 19–32.

Fineman, S. (1999). 'Emotion and Organizing', in S. R. Clegg and C. Hardy (eds.), *Organization: Theory and Method.* London: Sage, 289–310.

—— (2000) (ed.). *Emotion in Organizations.* 2nd edn. London: Sage.

Firat, A. (1994). 'Gender and Consumption: Transcending the Feminine?', in J. Costa (ed.), *Gender Issues and Consumer Behavior.* Thousand Oaks, Calif.: Sage, 205–25.

Ford, D. (1990) (ed.). *Understanding Business Markets.* London: Academic Press.

Forman, F. J., and Sowton, C. (1989) (eds.). *Taking our Time: Feminist Perspectives on Temporality.* Oxford: Pergamon.

Foucault, M. (1973a). *Madness and Civilization*, abridged and trans. Richard Howard. New York: Random House.

—— (1973b). *The Order of Things.* London: Tavistock.

—— (1979). *Discipline and Punish: The Birth of the Prison*, trans. Alan Sheridan. New York: Vintage Press.

—— (1980). *Power/Knowledge, Selected Interviews and Other Writings 1972–1977*, ed. Colin Gordon. Hemel Hempstead: Harvester.

—— (1982). 'The Subject and Power', in H. L. Dreyfus and R. Rabinow (eds.), *Michel Foucault: Beyond Structuralism and Hermeneutics.* Chicago: University of Chicago Press, 208–26.

—— (1988). 'Technologies of the self', in L. H. Martin, H. Gutman, and P. H. Hutton (eds.), *Technologies of the Self: A Seminar with Michel Foucault.* Amherst, MA: University of Massachusetts Press.

Foxall, G. (1986). 'The Role of Radical Behaviourism in the Explanation of Consumer Choice'. *Advances in Consumer Choice,* 13: 187–91.

—— (1987). 'Consumer Choice in Behaviourism and Consumer Research: Theoretical Promise and Empirical Process'. *International Journal of Research Marketing,* 4: 111–29.

—— (1990). *Consumer Psychology in Behavioural Perspective.* London: Routledge.

Fraisse, P. (1963). *The Psychology of Time.* New York: Harper & Row.

Frow, J. (1997). *Time and Commodity Culture: Essays in Cultural Theory and Postmodernity.* Oxford: Oxford University Press.

Fruin, W. Mark (1992). *The Japanese Enterprise System: Competitive Strategies and Cooperative Structures.* Oxford: Oxford University Press.

Fucini, J., and Fucini, S. (1990). *Working for the Japanese: Inside Mazda's American Auto Plant.* New York: Free Press.

Gabriel, Y., and Lang, T. (1995). *The Unmanageable Consumer: Contemporary Consumption and its Fragmentations.* London: Sage.

Game, A. (1991). *Undoing the Social: Towards a Deconstructive Sociology*. Milton Keynes: Open University Press

Garfinkel, H. (1967). *Studies in Ethnomethodology*. Englewood Cliffs, NJ: Prentice Hall.

Gebser, Jean (1985). *The Ever-Present Origin*, trans. Noel Barstad and Algis Mickunas. Athens, Oh.: Ohio University Press.

Gell, A. (1992). 'Inter-Tribal Commodity Barter and Reproductive Gift-Exchange in Old Melanesia', in C. Humphrey and S. Hugh-Jones (eds.), *Barter, Exchange and Value*. Cambridge: Cambridge University Press, 142–68.

—— (1996). *The Anthropology of Time*. Oxford: Berg.

Gergen, K. J. (1991). *The Saturated Self: Dilemmas of Identity in Contemporary Life*. New York: Basic Books.

—— (1999). *An Invitation to Social Construction*. London: Sage.

—— and Thatchenkery, T. J. (1996a). 'Developing Dialogue for Discerning Differences'. *Journal of Applied Behavioral Science*, 32/4: 428–33.

—— —— (1996b). 'Organization Science as Social Construction: Postmodern Potentials'. *Journal of Applied Behavioral Science*, 32/4: 356–77.

Gersick, C. (1988). 'Time and Transition in Work Teams: Toward a New Model of Group Development'. *Academy of Management Journal*, 31: 9–41.

—— (1989). 'Marking Time: Predictable Transitions in Task Groups'. *Academy of Management Journal*, 32: 274–309.

—— (1991). 'Revolutionary Change Theories: A Multilevel Exploration of the Punctuated Equilibrium Paradigm'. *Academy of Management Review*, 16: 10–36.

Gherardi, S., and Strati, A. (1988). 'The Temporal Dimension in Organization Studies'. *Organization Studies*, 9: 149–64.

Gibbs, P. (1993). *Time as a Dimension of Consumption in Financial Services*. Bournemouth Working Paper Series. Bournemouth: Bournemouth University.

Giddens, A. (1979). *Central Problems in Social Theory*. London: Macmillan.

—— (1981). *A Contemporary Critique of Historical Materialism, i. Power, Property and the State*. London: Macmillan.

—— (1984). *The Constitution of Society*. Cambridge: Polity.

—— (1990). *The Consequences of Modernity*. Cambridge: Polity.

—— (1991). *Modernity and Self-Identity: Self and Society in the Late Modern Age*. Cambridge: Polity.

—— (1999). *Reith Lecture 2: Risk*. London: BBC.

Gjesme, T. (1981). 'Some Factors Influencing Perceived Goal Distance in Time: A Preliminary Check'. *Perceptual Motor Skills*, 53 (Aug.), 175–82.

Gleick, J. (1999). *Faster: The Acceleration of Just about Everything*. New York: Pantheon Books.

Glennie, P., and Thrift, N. (1996). 'Reworking E. P. Thompson's "Time, Work-Discipline and Industrial Capitalism"'. *Time and Society*, 5/3: 275–99.

Goffman, E. (1959/1990). *The Presentation of Self in Everyday Life*. Harmondsworth: Penguin.

Goldthorpe, J. H., Lockwood, D., Bechhofer, F., and Platt, J. (1968). *The Affluent Worker*. Cambridge: Cambridge University Press.

Gordon, A. (1993). 'Contests for the Workplace', in Andrew Gordon (ed.), *Postwar Japan as History*. Berkeley and Los Angeles: University of California Press, 373–94.

Gould, S. J. (1987). *Time's Arrow, Time's Cycle*. Cambridge, Mass.: Harvard University Press.

Graham, L. (1995). *On the Line at Subaru-Isuzu: The Japanese Model and the American Worker*. New York: ILR/Cornell University Press.

Graham, R. (1981). 'The Role of Perception of Time in Consumer Research'. *Journal of Consumer Research*, 7: 335–42.

Grant, D., Keenoy, T., and Oswick, C. (1998) (eds.). *Discourse and Organisation*. London: Sage.

Grant, R. (1998). *Contemporary Strategy Analysis*. Oxford: Blackwell.

Greiner, L. E. (1972). 'Evolution and Revolution as Organizations Grow'. *Harvard Business Review*, 50/4: 37–46.

Griffiths, J. (1999). *Pip Pip: A Sideways Look at Time*. London: HarperCollins.

Gronomo, S. (1989). 'Concepts of Time: Some Implications for Consumer Research'. *Advances in Consumer Research*, 16: 339–45.

Grossin, W. (1974). *Les Temps de la vie quotidienne*. Berlin: De Gruyter.

Guillet de Monthoux, P. (1983). *Action and Existence: Anarchism for Business Administration*. Munich: Accedo.

Gurvitch, G. (1964). *The Spectrum of Social Time*. Dordrecht: Reidel.

Hacking, I. (2000). *The Social Construction of What?* Cambridge, Mass.: Harvard University Press.

Hägerstrand, T. (1975). *Dynamic Allocation of Urban Space*. Farnborough: Saxon House.

Håkansson, H., and Snehota, I. (1995). *Developing Relationships in Business Networks*. London: Routledge.

Halinen, Aino, and Törnroos, J.-Å. (1995). 'The Meaning of Time in the Study of Industrial Buyer–Seller Relationships', in K. E. Möller and D. T. Wilson (eds.), *Business Marketing: An Interaction and Network Perspective*. Boston: Kluwer Academic Publishing, 493–529.

Hall, E. T. (1983). *The Dance of Life—the Other Dimension of Time*. New York: Doubleday.

Handy, C. (1994). *The Empty Raincoat: Making Sense of the Future*. London: Hutchinson.

—— (1995). 'Trust and the Virtual Organization'. *Harvard Business Review* (May–June), 40–8.

Handy, C. (1998). *The Hungry Spirit: Beyond Capitalism – A Quest for Purpose in the Modern World*. London: Random House.

Harvey, M. (1999). 'Economies of Time: A Framework for Analysing the Restructuring of Employment Relations', in A. Felstead and N. Jewson (eds.), *Global Trends in Flexible Labour*. Basingstoke: Macmillan, 21–42.

Harvey, D. (1989). *The Condition of Postmodernity*. Oxford: Blackwell.

—— (1991). *The Condition of Postmodernity: An Inquiry into the Origins of Cultural Change*. Oxford: Blackwell.

Hassard, J. (1989). 'Time and Industrial Sociology', in P. Blyton, J. Hassard, S. Hill, and K. Starkey (eds.), *Time, Work and Organization*. London: Routledge, 13–34.

—— (1990). (ed.), *The Sociology of Time*. Basingstoke: Macmillan.

—— (1991). 'Aspects of Time in Organization'. *Human Relations*, 44: 105–24.

—— (1996). 'Images of Time in Work and Organization', in R. Clegg, C. Hardy, and W. Nord (eds.), *Handbook of Organizations*. London: Sage, 581–98.

Hatch, M. (1999). 'Exploring the Empty Spaces of Organizing: How Improvisational Jazz Helps Redescribe Organizational Structure'. *Organization Studies*, 20: 75–100.

Hedaa, L. (1997). *Sat ud af spillet. Case: Tele Danmark Forlag—Personal Management Institute*. Copenhagen: Samfundslitteratur.

—— (1999). 'Black Holes in Networks', in Pervez N. Ghauri (ed.), *Advances in International Marketing*, 9: 131–45.

—— and Törnroos, J.-Å. (1997). 'Understanding Event-Based Business Networks'. Working Paper, 10. Copenhagen: Copenhagen Business School, Department of Management, Politics and Philosophy.

Heidegger, M. (1926/1962). *Being and Time*, trans. J. Macquarre and E. Robinson. New York: Harper & Row.

—— (1971). *Poetry, Language, Thought*, trans. A. Hofstadter. New York: Harper Row.

Hein, L. E. (1993). 'Growth versus Success: Japan's Economic Policy in Historical Perspective', in A. Gordon (ed.), *Postwar Japan as History*. Berkeley and Los Angeles: University of California Press, 99–122.

Heirich, M. (1964). 'The Use of Time in the Study of Social Change'. *American Sociological Review*, 29: 386–97.

Hekman, S. (1990). *Gender and Knowledge: Elements of a Postmodern Feminism*. Cambridge: Polity.

—— (1995). *Moral Voices, Moral Selves: Carol Gilligan and Feminist Moral Theory*. Cambridge: Polity.

Helprin, M. (1999). 'The Acceleration of Tranquility'. *FORBES ASAP*, 4 Oct., 263–7.

Hendrix, P. (1980). 'Subjective Elements in the Examination of Time Expenditure', in W. Wilkie (ed.), *Advances in Consumer Research*. Ann Arbor: Association for Consumer Research, vi. 38–44.

Hewitt, P. (1993). *About Time: The Revolution in Work and Family Life*. London: Rivers Oram Press.

Heyes, J. (1997). 'Annualised Hours and the Knock: The Organisation of Working Time in a Chemicals Plant'. *Work, Employment and Society*, 11/1: 65–81.

Hickson, D., Butler, R., Gray, D., Mallory, G., and Wilson, D. (1986). *Top Decisions: Strategic Decision-Making in Organizations*. Oxford: Blackwell

Hirschman, E. (1987). 'Theoretical Perspectives of Time Use: Implications for Consumer Behaviour Research'. *Research in Consumer Behaviour*, 2: 55–81.

—— and Holbrook, M. (1992). *Postmodern Consumer Research*. London: Sage.

Hoch, S., and Loewenstein, G. (1991). 'Time-Inconsistent Preferences and Consumer Self-Control'. *Journal of Consumer Research*, 17 (Mar.), 492–507.

Holman, R. (1981). 'The Imagination of the Future: A Hidden Concept in the Study of Time', in K. B. Monroe (ed.), *Advances in Consumer Research*. Ann Arbor: Association for Consumer Research, viii. 187–91.

Homer, S. (1994). *Fredric Jameson and the Limits of Postmodern Theory*. Center for Psychotherapeutic Studies, University of Sheffield. http://www.shef.ac.uk/uni/academic/N-Q/psysc/staff/sihomer/limits.html.

Hornik, J. (1984). 'Subjective versus Objective Time Measures: A Note on the Perception of Time in Consumer Behaviour'. *Journal of Consumer Research*, 11 (June), 615–18.

Howard, J., and Sheth, J. (1969). *The Theory of Buyer Behaviour*. New York: John Wiley & Sons.

Hunt, S. (1983). 'General Theories and the Fundamental Explanda of Marketing'. *Journal of Marketing*, 47 (Fall), 9–17.

Husserl, E. (1928/1964). *The Phenomenology of Internal Time-Consciousness*, ed. M. Heidegger, trans. J. Churchill. The Hague: Nijhoff.

IDS (1996). Income Data Services, *Annual Hours*, 604 (June).

IDS (1999). *Annual Hours*, 647 (Aug.).

Ilinitch, A. Y., d'Aveni, R. A., and Lewin, A. Y. (1996). 'New Organizational Forms and Strategies for Managing in Hypercompetitive Environments'. *Organization Science*, 7: 211–20.

——Lewin, A., and d'Aveni, R. (1998) (eds.). *Managing in Times of Disorder: Hypercompetitive Organizational Responses*. Thousand Oaks, Calif.: Sage.

Ingold, T. (1986). *Evolution and Social Life*. Cambridge: Cambridge University Press.

——(1993). 'The Temporality of Landscape'. *World Archaeology*, 25: 152–74.

——(1995). 'Work, Time and Identity', *Time and Society*, 4/1: 5–28.

Ishaya, T., and Macaulay, L. (1999). 'The Role of Trust in Virtual Teams'. *Electronic Journal of Organizational Virtualness*, 1/1: 140–57.

Jackson, P., and Thrift, N. (1995). 'Geographies of Consumption', in D. Miller (ed.), *Acknowledging Consumption: A Review of New Studies*. London: Routledge.

Jacoby, J., Szybillo, G., and Berning, C. (1976). 'Time and Consumer Behaviour: An Interdisciplinary Overview'. *Journal of Consumer Research*, 2: 320–39.

Jameson, F. (1984). *Postmodernism, or the Cultural Logic of Late Capitalism*. London: Verso.

——(1997). *Postmodernism, or the Cultural Logic of Late Capitalism*. Durham, NC: Duke University Press.

Jaques, E. (1982). *The Form of Time*. London: Heinemann.

Kaempfer, W. (1996). *Zeit des Menschen*. Frankfurt/Main: Insel.

Kamata, S. (1983). *Japan in the Passing Lane: An Insider's Account of a Life in a Japanese Auto Factory*. London: George Allen & Unwin.

Kant, I. (1788/1956). *Critique of Pure Reason*, trans. N. Kemp Smith. London: Macmillan.

Katz, D., and Kahn, R. L. (1966). 'Common Characteristics of Open Systems', in *The Social Psychology of Organizations*. New York: John Wiley & Sons, 14–29.

Kauffman, S. (1995). *At Home in the Universe: The Search for the Laws of Self-Organization and Complexity*. Oxford: Oxford University Press.

Keenoy, T. (1999). 'HRM as Hologram: A Polemic'. *Journal of Management Studies*, 36/1: 1–23.

——Oswick, C., and Grant, D. (1997). 'Organizational Discourse: Text and Context'. *Organization*, 4/2: 147–57.

——Anthony, P., Grant, D., Mangham, I., and Oswick, C. (1999). 'Reconfiguring Academic Values: Documenting the Complex and Dramatising the Chaotic—a Position Paper', paper for 2nd International 'Organization' Conference on Re-Organising Knowledge: Transforming Institutions, Knowing, Knowledge and the University in the XXI Century, University of Massachusetts, Ang.

——Oswick, C., and Grant, D. (2000). 'Discourse, Epistemology and Organization: A Discursive Footnote'. *Organization*, 7/3: 542–5.

Kelm, K. M., Narayanan, V. K., and George, E. P. (1995). 'Shareholder Value Creation during R & D Innovation and Commercialization'. *Academy of Management Journal*, 38/3: 770–86.

Kelman, H. (1969). 'Kairos—the Auspicious Moment'. *American Journal of Psychoanalysis*, 29: 59–83.

Kendall, L. (1998). 'Meaning and Identity in Cyberspace: The Performance of Gender Class and Race On-Line'. *Symbolic Interaction*, 21/2: 129–53.

Kern, S. (1983). *The Culture of Time and Space 1880–1919*. London: Weidenfeld & Nicolson.

Kirkeby, O. F. (2000). *Management Philosophy: A Radical-Normative Perspective.* Heidelberg: Springer Verlag.

Klein, B., and Leffler, K. B. (1981). 'The Role of Market Forces in Assuring Contractual Performance'. *Journal of Political Economy,* 89 (Aug.), 615–41.

Knights, D. (1997). 'Fear of the "Empty Space": The Threat of Postmodern Feminism'. Paper delivered at the 15th SCOS International Conference, Warsaw, 9–12 July.

—— (forthcoming). 'Writing Organizational Analysis into Foucault', in S. Linstead (ed.), *Postmodern Organizations.* London: Sage.

—— and Morgan, G. (1993). 'Organisation Theory and Consumption in a Postmodern Era'. *Organisation Studies,* 14/2: 211–34.

—— and Odih, P. (1995). 'It's about Time: The Significance of Gendered Time for Financial Services Consumption'. *Time and Society,* 14/2: 205–31.

—— —— (1997). '"From here to Eternity"—A Masculine Project Theorising Time, Space and Risk within the Classical, Modern and Postmodern Epistemological Regimes', in H. Rasmussen (ed.), *Proceedings of the AOS, Accounting Time and Space Conference.* Copenhagen: Copenhagen Business School, 1–25.

—— —— (1999). 'What's in a Name? The Dynamics of Branding Personal Financial Services'. *Financial Services Marketing,* 4/2: 163–77.

—— and Sturdy, A. (1997). 'Marketing the Soul: From the Ideology of Consumption to Consumer Subjectivity'. Paper delivered at the EGOS 11th Colloquium, Paris, 6–8 July.

—— and Willmott, H. (1989). 'Power and Subjectivity at Work: From Degradation to Subjugation in Social Relations'. *Sociology,* 23/4: 535–58.

—— and Willmott, H. (1999). *Management Lives: Power and Identity in Work Organizations.* London: Sage.

Kochan, T., Lansbury, A., Russel D., and MacDaffie, J. P. (1997). *After Lean Production: Evolving Employment Practice in the World Auto Industry.* New York: ILR/Cornell University Press.

Koestler, A. (1970). *The Act of Creation.* New York: Pan Books.

Kohli, R., Lehmann, D. R., and Pae, J. (1999). 'Extent and Impact of Incubation Time in New Product Diffusion'. *Journal of New Product Innovations Management,* 16/2: 131.

Koku, P. S., Jagpal, S. H., and Viswanath, P. V. (1997). 'The Effect of New Announcements and Preannouncements on Stock Prices'. *Journal of Market-Focused Management,* 2/2: 183–99.

Koot, W., and Sabelis, I. (2000). *Over-Levenaan de Top. Top managers in complexe tijden.* Utrecht: Lemma Publishers. Trans. as *Surviving at the Top: Top Managers in Complex Times* (forthcoming).

Langlois, R. (1986) (ed.). *Economics as Process: Essays in the New Institutional Economics.* Cambridge: Cambridge University Press.

Lash, S., and Urry, J. (1994). *Economics of Sign and Space.* London: Sage

Latour, B. (1991). *Nous n'avons jamais été moderne.* Paris: La Découverte.

Lauer, R. H. (1981). *Temporal Man: The Meaning and Uses of Social Time.* New York: Praeger.

Leccardi, C. (1996). 'Re-Thinking Social Time: Feminist Perspectives'. *Time and Society,* 5/2: 169–86.

Lee, H. (1999). 'Time and Information Technology: Monochronicity, Polychronicity and Temporal Symmetry'. *European Journal of Information Systems,* 8: 16–26.

Lee, H., and Liebenau, J. (1999). 'Time in Organizational Studies: Towards a New Research Direction'. *Organization Studies*, 20/6: 1035–58.

—— —— (2000). 'Temporal Effects of Information Systems on Business Processes: Focusing on the Dimensions of Temporality'. *Accounting, Management and Information Technologies*, 10/3: 157–85.

Lee, J. (1999a). 'Lean Manufacturer's Role during the Crisis: The Case of Fire at Aisin's Factory'. *Economy Review*, 163/5–6: 572–90 (in Japanese).

—— (1999b). 'Lean Production System and Flexible Work Force during the Crisis: The Case of Fire at Aisin's Factory'. *Economy Review*, 164/2: 45–65 (in Japanese).

Lefèbvre, H. (1991). *The Production of Space*, trans. D. Nicholson-Smith. Oxford: Blackwell.

Le Goff, J. (1980). *Time, Work and Culture in the Middle Ages*. Chicago: Chicago University Press.

Leroi-Gourhan, A. (1988). *Hand und Wort*. Frankfurt/Main: Suhrkamp.

Levine, R. (1997). *A Geography of Time: The Temporal Misadventures of a Social Psychologist*. New York: Basic Books.

Lewis, J. D., and Weigert, A. J. (1981). 'The Structures and Meanings of Social Time'. *Social Forces*, 60: 432–62.

Lightman, A. (1993). *Einstein's Dreams: A Novel*. New York: Warner Books.

Lindblom, C. E. (1959). 'The Science of "Muddling Through"'. *Public Administration Review*, 19 (Spring), 79–88.

Lloyd Smith, S., and Wilkinson, B. (1996). 'We are our own Policemen! Organizing without Conflict', in S. Linstead, R. Grafton-Small, and P. Jeffcut (eds.), *Understanding Management*. London: Sage, 130–44.

Luce, G. G. (1973). *Body Time: The Natural Rhythms of the Body*. St Albans: Paladin.

Luhmann, N. (1976). 'The Future Cannot Begin: Temporal Structures in Modern Society'. *Social Research*, 43: 130–52.

—— (1978). 'Temporalization of Complexity', in R. F. Geyer and J. van der Zouwen (eds.), *Sociocybernetics*. Leiden: Martinus Nijhoff, ii. 95–111.

—— (1982). *The Differentiation of Society*. New York: Columbia University Press.

—— (1990). *Essays on Self-Reference*. New York: Columbia University Press.

—— (1995). *Social Systems*. Stanford, Calif.: Stanford University Press.

—— (1997). 'Limits of Steering'. *Theory, Culture and Society*, 14/1: 41–57.

Lyles, M. (1990). 'A Research Agenda for Strategic Management in the 1990s'. *Journal of Management Studies*, 27/4: 363–75.

Lyotard, J. F. (1984). *The Postmodern Condition*. Minneapolis: University of Minneapolis Press.

McCracken, G. (1990). 'Culture and Consumer Behaviour'. *Journal of the Market Research Society*, 32/1: 3–11.

McGrath, J. (1988). 'Time and Social Psychology', in J. McGrath (ed.), *The Social Psychology of Time*. Newbury Park, Calif.: Sage, 255–67.

—— and Kelly, J. (1986). *Time and Human Interaction: Toward a Social Psychology of Time*. New York: Guilford Press.

—— and Rotchford, N. L. (1983). 'Time and Behavior in Organizations', in B. Staw and L. Cummings, (eds.), *Research in Organizational Behavior*. Greenwich, Conn.: JAI Press, 57–101.

McKenna, R. (1997). *Real Time*. Boston: Harvard Business School Press.

Mangham, I. L. (1986). *Power and Performance in Organizations*. Oxford: Blackwell.

——and Overington, M. A. (1987). *Organizations as Theatre: A Social Psychology of Dramatic Appearances*. Chichester: Wiley.

March, J. G. (1994). *A Primer on Decision Making: How Decisions Happen*. New York: Free Press.

——and Olsen, J. (1976). *Ambiguity and Choice in Organizations*. Bergen: Universitetsforlaget.

——and Simon, H. A. (1958). *Organizations*. New York: Wiley.

——Sproull, L. S., and Tamuz, M. (1996). 'Learning from Samples of One or Fewer', in Michael D. Cohen and Lee S. Sproull (eds.), *Organizational Learning*. Thousand Oaks, Calif.: Sage, 1–19.

Marion, R. (1999). *The Edge of Organization: Chaos and Complexity Theories of Formal Social Systems*. Thousand Oaks, Calif.: Sage.

Marshak, R., Keenoy, T., Oswick, C., and Grant, D. (2000). 'From Outer Words to Inner Worlds'. *Journal of Applied Behavioral Science*, 36/2: 245–58.

Marx, K. (1857/1973). *Grundrisse*. Harmondsworth: Penguin.

——(1867/1976). *Capital*, i. Harmondsworth: Penguin.

Maturana, H., and Varela, F. (1980). *Autopoiesis and Cognition: The Realization of the Living*. London: Reidl.

Mayo, E. (1945). *The Social Problems of an Industrial Civilization*. Boston: Division of Research, Graduate School of Business Administration, Harvard University.

Mead, G. H. (1932/1959). *The Philosophy of the Present*, ed. A. E. Murphy, Preface by J. Dewey. La Salle: Open Court.

——(1932/1980). *The Philosophy of the Present*, ed. A. E. Murphy, Preface by John Dewey. Chicago: Chicago University Press.

——(1938/1950). *The Philosophy of the Act*. 3rd edn. Chicago: University of Chicago Press.

——(1963). 'Relative Space-Time and Simultaneity'. *Review of Metaphysics*, 17: 514–35.

Melbin, M. (1987). *Night as Frontier: Colonizing the World after Dark*. New York: Free Press.

Melucci, A. (1996). *The Playing Self*. Cambridge: Cambridge University Press.

Merleau-Ponty, M. (1945). *The Phenomenology of Perception*. New York: Humanities Press.

Meyerson, D., Weick, K., and Kramer, R. (1996). 'Swift Trust and Temporary Groups', in R. Kramer and T. Tyler (eds.), *Trust in Organizations: Frontiers of Theory and Research*. Thousand Oaks, Calif.: Sage, 166–95.

Miller, C. R. (1994). 'Opportunity, Opportunism and Progress: Kairos in the Rethoric of Technology'. *Argumentation*, 8: 81–96.

Miller, D. (1993). 'The Architecture of Simplicity'. *Academy of Management Review*, 18: 116–38.

Mintzberg, H. (1973). *The Nature of Managerial Work*. New York: Harper & Row.

——(1978). 'Patterns in Strategy Formation'. *Management Science*, 24: 934–48.

——(1979). *The Structuring of Organizations*. Englewood Cliffs, NJ: Prentice Hall.

——(1994). *The Rise and Fall of Strategic Planning*. New York: Free Press.

——and McHugh, A. (1985). 'Strategy Formation in an Adhocracy'. *Administrative Science Quarterly*, 30/2: 160–97.

——Waters, J., Pettigrew, A. M., and Butler, R. (1990). 'Studying Deciding: An Exchange of Views between Mintzberg and Waters, Pettigrew, and Butler'. *Organization Studies*, 11/1: 1–6.

Möller, K. E., and Wilson, D. T. (1995) (eds.). *Business Marketing: An Interaction and Network Approach*. Boston: Klüwer Academic Publishers.

Monden, Yasuhiro (1981). 'What Makes the Toyota Production System Really Tick?', *Industrial Engineering* (Jan.), 36–46.

—— (1991). *Shin Toyota Shisutemu*. Tokyo: Kodansha.

Montesano, M. (1995). 'Kairos and Kerygma: The Rhetoric of Christian Proclamation'. *Rhetoric Society Quarterly*, 25: 164–78.

Moore, W. E. (1963). *Man, Time and Society*. New York: John Wiley & Sons.

Moore-Ede, M. (1993). *The 24-Hour Society: The Risks, Costs and Challenges of a World that Never Stops*. London: Piatkus.

Moorman, C., and Miner, A. S. (1998). 'Organizational Improvisation and Organizational Memory'. *Academy of Management Review*, 23: 698–723.

Morello, G. (1988). 'Business Requirements and Future Expectations in Comparative Bank Services: The Issue of Time Perceptions'. *Research for Financial Services Seminar*. Milan: ESOMAR, 235–45.

Morgan, G. (1997). *Images of Organization*. London: Sage.

Morley, D., and Robins, K. (1995). *Spaces of Identity: Global Media, Electronic Landscapes and Cultural Boundaries*. London: Routledge.

Morris-Suzuki, T. (1994). *The Technological Transformation of Japan: From the Seventeenth to the Twenty-First Century*. Cambridge: Cambridge University Press.

Morse, M. (1990). 'An Ontology of Everyday Distraction: The Freeway, the Mall and Television', in P. Mellencamp (ed.), *Logics of Television Essays in Cultural Criticism*. Bloomington, Ind.: Indiana University Press, 191–221.

—— (1998). *Virtualities: Television, Media Art, and Culture*. Bloomington, Ind.: Indiana University Press.

Mort, F. (1988). 'Boys Own? Masculinity, Style and Popular Culture', in R. Chapman and J. Rutherford (eds.), *Male Order: Unwrapping Masculinity*. London: Lawrence & Wishart, 193–224.

Mosakowski, E., and Earley, C. (2000). 'A Selective Review of Time Assumptions in Strategy Research'. *Academy of Management Review*, 25/4: 796–812.

Mumford, L. (1934/1955). 'The Monastery and the Clock', in *The Human Prospect*. Boston: Beakon Press, 3–10.

Nash, W. (1993). *Jargon: Its Uses and Abuses*. Oxford: Blackwell.

Near, J. P., Rice, R. W., and Hunt, R. G. (1980). 'The Relationship between Work and Nonwork Domains: A Review of Empirical Research'. *Academy of Management Review*, 5/3: 415–29.

Negroponte, N. (1995). *Being Digital*. London: Hodder & Stoughton.

Nicosia, F., and Myer, R. (1976). 'Towards a Sociology of Consumption'. *Journal of Consumer Research*, 3 (Sept.), 65–75.

Nishimoto, I. (1997). 'The "Civilization" of Time: Japan and the Adoption of the Western Time System'. *Time and Society*, 6/2–3: 237–60.

—— (1999). '"Harmony" as Efficiency: Is "Just-In-Time" a Product of Japanese Uniqueness?' *Time and Society*, 8/1: 119–40.

Noon, M., and Blyton, P. (1997). *The Realities of Work*. Basingstoke: Macmillan.

Noss, C. (1998). '*Problems of Time in the Management of Organizations: Towards a Conceptual Integration of Temporal Complexity*'. Paper presented at EGOS 14th Colloquium, Maastricht University, The Netherlands, 9–11 July.

Nowotny, H. (1988). 'From the Future to the Extended Present: Time in Social Systems', in G. Kirsch, P. Nijkamp, and K. Zimmermann (eds.), *The Formation of Time Preferences in Multidisciplinary Perspectives*. Aldershot: Gower, 17–31.

—— (1989). 'Mind, Technologies, and Collective Time Consciousness: From Future to Extended Present', in J. T. Frazer (ed.), *The Study of Time VI*. Madison, Conn.: International Universities Press, 197–213.

—— (1989/1994). *Time: The Modern and Postmodern Experience*, trans. Neville Plaice. Cambridge: Polity.

—— (1992). 'Time and Social Theory: Towards a Social Theory of Time'. *Time and Society*, 1/3: 421–54.

—— (1993). *Eigenzeit: Entstehung und Strukturierung eines Zeitgefühls*. Frankfurt/Main: Suhrkamp.

Odih, P. (1998). 'Gendered Time and Financial Services Consumption'. Ph.D. thesis. Manchester: FSRC Manchester School of Management, UMIST.

—— (1999). 'Gendered Time in the Age of Deconstruction'. *Time and Society*, 8/1: 9–39.

—— and Knights, D. (2000).' "Just in Time". The Prevalence of Representational Time to Marketing Discourses of Consumer Buyer Behaviour', in P. Daniels, J. Bryson *et al.* (eds.), *Knowledge, Space and Economy*. London: Routledge, 79–101.

Ohmae, K. (1995). *The End of the Nation State*. London: Harper & Row.

Ohno, T. (1988). *Toyota Production System: Beyond Large-Scale Production*. Cambridge, Mass.: Productivity Press.

Onians, R. B. (1951/1973). *The Origins of European Thought about the Body, the Mind, the Soul, the World, Time, and Fate*. New York: Arno.

O'Rouke, P. (1990). 'Past Imperfect'. *Leisure Measurement* (May), 12–14.

Oswick, C., and Keenoy, T. (2001). 'Cinematic Re-Presentations of Las Vegas: Reality, Fiction and Compulsive Consumption'. *M@n@gment*.

Oswick, C., Anthony, P., Grant, D., Keenoy, T., and Mangham, I. L. (2000). 'A Dialogic Analysis of Organisational Learning'. *Journal of Management Studies*, 37/6: 887–901.

Ouchi, W. G. (1981). *Theory Z: How American Business can Meet the Japanese Challenge*. Reading, Mass.: Addison-Wesley.

Pahl, R. (1995). *After Success: Fin-de-siècle Anxiety and Identity*. Cambridge: Polity.

Panorama (2000). 'Back to the Kitchen Sink'. BBC 1, 24 Jan.

Papows, J. (1999). *Enterprise.com Market Leadership in the Information Age*. London: Nicholas Brealey Publishing.

Perlow, L. (1999). 'The Time Famine: Toward a Sociology of Work Time'. *Administrative Science Quarterly*, 44: 57–81.

Pettigrew, A. (1977). 'Strategy Formulation as a Political Process'. *International Studies of Management and Organization*, 7/2: 78–87.

Pfeffer, J., and Salancik, G. R. (1978). *The External Control of Organizations: A Resource Dependence Perspective*. New York: Harper & Row.

Poster, M. (1990). *The Mode of Information*. Cambridge: Polity.

—— (1995). *The Second Media Age*. Cambridge: Polity.

Postman, N. (1993). *Technopoly: The Surrender of Culture to Technology*. New York: Vintage Books.

Pratchett, T. (1998). *The Bromeliad. Truckers—Diggers—Wings*. London: Doubleday.

Prigogine, I. (1994). *Les Lois du Chaos*. Paris: Flammarion.

Propp, V. (1958). *The Morphology of the Folktale*. Austin, Tex.: University of Texas Press.

Purser, R., Pasmore, W., and Tenkasi, R. (1992). 'The Influence of Deliberations on Learning in New Product Development Teams'. *Journal of Engineering and Technology Management*, 9/1: 1–28.

Quarantelli, E. L. (1988). 'Disaster Crisis Management: A Summary of Research Findings'. *Journal of Management Studies*, 25: 373–85.

Quinn, R. E., and Cameron, K. (1983). 'Organizational Life Cycles and Shifting Criteria of Effectiveness: Some Preliminary Evidence'. *Management Science*, 29/1: 33–51.

Ramaprasad, A., and Stone, W. (1992). 'The Temporal Dimension of Strategy'. *Time and Society*, 1/3: 359–77

Rappaport, H. (1990). *Marking Time*. New York: Simon & Schuster.

Ray, C. (1991). *Time Space and Philosophy*. London: Routledge.

Reeves, C. A., and Bednar, D. A. (1995). ' "Quality as Symphony": Cornell Hotel and Restaurant'. *Administration Quarterly*, 36: 72–80.

Reeves, R. (2001). 'Business Turns Clockwise'. *Industry Standard*, 21 Feb. http://europe.thestandard.com/article/display/0,1151,14968,00.html.

Rifkin, J. (1987). *Time Wars*. New York: Henry Holt.

—— (2000). *The Age of Access: The New Culture of Hypercapitalism where All of Life is a Paid-for Experience*. New York: Jeremy Tarcher.

Rodaway, P. (1995). 'Exploring the Subject in Hyper-Reality', in S. Pile and N. Thrift (eds.), *Mapping the Subject*. London: Routledge, 241–61.

Roger, E. M. (1983). *Diffusion of Innovations*. 3rd edn. New York: Free Press.

Rojek, C. (1993). 'Disney Culture'. *Leisure Studies*, 12: 121–35.

Romanelli, E., and Tushman, M. L. (1994). 'Organizational Transformation as Punctuated Equilibrium: An Empirical Test'. *Academy of Management Journal*, 37: 1141–66.

Rorty, R. (1979). *Philosophy and the Mirror of Nature*. Princeton: Princeton University Press.

—— (1989). *Contingency, Irony, and Solidarity*. Cambridge: Cambridge University Press.

—— (1998). *Truth and Progress*. Cambridge: Cambridge University Press.

Rothenberg, D. (1993). *Hand's End: Technology and the Limits of Nature*. Berkeley and Los Angeles: University of California Press.

Roy, D. F. (1960). 'Banana Time: Job Satisfaction and Informal Interaction'. *Human Organization*, 18: 158–68.

Sabelis, I. (1996). 'Temporal Paradoxes: Working with Cultural Diversity in Organizations', in W. Koot, I. Sabelis, and S. Ybema (eds.), *Contradictions in Context: Puzzling over Paradoxes in Contemporary Organizations*. Anthropological Studies, 19. Amsterdam: Free University Press, 171–92.

Sakuma, S., and Ohmori, H. (1991). 'The Auto Industry', in National Defense Council for Victims of Karoshi (ed.), *Karoshi: When the 'Corporate Warrior' Dies*. Tokyo: Mado-sha.

Sarup, M. (1996). *Identity Culture and the Postmodern World*. Edinburgh: Edinburgh University Press.

Sastry, M. A. (1997). 'Problems and Paradoxes in a Model of Punctuated Organizational Change'. *Administrative Science Quarterly*, 42: 237–75.

Saxonhouse, G. (1983). 'Economic Relations with the United States, 1945–1973', in *Kodansha Encyclopedia of Japan*. Tokyo: Kodansha, viii. 161–4.

Schein, E. H. (1992). *Organizational Culture and Leadership*. San Francisco: Jossey-Bass.

Schendel, D. E., and Hofer, C. W. (1979). 'Introduction', in D. E. Schendel and C. W. Hofer (eds.), *Strategic Management*. Boston: Little, Brown Company, 1–22.

Schonburger, R. (1982). *Japanese Manufacturing Techniques: Nine Hidden Lessons in Simplicity*. New York: Free Press.

Schreyögg, G., and Noss, C. (2000). 'Reframing Change in Organizations: The Equilibrium Logic and Beyond', in S. J. Havlovic (ed.), *Academy of Management Best Paper Proceedings of the AOM's Toronto 2000 Conference*. Toronto: Academy of Management (CDROM). See also http://aom.pace.edu/odc/papers.html#2000bp.

——and Steinmann, H. (1987). 'Strategic Control: A New Perspective'. *Academy of Management Review*, 12: 91–103.

Schriber, J. B. (1986). 'An Exploratory Study of the Temporal Dimensions of Work Organizations'. Unpublished doctoral dissertation. Claremont Graduate School.

——and Gutek, B. A. (1987). 'Some Time Dimensions of Work: The Measurement of an Underlying Aspect of Organization Culture'. *Journal of Applied Psychology*, 72/4: 642–50.

Schutz, A. (1967). *The Phenomenology of the Social World*. Evanston, Ill.: North Western University Press.

——(1971). 'The Problem of Social Reality', in *Collected Papers*, i, ed. M. Natanson. The Hague: Martinus Nijhoff.

Searle, J. (1999). *Mind, Language and Society*. London: Phoenix.

Sennett, R. (1998). *The Corrosion of Character: The Personal Consequences of Work in the New Capitalism*. New York: W. W. Norton.

Serres, M. (1982/1995). *Genesis*, trans. Genevieve James and James Nielson. Michigan: University of Michigan Press.

Sewell, G., and Wilkinson, B. (1992). '"Someone to Watch over Me": Surveillance, Discipline and the Just-in-Time Labour Process'. *Sociology*, 26/2: 271–89.

Shackle, G. L. S. (1972). *Epistemics and Economics: A Critique of Economic Doctrines*. Cambridge: Cambridge University Press.

Sheth, J. N., and Gardner, M. (1986). 'History of Marketing Thought: An Update', in J. N. Sheth and D. E. Garrett (eds.), *Marketing Theory: Classic and Contemporary Readings*. Cincinnati: South-Western Publishing Co., 211–26.

——and Garrett, D. E. (1986) (eds.). *Marketing Theory: Classic and Contemporary Readings*. Cincinnati: South-Western Publishing Co.

——and Sisodia, R. (1997). 'Consumer Behaviour in the Future', in Robert Peterson (ed.), *Electronic Marketing and the Consumer*. Thousand Oaks, Calif.: Sage, 17–37.

Shields, R. (1992). *Lifestyle Shopping: The Subject of Consumption*. London: Routledge.

Shrivastava, P. (1987). *Bhopal: Anatomy of a Crisis*. Cambridge, Mass.: Ballinger.

Sievers, B. (1990). 'The Diabolization of Death: Some Thoughts on the Obsolescence of Mortality in Organization Theory and Practice', in J. Hassard and D. Pym (eds.), *The Theory and Philosophy of Organizations*. London: Routledge, 125–36.

Simpson, L. (1995). *Technology, Time and the Conversations of Modernity*. New York: Routledge.

Sköldberg, K. (1998). 'Heidegger and Organization: Notes towards a New Research Programme'. *Scandinavian Journal of Management*, 14/1–2: 77–102.

Smith, T. C. (1988). *Native Source of Japanese Industrialization 1750–1920*. Berkeley and Los Angeles: University of California Press.

Smith, W. R. (1956). 'Product Differentiation and Market Segmentation as Alternative Strategies'. *Journal of Marketing* (July), 3–8.

Sobchack, V. (1991). *Screening Space*. New York: Ungar.

Sorokin, P. (1964). *Socio-Cultural Causality, Space and Time: A Study of Referential Principles of Sociology and Social Science.* New York: Russell & Russell.

—— and Merton, R. K. (1990). 'Social Time: A Methodological and Functional Analysis', in J. Hassard (ed.), *The Sociology of Time.* Basingstoke: Macmillan, 56–66.

Springer, C. (1996). *Electronic Eros: Bodies and Desire in the Postindustrial Age.* London: Athlone.

Stacey, R. (1992). *Managing the Unknowable.* San Francisco: Jossey-Bass.

Staines, G. L. (1980). 'Spillover versus Compensation: A Review of the Literature on the Relationship between Work and Nonwork'. *Human Relations,* 33/2: 111–29.

Starbuck, W. H. (1976). 'Organizations and their Environments', in M. D. Dunnette (ed.), *Handbook of Industrial and Social Psychology.* Chicago: Rand McNally, 1069–123.

—— and Milliken, F. J. (1988). 'Challenger: Fine-Tuning the Odds until Something Breaks'. *Journal of Management Studies,* 25: 319–40.

Starkey, K. (1988). 'Time and Work Organization: A Theoretical and Empirical Analysis', in M. Young and T. Schuller (eds.), *The Rhythms of Society.* London: Routledge, 95–117.

Strauss, E. (1966) (ed.). *Phenomenological Psychology: Selected Papers,* trans. E. Eng. New York: Basic Books.

Sullivan, Dale L. (1992). 'Kairos and the Rhetoric of Belief'. *Quarterly Journal of Speech,* 78: 317–32.

Taschdjian, E. (1977). 'Time Horizon: The Moving Boundary'. *Behavioral Science,* 22: 41–8.

Taylor, F. W. (1911/1947). 'The Principle of Scientific Management', in *Scientific Management.* New York: Harper & Row.

—— (1912/1947). 'Testimony before the Special House Committee', in *Scientific Management.* New York: Harper & Row.

Thompson, E. P. (1967). 'Time, Work-Discipline and Industrial Capitalism', *Past and Present,* 38: 56–97.

Thrift, N. (1981). 'Owners' Time and Own Time: The Making of a Capitalist Time Consciousness, 1300–1800', in A. R. Pred (ed.), *Space and Time in Geography.* Lund: Gleerup, 56–84.

—— (1988). 'Vicos Voco: Ringing the Changes in Historical Geography of Time Consciousness', in M. Young and T. Schuller (eds.), *The Rhythms of Society.* London: Routledge, 53–94.

—— (1996). *Spatial Formations.* London: Sage.

Tillich, P. (1963). *Systematic Theology,* iii. Chicago: University of Chicago Press.

Tillman, M. K. (1970). 'Temporality and Role Taking in G. H. Mead'. *Social Research,* 37: 533–46.

Toffler, A. (1970). *Future Shock.* London: Bantam Books.

Toyota (1988). *A History of the First 50 Years.* Toyota: Toyota Motor Corporation.

Tribe, M. (1993). *Postmodern Time.* http://www.thetribes.com/mark/time/index.html.

Tsutsui, W. M. (1998). *Manufacturing Ideology: Scientific Management in Twentieth-Century Japan.* Princeton: Princeton University Press.

Tuckman, A. (1998). ' "All Together Better?" Single Status and Union Recognition in the Chemical Industry'. *Employee Relations,* 20/2: 132–47.

—— (2000). 'Space for Conflict in New Work Time Disciplines? Security and the Resurgence of Workplace Organization'. Paper presented at the EGOS 16th Colloquium, Helsinki School of Economics and Business Administration, Finland, 2–4 July.

——and Whittall, M. (2002). 'Affirmation, Games, and Insecurity: Cultivating Consent within a New Workplace Regime', *Capital and Class*, 76: 65–93.

Turkle, S. (1995). *Life on the Screen: Identity in the Age of the Internet*. New York: Simon & Schuster.

Urry, J. (1995). *Consuming Places*. London: Routledge.

——(2000). *Sociology beyond Societies: Mobilities for the Twenty-First Century*. London: Routledge

Van de Ven, A. H., and Poole, M. S. (1995). 'Explaining Development and Change in Organization'. *Academy of Management Review*, 20: 510–40.

van den Bosch, F. (2001). 'What Makes Time Strategic?', in H. Volberda and T. Elfring (eds.), *Rethinking Strategy*. London: Sage.

van Dijk, T. (1985). *Handbook of Discourse Analysis*, i–iv. London: Academic Press.

Vattimo, G. (1988). *The End of Modernity: Nihilism and Hermeneutics in Postmodern Culture*, trans. and intro. J. Synder. Cambridge: Cambridge University Press.

Venkatesh, A., Meamber, L., and Firat, F. (1998). 'Cyberspace as the Next Marketing Frontier(?)—Questions and Issues', in S. Brown and D. Turley (eds.), *Consumer Research: Postcards from the Edge*. London: Routledge, 300–22.

Virilio, P. (1977/1986). *Speed and Politics: An Essay on Dromology*, trans. M. Polizotti. New York: Columbia University Press/Semiotext(e). *Vitesse et Politique*. Paris: Editions Galileé, 1977.

——(1980/1991). *The Aesthetics of Disappearance*. New York: Semiotext(e).

——(1991). *La Vitesse*. Paris: Éditions Flammarion.

——(1995*a*). *La Vitesse de liberation*. Paris: Galilée.

——(1995*b*). *The Art of the Motor*. Minneapolis: University of Minnesota.

——(1995*c*). 'Speed and Information: Cyberspace alarm!', in A. Kroker and M. Kroker (eds.). *CTHEORY*, 18/3: 1–5.

——(1997). *Open Sky*, trans. Julie Rose. London: Verso.

——(1999). *Fluchtgeschwindigkeit*. Frankfurt/Main: Fischer.

——(2000). *The Information Bomb*, trans. Chris Turner. London: Verso.

Vogel, E. F. (1979/2001). *Japan as Number One: Lessons for America*. San Jose: iUniverse.Com.

——(1991). *The Four Little Dragons*. Cambridge, Mass.: Harvard University Press.

Volberda, H. K. (1998). *Building the Flexible Firm: How to Remain Competitive*. New York: Oxford University Press.

von Foerster, H. (1981). *Observing Systems*. Seaside, Calif.: Intersystems.

Vreiling, L. (1998). *The Pathfinder: Strategy Paths and Resources in their Territory through Time*. Capelle a/d IJssel: Labyrint Publication.

Walsh, J. P., and Ungson, G. R. (1991). 'Organizational Memory'. *Academy of Management Review*, 16: 57–91.

Watson, T. (1994). *In Search of Management*. London: International Thomson Business Press.

——and Harris, P. (1999). *The Emergent Manager*. London: Sage.

Weber, M. (1904–5/1958). *The Protestant Ethic and the Spirit of Capitalism*. New York: Scribners.

——(1904–5/1989). *The Protestant Ethic and the Spirit of Capitalism*. London: Unwin Hyman.

Webster's (1991). *Webster's Dictionary of the English Language*. New York: Lexicon Publication Inc.

Webster's (1993). *Merriam Webster's Collegiate Dictionary*. 10th edn. Springfield, Mass.

Weick, K. E. (1987). 'Substitutes for Strategy', in D. J. Teece (ed.), *The Competitive Challenge*. New York: Harper & Row, 221–33.

—— (1995). *Sensemaking in Organizations*. Thousand Oaks, Calif.: Sage.

—— (1998). 'Improvisation as a Mindset for Organizational Analysis'. *Organization Science*, 9: 543–55.

Weihrich, H., and Koontz, H. (1993). *Management—A Global Perspective*. 10th edn. New York: McGraw Hill.

Wendorff, R. (1980). *Zeit und Kultur*. Wiesbaden: Westdeutscher Verlag.

—— (1991). *Die Zeit mit der wir leben*. Herne: Heitkamp.

Wheatley, M. (1999). *Leadership and the New Science: Discovering Order in a Chaotic World*. San Francisco: Berrett-Koehler.

Whipp, R. (1987). ' "A Time to Every Purpose": An Essay on Time and Work', in P. Joyce (ed.), *The Historical Meanings of Work*. Cambridge: Cambridge University Press, 210–307.

—— (1990). *Patterns of Labour: Work and Social Change in the Pottery Industry*. London: Routledge.

—— (1994). 'A Time to be Concerned: A Position Paper on Time and Management'. *Time and Society*, 3/1: 99–116.

—— (1996). 'Creative Deconstruction: Strategy and Organizations', in S. Clegg, C. Hardy, and W. Nord (eds.), *Handbook of Organization Studies*. London: Sage, 261–75.

—— (2002). 'Managing Strategic Change', in D. Faulkner and A. Campbell (eds.), *The Oxford Handbook of Strategic Management*. Oxford: Oxford University Press.

—— and Clark, P. A. (1986). *Innovation and the Auto Industry: Product, Process and Work Organization*. London: Frances Pinter.

Whitehead, A. N. (1929). *Process and Reality*. New York: Macmillan.

Whittington, R. (1989). *Corporate Strategies in Recession and Recovery: Social Structures and Strategic Choice*. London: Unwin Hyman.

Wigand, R. (1996). 'Electronic Commerce: Definition, Theory and Context'. *Information Society*, 13: 1–16.

Wildavsky, A. (1973). 'If Planning is Everything, Maybe it's Nothing'. *Policy Sciences*, 4: 127–53.

Willis, P. (1979). 'Shop Floor Culture, Masculinity and the Wage Form', in J. Clarke, C. Critcher, and R. Johnson (eds.), *Working Class Culture: Studies in History and Theory*. London: Hutchinson, 185–98.

Wilson, D. (1992). *A Strategy of Change: Concepts and Controversies in the Management of Change*. London: Routledge.

Wilson, D. T., and Holman, R. (1980). 'Economic Theories of Time in Consumer Behaviour', in C. W. Lamb and P. M. Dunne (eds.), *Theoretical Developments in Marketing: Advances in Consumer Research*. Chicago: American Marketing Association, 265–8.

Wittgenstein, L. (1973). *The Blue and Brown Books*. Oxford: Blackwell.

Wittink, D., Ryans, A., and Burrus, N. (1982). 'New Products and Security Prices'. Working paper. Ithaca, NY.: Cornell University.

Womack, J. P., Jones, D. T., and Roos, D. (1990). *The Machine that Changed the World*. New York: Rawson Associates.

Wood, J. (1998). 'Redesigning the Present', in J. Wood (ed.), *The Virtual Embodied*. London: Routledge: 88–101.

Wright, P., and Weitz, B. (1977). 'Time Horizon Effects on Product Evaluation Strategies'. *Journal of Marketing Research*, 14 (Nov.), 429–43.

Young, M. (1988). *The Metronomic Society: Natural Rhythms and Human Timetables*. London: Thames & Hudson.

—— and Schuller, T. (1988) (eds.). *The Rhythms of Society*. London: Routledge & Kegan Paul.

—— —— (1991). *Life after Work: The Arrival of the Ageless Society*. London: HarperCollins.

Zaheer, S., Albert, S., and Zaheer, A. (1999). 'Time Scales and Organizational Theory'. *Academy of Management Review*, 24/4: 725–41.

Zerubavel, E. (1979*a*). *Patterns of Time in Hospital Life*. Chicago: University of Chicago Press.

—— (1979*b*). 'Private Time and Public Time: The Temporal Structure of Social Accessibility and Professional Commitments'. *Social Forces*, 58/1: 38–58.

—— (1981). *Hidden Rhythms: Schedules and Calendars in Social Life*. Chicago: Chicago University Press.

—— (1985). *The Seven Day Cycle. The History and Meaning of the Week*. New York: Free Press.

Zimbardo, P., Marshall, G., and Moslach, C. (1971). 'Liberating Behaviour from Time Bound Control'. *Journal of Applied Social Psychology*, 1: 305–23.

INDEX